What People Are Saying about
Valerie Geller's *Creating Powerful Radio*

"If you want to understand what makes radio work, read this, then read it again."
— Jon Faine, Air Personality
ABC Radio 774, Melbourne, Australia

"It should be a textbook."
— Chris Berry, General Manager
WMAL, Washington, DC

"If you want to achieve compelling radio and increase audiences, read this book immediately! LBC 97.3 in London has experienced massive growth using its methods."
— Scott Solder, Programme Controller
LBC Radio, London

"Making it in broadcasting takes more than just luck. Think of *Creating Powerful Radio* as your 'Road Guide' to success in radio."
— Andy Vierra, Program Director
KNUU, Las Vegas

"This book will help your show get better."
— Al Rantel, Talk Show Host
KABC, Los Angeles

"Wonderful."
— Paul Fisher, Vice President
Rogers Radio
Vancouver, BC, Canada

"Valerie Geller's first book was a triumph. It has proved to be an excellent primer for my staff. Valerie is an inspiration. If you can't get her for your station, buy this book."
— John Ryan, Managing Director
BBC Radio Manchester, Manchester, UK

"*Creating Powerful Radio* is a fine guide for people inside the radio biz and an explanation of that biz to people outside, including the people who would like to get in. It's the kind of book where the reader thinks, 'Oh that's why they do that.'"
— David Hinckley
New York Daily News

"*Creating Powerful Radio* might eventually make an executive's job at a satellite formatted affiliate much tougher."
— Professor Peter Hunn
Communications Studies Department
State University of New York, Oswego

"It's great. Read it!"
— Kim Komando,
Syndicated Air Personality

"I recommend it to everyone and I use it in my classes. I love this book."
— Jo Maeder (The Rock 'N Roll Madame)
   Air Personality and Instructor
   New York University

"Packed with insights, well written, and fun to read. It's obvious why so many radio people consider this book 'a must'!"
— John Sawatsky, Professor of Journalism
   Carleton University, Ottawa, ON, Canada

"Brilliant."
— Phil Taylor
   BBC, Scotland

"Creating *Powerful Radio* contains valuable tips and information for presenters, managers, and programmers."
— Julia Sullivan
   Music & Media

"Useful and practical."
— Jan Ørskov, Journalist
   Danmarks Radio, Denmark

"It's my bible!"
— Åsa Paborn, Program Director
   SBS Radio, Stockholm, Sweden

"We gave copies to the entire staff."
— Viktor Worms, Antenne Bayern
   Munich, Germany

"Anyone even considering a career in radio should read this!"
— Adele Scheele, Ph.D, Career Strategist
   Author of *Skills for Success*

"Techniques for the beginner all the way up to the most seasoned pro. Offers ways to think about ratio as a larger medium, using the airwaves as a canvas, as an art. I highly recommend this and all of Valerie Geller's books to anyone interested in radio broadcasting. These [books] should be in every station and in every broadcast school. We all need reminding of how to create powerful radio."
— Rusty Humphries
   Syndicated Talk Host

"The real things that make radio the special and deeply personal medium are simple: emotion, intimacy and telling a story. In the end we are not much different from cave dwellers of thousands of years ago who were enthralled by one man's ability to tell a story. All that changes are the outfits, but basically we respond the way the cave men did ... [Valerie Geller is] a person who really gets it. These writings are an instruction manual on how to create compelling radio, step-by-step"
— Nick Michaels
   Nick Michaels Productions

"A fantastic book, a triumph, a cornucopia of wisdom for anyone who works in radio."
— Carol Archer
   Smooth Jazz Editor, Radio & Records

Creating Powerful Radio

Getting, Keeping & Growing Audiences

News, Talk, Information & Personality
Broadcast, HD, Satellite & Internet

VALERIE GELLER

Edited by Turi Ryder

ELSEVIER

AMSTERDAM • BOSTON • HEIDELBERG • LONDON
NEW YORK • OXFORD • PARIS • SAN DIEGO
SAN FRANCISCO • SINGAPORE • SYDNEY • TOKYO

Focal Press is an imprint of Elsevier

Focal
Press

Focal Press is an imprint of Elsevier
30 Corporate Drive, Suite 400, Burlington, MA 01803, USA
Linacre House, Jordan Hill, Oxford OX2 8DP, UK

Library of Congress Cataloging-in-Publication Data

Geller, Valerie.
    Creating Powerful Radio: Getting, Keeping, & Growing Audiences for News, Talk, Information, and Personality / Valerie Geller; edited by Turi Ryder.
        p.   cm.
    Includes bibliographical references and index.
    ISBN-13: 978-0-240-51928-9 (alk. paper)
    ISBN-10: 0-240-51928-0 (alk. paper)
1. Radio broadcasting   2. Communications   3. Radio/Television
4. Journalism   5. Broadcast News   6. Title
I. Ryder, Turi.   II. Title.
    PN1991.5.G45 2007
    384.54—dc22

                                                                    2007023957

First published 2007
Reprinted 2007

British Library Cataloguing-in-Publication Data
A catalogue record for this book is available from the British Library.

ISBN: 978-0-240-51928-9

For information on all Focal Press publications,
visit our website at *www.books.elsevier.com*

07 08 09 10 11   5 4 3 2

Printed in the *Hungary*

A full and complete instructor manual is available with this text.
www.creatingpowerfulradio.com/textbook

Working together to grow
libraries in developing countries

www.elsevier.com | www.bookaid.org | www.sabre.org

ELSEVIER   BOOK AID
            International   Sabre Foundation

For Lyla and Fred

Other Books by Valerie Geller

Creating Powerful Radio: A Communicator's Handbook for News, Talk, Information & Personality

The Powerful Radio Workbook: The Prep, Performance & Post Production Planning

Contents

Permissions

Grateful acknowledgment is given to the following people and organizations for permission to reprint previously published materials.

Bonus Books: Excerpts from *Writing Broadcast News*. © Copyright 1987 by Mervin Block. Reprinted with permission of Bonus Books.

Leo Cullum cartoon: "That's not *my* political opinion. That's just stuff I hear on the radio." © The New Yorker Collection, 2003. Leo Cullum from cartoonbank.com. All rights reserved. Reprinted with permission.

Leo Cullum cartoon: "It's always 'Get me a Godzilla type,' never, 'Get me Godzilla!'" © The New Yorker Collection, 2004. Leo Cullum from cartoonbank.com. All rights reserved. Reprinted with permission.

Leo Cullum cartoon: "That's not what you told my screener you wanted to talk about." © The New Yorker Collection, 2001. Leo Cullum from cartoonbank.com. All rights reserved. Reprinted with permission.

Leo Cullum cartoon: "It's come to my attention that you have a life outside the office." © Copyright 1992. Reprinted with permission of Leo Cullum, Sandhill Arts.

Leo Cullum cartoon: "They say the early forties is the new late thirties." © The New Yorker Collection, 2005. Leo Cullum from cartoonbank.com. All rights reserved. Reprinted with permission.

Pantheon Press: Excerpt from *Bird by Bird: Some Instructions on Writing and Life*. © Copyright 1994 by Anne Lamott. Reprinted with permission of Pantheon Books.

Perseus Press: Excerpt from *On Listening*. © Copyright 1976 by Carl A. Faber, Ph.D. Reprinted with permission of Carl A. Faber.

The Radio Store: Excerpts from *Write Good Copy Fast: The Broadcast Professional's Guide to Writing Effective Copy for Direct Advertisers*. © Copyright 2003 by Maureen Bulley.

Foreword

Opinions regarding the future prospects of broadcast radio have been, to say the least, mixed, if not disconcerting, in recent years. Traditional radio's popularity and audience shares have taken a hit as the result of the rollout of satellite and Web radio, and the most significant impact on the fortunes of the eldest electronic mass medium has come from music downloading. Young people have been abandoning music radio in droves in favor of their MP3 and iPod players. These recently evolved audio services have taken considerable luster away from over-the-air radio, and station consolidation has added to its listening audience's disenchantment as well.

Critics claim media conglomeration has bred more sameness on the radio dial and has fostered an intensification of commercial clutter. Many of these same detractors point to the decline in localism in favor of voice tracking and music playlists originating from faraway studios as yet another reason for terrestrial radio's mounting woes.

However, to paraphrase Samuel Langhorne Clemens, stories in the press about radio's so-called death have been greatly exaggerated. The "talking box," as radio legend Fred Allen once called it, still claims more listeners in an average week than all of the new audio technologies combined, and then some; but this does not mean that broadcast radio can rest on its fading laurels. The contrary is true. It is an undeniable fact that the medium's audience numbers are eroding, and if it treads water (as many contend it has been doing for a long time), it will lose its dominance and end up as just another store in the burgeoning audio mall. Indeed, radio is not dead, nor is it moribund, but it is in need of some major first aid by talented professionals who have a genuine passion and appreciation for the medium and the expertise to restore its flagging health.

Enter Valerie Geller. Never has the medium needed someone with her vision and knowledge more. For years she has been reinvigorating stations around the globe by focusing on the development of on-air talent—radio's eternal mainstay—as well as by providing dynamic workshops on creativity in programming, news, promotion, and sales, among a host of other areas. In nearly every instance, her extraordinary consultancy has resulted in vastly improved ratings. Valerie knows radio and knows how to help it realize its fullest potential, and that is what the medium needs to do in an audio marketplace that is more competitive than ever. The challenges confronting broadcast radio are greater than at any time in its one hundred year history, which is saying a lot, because the medium is no stranger to challenges.

In this new and vastly enhanced edition of *Creating Powerful Radio*, the reader will find a comprehensive and incisive schematic for achieving success in every aspect of station operations. Valerie Geller provides professionals and students alike with an invaluable resource at a time when radio is about to transition to digital. A new age of broadcast radio is upon us — one that will require great communicators, programmers, and managers more than ever. Toward that end, this book constitutes a precious tool.

— *Michael C. Keith*

– Michael C. Keith PhD, served as the inaugural chair of the Broadcast Education Association's Radio Division and is an associate professor in the Communications Department at Boston College. He is the author of twenty books, including "Voices in the Air," "Talking Radio," and "Sounds in the Dark" and "The Radio Station," from Focal Press.

Acknowledgments

It is impossible to thank all the people whose friendship, insight, and talent have helped nurture, develop, and inspire this work. I am deeply grateful to those who have generously shared their ideas, wisdom, and experiences.

There are no words to thank my editor and friend, Turi Ryder, without whom this book would not exist.

Special thanks to Doug Harris and Maureen Bulley, both of whom created extensive sections for this book in their areas of expertise.

Many thanks also to contributors Michael C. Keith, Lee Harris, Sean Ross, Mike Sugerman, Jim Chenevey, Warren Levinson, Michael Haas, Dave Ross, Sharon Katchen, Phil Hendrie, Mervin Block, Scott Shannon, John Catchings, Lynn Jimenez Catchings, Denise Jimenez Adams, Christine Lavin, Howard Price, Bob Christopher, Sheri Inglis-Schmickl, Jerry Bell, Dan Vallie, Bernard Gershon, Mackie Morris, Jaye Albright, Tom Zarecki, Guy Zapoleon, Randy Lane, Denise McIntee, Alan Eisenson, Lorna Ozmon, Deborah Potter, Tommy Kramer, June Barnes, Kelli Grisez, Ed Walsh, Michael Hedges, Susanne Whatley, Scott Borden, Andy Beaubien, Jeremy Millar, Mike Siegel, Mark Howell, Dave Sholin, David Baronfeld, Ross Brittain, Matt Siegel, Caroline Feraday, Sam Litzinger, Pam Lontos, Matt Hudson, Steve Apel, Pat McCrummen, and Robert Unmacht.

And personal thanks to Melissa McConnell Wilson, J. Ruth Gendler, Anne Chaabane, Dr. Linwood Hagin, Dr. Adele Scheele, Kate McCallum, Elizabeth L. Dribben, Laurel Ornitz, Carol Archer, Jeff Neuman, Don Barrett, Marie Sandgren, Marian O'Brien, Gillien Goll, Christine Henrich, Rhonda Funes, Ron and Alice Lando, Bonnie Aylesworth, Wendy McLeod, Scott Adams, Colman Adams, Simon Adams, Nic and Becky Gaunt, Dr. Evian Gordon, and Doug Kaplan.

Finally, a sincere thank you to all my client stations and to the talented broadcasters, around the world, who have taken these ideas to heart, have believed in this material, have risked much, and have succeeded by using the methods in *Creating Powerful Radio*, currently and in years past.

Introduction

One of the curses of radio is that it seems so easy. Everyone can talk, so everyone thinks that they are experts at radio and that just about anyone can do it. And the great on-air personalities always make their shows look effortless. But creating *powerful radio* that will get, keep, and grow audiences is very hard work. It takes craft, skill, desire, and training. If you have the desire and the talent for this work, this book will teach you methods that can help you succeed.

It has been well over a decade since the first edition of *Creating Powerful Radio* was published. At the time, I had no idea that it would find its way around the world. It was mostly intended for my clients as a sort of "written summary" of ideas we'd worked with to get stations and air personalities up to the next level. I wanted to leave them with something tangible and permanent that would last after a Creating Powerful Radio Workshop was over—something to avoid that "back-to-normal slump" that hits a few weeks after the consultant leaves. But *Creating Powerful Radio* has become so much more than that. It has served as a calling card in 27 countries at more than 500 stations, all of which have increased listenership by learning and working with the book's methods. It has helped thousands of broadcasters and students in dozens of countries with techniques to get, keep, and grow audiences.

The Creating Powerful Radio techniques work in every language and every country because they are based on the common denominator of human connection and communication. The three basic *Creating Powerful Radio* principles are: Tell the truth. Make it matter. Never be boring. The way you create powerful radio is a highly personal effort. Your show is unique. No one can tell you how to do it. You have to find your own way.

Wherever you are in your broadcast career, this book can help you. It is intended for people at every level of broadcasting whose jobs are to face the blank page and create compelling programming using their personalities, listening skills, and powers of observation and communication.

The nature of radio is to capture and chronicle. Much of its power comes from its immediacy. Powerful radio holds up a mirror and *reflects* life as it is at the moment. Broadcasting stays interesting because, just as in life, it is in a state of constant change.

Since the first edition of *Creating Powerful Radio* was published, satellite delivery and digital technologies have emerged that let us work cleaner, faster, and better. The Internet also plays a bigger role in broadcasting. But no matter the delivery system, there will always need to be a story, *and* a storyteller who makes it matter.

If you have a copy of the first edition, you will find that this is a completely updated and revised book, with several new chapters based on what I've learned from working with the Creating Powerful Radio techniques over the years. I've also asked some people whose work I respect to contribute to this edition of *Creating Powerful Radio*.

You'll find much more on talent development and airchecking and see expanded sections on creating powerful news, show prep, producers, on-air performing, selling, and effective promoting and marketing. You'll also learn more about your audience, how they react to and take in information in new chapters on Research and LifeStage Demographics.

A colleague of mine, David G. Hall, once paid me a very high compliment when he said: "This is the book I wish someone had given me when I first got into radio." So, here it is in writing. Do your best. Make it count. Learn the techniques. Don't waste a moment of it.

If you would like further information about Geller Media International or the Creating Powerful Radio Workshops, contact:

Geller Media International
Phone: 212-580-3385
Email: vgeller@aol.com
www.gellermedia.com

CHAPTER 1

Creating Powerful Radio

"The experimental test of whether this art is great or good,
or minor or abysmal is the effect it has on your own sense
of the world and of yourself. Great art changes you."
— *Art historian Sister Wendy Beckett*

"Art is accusation, expression, passion."
— *Gunter Grass*

Sitting on a shelf or in a car dashboard, it's merely a box full of wires and silicon chips. It may or may not look handsome, the outward appearance gives little indication of the magic contained within. The radio is clearly one of the most ingenious devices ever created, yet to understand its power fully, it may help to view radio with primitive eyes.

You may have heard the story of natives in Papua, New Guinea, who, upon seeing and hearing their first radio, demanded to see the little man inside. A magic man, obviously, to fit inside so small a box. In the Pidgin of Papua, radio is in fact known as "Bokis, he cry," or "the box that cries." Primitive, perhaps, but accurate in a philosophical sense.

The radio is a magical extension of the human spirit. It can "cry out" and make a listener feel, laugh, and think. Powerful radio rings true and evokes a reaction. It also makes the listener want to keep listening in the hope that this will happen again.

Radio is very, very personal. People no longer sit around in groups listening to it. Today, much listening is done alone, almost in secret, through headphones, computers, or in the steel-and-glass-enclosed privacy of a car.

One by one, the listeners are hunting for that connection, that powerful magic which is often missing from radio today. Watching an average listener punch through the buttons on the car radio is proof of that. One station after another is rejected. Many of these stations are simply unknown to the listener. In the United States, often the entire AM band is unknown to the listener. Once that magic contact is made, listeners won't go unless given a reason to leave. Your job as a radio professional is to entice the listener through the radio door, and then keep him or her coming back. This calls for powerful radio.

What is powerful radio? "I always know it when I hear it" is the answer most programmers give when asked to define it. But when asked to break down the specific elements, they often cannot express it in words.

In working with stations around the world, I've noticed that certain common threads run through each great radio moment, whether on satellite, HD, online, or on terrestrial radio. First, the audience must care about what is said. It must matter to them. It must touch their lives. The content or topic must reach them in a real and true way. And the topic can never be boring, or the audience will tune out.

Before anything goes on air, ask yourself:

- Is it *relevant*?
- Does it *matter*?
- Do you *care*?
- Do your *listeners* care?

While it may be the music or the news that first touches a listener, I believe the richest source of powerful radio comes from the personalities of the performers.

The key to personality radio is, logically, having a personality. This means having a rich, full life and drawing on all of your experiences. How you relate to life is how your audience will relate to you. The best broadcasters are great observers of life. They filter what they see going on around them through their unique creative process, and send it back out to the world. They talk about what they see, notice, think, and feel. They share their *real* selves. They mention what irritates them, what excites them, what saddens them. They react honestly to the news, current events, and the music they play. They are good storytellers.

If an air personality is doing the job right, audience members will feel that they are being addressed individually. The words "Hello, everybody" or "Good morning, St. Louis" will likely not be heard. The listener should feel that the person behind the microphone is like a friend. The air personality won't seem like a star but more like someone they would know in real life—a person with daily struggles, life experiences, and problems. Humor helps. You don't have to be a funny person to recognize a funny moment. This is a key element in creating powerful radio.

The points in the list on the following page are a basic recipe for Creating Powerful Radio. You will read more about each of them in the rest of this book.

Every element of Creating Powerful Radio relates back to these ideas. You can apply them to all facets of on-air work, including music presentation, talk shows, news, commercials, public service announcements, promotions, and more.

Let It Grow

Even the most powerful radio programming will take time to build an audience. Growing tomatoes takes a certain amount of time. So does building a news-talk radio station. Music stations tend to grow a little faster. Obviously standing over the tomatoes yelling "hurry up" is futile. Though it may seem ridiculous, it's amazing how many people expect that approach to be effective with creative talent and sales. Managers and owners hate to hear this, but in my experience, with few exceptions, it takes about three years to build a talk station.

The "overnight success" of Los Angeles Talk Station KFI is a good example: In 1988 every single bus board in traffic-infested Southern California was plastered with KFI ads. You could hear the station playing everywhere. People were talking about then-newcomer Rush Limbaugh. The *Los Angeles Times* printed six huge cover stories in its entertainment

Valerie Geller's Guidelines
for Creating Powerful Radio

- Speak in terms your listener can "picture." Use details. Describe the little things so your audience can "see" what you are talking about.

- Always start your show with something *very* interesting. This ought to be obvious but often isn't.

- Tell the truth. Listeners can tell when you don't.

- Never be boring. If you are bored, your audience will be too.

- If something big or important is happening today, go with it. It may be a pain to change your program or reschedule a guest, but it's worth the trouble.

- Listen to your station, even when you are not on.

- Make your program matter. Use your own life as a show resource. Always answer: "Why is this on air? Why should someone listen to this?"

- Bury the dead. If a topic is overdone, drop it.

- If you are live on-air, anything goes! But anything pre-recorded should be perfect.

- It is okay to brag about your stuff—if it's good. Promote it.

- Brag about other people's stuff. If another host on your station had a "magic moment," talk about that too.

- If you don't know something, it's okay to say so. Actually, audiences love it when they sense that you are like them.

- Do smooth and interesting segue-ways and transitions to other hosts and shows. Support them sincerely.

- Be who you are on the radio.

- Risk. Try things. Dare to be great!

section about the various KFI hosts. Still the numbers hardly budged. Former owner Cox Broadcasting persevered. The company had spent money on programming, talent, promotion, and an award-winning news department, so they hung on without making major changes. Three years, or about a thousand days after it signed on, KFI became an "overnight success." Years later it remains one of the most listened to news-talk stations in the USA.

Give It Time

It is appalling to observe various local stations and networks hire and fire an on-air personality in haste if the show is not a "two-book wonder." One of the problems with our industry is a lack of commitment to talent on the part of management.

Brain researcher Dr. Evian Gordon writes, "It takes a thousand times of doing a repeated behavior to rewire the human brain to change a habit," including changing the listener's habits. Building an audience for both talent and a format is a process. It is tempting to pull the plug if results are not immediate, but a little patience and consistency can go a long way toward success.

The original *Star Trek* TV series was canceled after just three seasons, because it had "failed." It took reruns for the audience to discover the starship Enterprise and get hooked on the show. *Star Trek* in television spin-off shows, movies, and books has been breaking records for decades.

American comedy star Jerry Seinfeld exhibits a framed memo from NBC-TV declaring that the initial research on his then new situation comedy showed a weak response, a poor supporting cast, and that most viewers who had seen the test pilot would not want to watch it again. The network ordered only four episodes. But somebody had faith in the series, and it paid off with years of success for the network. Broadcasting is filled with stories like these.

If you can create quality programming, and consistently stick with a host, program, or format over the time it takes to find its audience, you will likely have your own success story.

CHAPTER 2

Creating Powerful Radio
Finding and Developing Talent

"Sometimes when you are leading [an expedition] you have
to say whatever you can to keep people on your side. It
doesn't matter if people believe what you say or not. They
need to see you believe it. That's what leadership is about."
— *Philip Kerr (on leadership and mountain climbing)*

Where Do We Find Tomorrow's Talent?

In her novel *Star Country,* Jill Robinson suggests that "star potential," or
raw talent, is easy to spot: "Long before the fame hits, the star's the different one. The leader—or the weird one. The motor's there. You want to feed
off it; use its heat."

The stars of broadcasting share certain traits. Genuine talent are true
individuals, gifted storytellers, and good listeners, as well as articulate communicators. They have original thought, intelligence, and passion. These
people have a spark of life and a sense of humor. They get a kick out of
things. They burn with curiosity. Some have a formal academic education;
all have a lot of life experience. These are people who naturally connect
with others—individuals with ideas and things to say. They tend to be a little
ahead of popular trends. They have a strong need to be seen and heard.

Developing talent, product, and content requires another element: faith. There must be someone on staff—a manager, producer, or programmer—who has the ability to find the right people and bring them into the fold. The ability to recognize talent is a talent in itself.

General managers and program directors would love to have a crystal ball they could consult to find out which personalities will work and which will flop. But there's just no way to do it with a new person the public has not experienced.

Take a chance. Give a talented prospect a shot on the air. Make it a weekend or fill-in slot. See how he or she sounds and trust your instincts. Don't pull the plug too soon. If you believe in a talent, hold on, even if not everyone in the building shares your belief.

A tip that can save you two ways: Never judge the talent on just one show. A talented host should be versatile and able to switch from light to heavy topics. I once heard a guy do a pretty decent show on the right way to hang the toilet paper. The next day he was interviewing the Secretary of State. It's just as important to know that the quality is consistent even if the topics vary wildly.

Finding Talent

Station managers constantly complain that fresh, up-and-coming talent is hard to find. Where are the syndication superstars of the future? Because talent is born, not created, how do we spot it? Then how do we develop and keep talent once we have them?

Despite the spectacular growth of syndicated and satellite radio, only a handful of people have developed at the network level. Most successful national talent started on a much smaller scale, with daily or weekend shows in small to medium markets. When network talk or music shows are given to individuals who don't have much training or talent, they usually have some degree of fame, particularly in politics or acting. A lot of programmers get seduced by using a "big name" to draw an audience. Usually, this doesn't work out. Most successful hosts are people with strong backgrounds in radio. They've worked hard to learn their craft and often make the job look easier than it is. That illusion of ease is one of the reasons many managers think they can put any famous person on the air and have him succeed.

As more and more stations turn to syndicated programming, there is concern that the smaller-market, "farm team" method of growing tomorrow's talent is disappearing. Using a syndicated show may be cheaper in the short run, but developing your own talent can pay off down the line in ratings, revenue, and goodwill.

Programming executive Denise McIntee has years of experience finding and developing new radio talent. She advises:

> Be on the lookout for colorful characters in your everyday life. Ask friends, business associates, relatives, and neighbors. Often, they can tell you about an obscure cable-TV host on at 4:30 in the morning who was totally entertaining, or a local stand-up comic who had the patrons in stitches. Teenagers are a valuable resource as well. They hear about the latest trends or hottest acts about a year ahead of everybody else.
>
> Radio stations are loaded with born entertainers, and not just the people on the air.
>
> Look closely for the [off-air] employees who are surrounded by staff when they walk in the office. These are the people everyone looks to for entertainment. Their electricity may translate onto the airwaves.
>
> Sadly, most programmers will not give an audition to anyone without an established track record or who has not honed his or her craft in a smaller market. These programmers lack confidence in their ability to discover a "diamond-in-the-rough."

Sometimes looking at the people working or just "hanging around" your radio station can bring big benefits. I have found and developed radio personalities who literally landed on my doorstep. At WABC/New York, we did a huge, nationwide talent search, looking for somebody fun, interesting, topical, and loaded with personality. I listened to hundreds of tapes from all over the country and auditioned several people. None of them proved right for the specific profile of the station we were building.

When our afternoon call screener/board operator expressed interest in hosting a show, no one took him seriously. Then we talked to him. He had studied acting at Yale and had a real feel for radio and a wonderful ability to do impressions. He could sing and write parody songs, was original and creative, and was up on current events. He was also funny. His idol was the afternoon host, for whom he was running the board. We tried him out. He was hilarious. The show was a success.

Syndicated host Lionel was a lawyer who called talk shows. He was so talented, verbal, and funny that the PD of a Florida station gave him a shot on the air. He wound up drawing such huge audiences that he was offered a job in New York.

Another example is TV and radio personality Danny Bonaduce, a former child actor from the popular 1970s TV show *The Partridge Family*. Chicago air personality Jonathon Brandmeier had a regular "Where Are They Now?" feature on his show. Brandmeier located Danny Partridge, alias Danny Bonaduce, in Danny's own words, "broke and starving" as a maitre d' at an L.A. restaurant. Brandmeier thought Bonaduce such an engaging personality that he helped him land a radio shift. Watch for talent wherever it presents itself.

Real-life characters are another way to jazz up your show. Include interesting folks from your community in your on-air cast. Many of the big morning show hosts in America have made "stars" out of peculiar people they encountered in real life. Brandmeier got enormous mileage out of "Piranha Man," a Pakistani immigrant who operated a donut shop. "Piranha Man," with his thick accent and his foreign ways, was endlessly amusing, but he also helped to familiarize other Chicagoans with a rather misunderstood ethnic group. "Piranha Man" eventually had his own theme song and even came out with his own line of cologne.

One BBC station in England has used a New York City taxi driver, "The Gabby Cabby," to keep listeners up to date on what's going on in America. His reports deal with pop culture, weird people, and odd occurrences. How did the station find this guy? He's the cab driver who happened to pick up a visiting British program director.

Another station uses a former flight attendant as their regular consumer/travel expert. Twice each week, she gives her humorous inside tips on the travel industry, and like the cabby, she's developed into a genuine station personality. "Rita from the Beauty Parlor" is another "found" personality. She's funny and spirited. Rita reviews movies, gossips, and gives advice about love and relationships, all based on what she's learned while doing women's hair.

Don't exclude people who might be considered mentally ill. As it's known in politically correct circles, their "alternative reality" can offer a refreshing change from the everyday reality the rest of us have to deal with. If a listener insists that he is Napoleon, and seems sincere, give him a chance.

You can find unique characters everywhere. The only requirements are that they have lots of personality, are fun, and are good talkers. I've found talent in all kinds of unlikely places. I've worked with bartenders,

teachers, musicians, writers, scientists, lawyers, doctors, university profes-
sors, pet groomers, athletes, pro-team coaches, priests and ministers, cops
and housewives, all of whom had personality and original things to say.
Even those who did not work out were worth a try. The moral is: Always
be on the lookout for talent everywhere, from the experts who make guest
appearances on your station to the life of the next party you attend.

What to Look for in a Talent

So how do you get on the talent development track while continuing to
provide a decent level of programming today? There is no easy answer.
Asking experts in the field for help and advice is one way. Many PDs use
the weekend, fill-in, or late-night shifts to find and develop people. Another
tactic is to steal promising talent from the competition. Don't worry if your
prospective host isn't perfect. Allow faults to show. That's what makes
people interesting. Author Anne Lamott could easily be writing about air
personalities as she describes the traits of narrators in her book *Bird by
Bird: Some Instructions on Writing and Life*:

> A person's faults are what make him or her likable. I like [for narrators]
> to be like the people I would choose for friends, which is to say they have
> a lot of the same flaws as I do. Preoccupation with self is good. As is a ten-
> dency toward procrastination, self-delusion, darkness, jealousy, grovelling,
> greediness, addictiveness. They shouldn't be too perfect. Perfect means
> shallow and unreal and fatally uninteresting. I like for them to have a nice
> sick sense of humour and to be concerned with important things...politics
> and psychological and spiritual matters.

Look for people who are unique, bright, and articulate. Find good listeners, with strong personalities and opinions and a variety of interests about
which they are passionate. Most have a sense of joy and humor and are
big readers. Often they are rebels. They should be fascinating. Sometimes
they are angry. These are the "odd ducks." They can talk to anyone about
anything. Most of all, great personalities possess a quality that is at once
indefinable and compelling. Some call this quality the "X-Factor." Can you
remember the last time you stood shivering in your towel in the morning,
but couldn't turn on your shower because you *had* to hear what was
coming next on your radio? Find people who can make you do *that*.

Humor has a place on your station. You might be surprised to find that humor has a place on every radio station. You do not have to hire funny people, just people who have a sense of humor. It is important that your staff and your station have an appreciation for the odd, the strange, or the quirkier aspects of life. Moments of levity can be found in topical stories, news, or issues. Even the most serious news programs save a "kicker" or feature for the end of the newscast.

Hire storytellers. See if you can find someone who can tell a story three times, three different ways. Because many broadcasters work with subject matter that may not change very much over the course of days, weeks, or even months, they must be able to vary their storytelling. This keeps it interesting to an audience familiar with the material. It is as if you told your spouse a story. That night you have dinner guests and you tell the story again. The following day, you retell it to a friend over the phone. Your spouse has now heard the story three separate times. However, if you managed to vary your anecdote with different details or a new approach, it was not boring. If you have people on the air who can do this, you have the makings of a great radio station.

Finally, hire smart people. And when *you* find youself looking for work, try to find the smartest people you can and work for *them*. If you are just learning broadcast management or any other aspect of the broadcast business, apprentice yourself as you would in any other field, from medicine to plumbing. Learn from the best—it will set a standard for you.

Right Casting

It is important when you have assembled a stable of on-air talent to make sure that each one is positioned to achieve maximum success. In my work, I call this "right casting." Understanding right casting is vital. If you were a movie director, you would not cast Arnold Schwarzenegger in the part of an old, bald, chemistry professor. He could play the part, but he is better playing his "strengths."

Once you've decided that someone has what it takes to be on your station, you still have some assessing ahead. I have found that talent tends to fall into one of two categories; you can read about them in Chapter 3, "Generators and Reactors."

Knowing the type of performer you have lets you guide toward his or her maximum performance. The programmer or manager is then able to design a powerful radio program by building a show around the strengths of the personality instead of trying to do it the other way around by stuffing your performer into a role that does not fit. Broadcasters also need to know what roles they play best when they are looking for work. As a manager, the first and maybe best thing you can do to help talent do their jobs well is to make sure they are correctly cast and given the tools they need to work effectively.

Managing Off-Air Staff

Most people get angry at anything they perceive as unfair. Radio is definitely a business in which, as George Orwell writes in *Animal Farm,* "some animals are more equal than others." A lot of radio performers are, at least on a local level, "stars." They get treated differently, with a lot of extra privileges. They are stars because of their talent, and talent is not distributed fairly.

It takes many people working behind the scenes to support a star. Some people would be better off going for an on-air position in a small market rather than working in an off-air capacity in a large one, because their need to be the star is huge. Others are far happier remaining out of the limelight.

Lots of people are drawn to this business and take supporting jobs until they can be on the air, but until that happens, they need to be at peace with the job they are doing. A producer, glaring across the booth and thinking, "I know I could do this show so much better" is not likely to be helping your program.

Management can compensate for some of the attention that gets directed to the star, but is really owed to the supporting cast, by acknowledging the cast members directly. Still, if you have a chorus line that is miserable not being in the main spotlight, they will be angry and dissatisfied and will do your station very little good.

There is nothing wrong with ambition, but the people you hire must have the talent and desire to do the job they are currently doing. When they have mastered that position and are eager to move up, managers owe it to them to look at whether or not they would now be well cast in another job. If such a position is not immediately available, give them the option, even the assistance, to move to another situation where they would be better able to fulfill their goals.

Radio is a highly demanding business. Often the hours are long and the pay is low. It would be nice if one could staff a station entirely with workaholics, heirs to large fortunes, or those who never need to go home. Many jobs in broadcasting really do require huge amounts of time and commitment. If you enjoy your job, but it never seems to be over, you might find that other stations set up their staffs differently, hire more people, and pay them better. It may not be the type of work you are doing that is causing you difficulty, but rather where you are doing it. In other words, you could be correctly cast doing the same job somewhere else.

Right Person, Wrong Show

Sometimes a talent has what it takes to succeed but has been put into a situation that is holding him or her back. Perhaps it's the venue that's to blame. Not everyone is right for every job. The talent may be GREAT, but the setting or the city or the station is wrong.

One example is funnyman Jay Thomas, a talented DJ and actor who never achieved substantial ratings in New York. But when he moved to Los Angeles, he became a top music radio personality.

The first incarnation of the *David Letterman Show* was actually in the middle of the day. It didn't work very well, but the folks at NBC felt they had *something* and the show metamorphosed into the hit *Late Night with David Letterman* show. Less resolute managers might have thrown Letterman on the heap of former TV talk hosts. Believe in talent and take the risk.

Part of the right casting is learning the abilities of each performer. Do not expect a serious interviewer or journalist to go on the air in morning drive and be a comedian. That is not the nature of the individual's talent. Right casting is also about risk. Allow talent to fully realize their roles even if, occasionally, they go to the extreme. Do not be upset if your funny, childlike jokesters make the occasional inappropriate remark. They are exploring the limits of the roles in which you have cast them.

Right Casting and the Passion Quotient

You and your staff should be listening to the station on your own time because you like to and because you are proud of it. Many managers who have moved up through the ranks of sales sometimes do not understand that although all on-air talent enjoy earning a good salary, their sole motivation is not always strictly a financial reward. On-air personalities are strongly motivated by the chance to do creative work and perform for an audience. So when you are thinking about whether you or your staff are rightly cast at your stations and jobs, look for passion about the station, its place in the community, and the audience it serves. A talent who does not like, respect, or value the listeners is not likely interested in working hard to get more of them.

Though most people have to work to earn a living, many broadcasters, if offered their same career track again today, say they would pursue it, even knowing in advance about the hardships and obstacles ahead. In fact, if asked how their jobs could be improved, other than with additional financial rewards, most on-air talent I've met list ways their show could be improved and the station could be promoted.

Meet with your staff. Ask each: "If I could offer you something to make your job easier, what would it be?" Those with a passion for their work often come up with ways they could do the job more efficiently, or better serve the listeners. They may surprise you. The following is from a news director's actual wish list: "Poor newsroom lighting and a dearth of natural light are creating lethargy. Proposed Solution: Reworking the lighting and hanging some drapes could improve the work environment and pay off in a more energized staff."

Notice this news director's commitment to the quality of product and the well-being of her staff. She is successful in part because she feels strongly about doing a good job with the tools she is given—just the sort of person who is right for her job.

By the way, it is possible to kill an employee's enthusiasm by consistently saying "no" to small but practical solutions to real station problems. Wherever possible, say "yes" and build passion for the station and your product.

Find out why each member of your staff *wanted* the job he or she now has. The answers may prove enlightening. While some may have thought broadcasting would be an easy paycheck, others fought hard for a chance to be part of the station or on the air.

A lot of prestige and power comes with our titles. It sounds good to be able to say, "I am a journalist" or "I run a radio station." The actual work is another matter. Did you become a program director because you thought that was the next job to take after hosting your own radio show and now find that you miss being on the air every day? You may have lost some of your passion for this work, due to wrong casting.

If you became a manager because you were offered a promotion and now find yourself in sales meetings when you would much rather be working with talent and marketing, your station is losing the benefit of a great PD who cared about the creative side of the organization.

Even if you have the most successful morning show in town on your station, if a DJ is burned out, or exhausted from getting up at 3:00 a.m., the numbers will soon reflect that. Keep checking in with your staff to make sure they are still happy. Just because all was well three months ago doesn't mean that everything is fine today, especially if there have been changes. For example, a member of a team show may have gotten a lot of inspiration from his or her co-host but may not enjoy working with the new partner.

There are a lot of reasons people choose a broadcast career. Perhaps in the beginning a DJ liked appealing to the opposite sex, seeing the country, and the music he played. But today, that same man is married, owns a house, and cannot bear listening to the music on his playlist. Clearly, as people grow and change, the challenge for a manager is to make sure they are cast in a role that is suitable for who they are today. That Top 40 DJ might be better cast playing hits on an Oldies station or Gold Format, or hosting a talk show.

Consolidation of broadcasting properties has made it easier to hang on to good people. Frequently, it's just a matter of moving someone to the sister station in the studio across the hall to rekindle their passion for the work.

Someone who likes to write comedy and create clever parody songs may end up producing commercials for mattress stores. The payoff for this person could have been when clients and sales people request his or her spots because they work so well. If that is the case, as a manager, you should also make sure that you are spotlighting your staff's achievements by submitting work for awards and industry commendations. But if that same production director envisioned being part of a morning team and is utterly miserable putting his or her creativity to use in a more anonymous and isolated setting, all the awards in the world can't substitute.

It is possible that a few modifications would make somebody's job right again. This may be as simple as hiring an assistant for a production director who feels overwhelmed or finding the right co-host for an uninspired morning host. Maybe a change of daypart would enable a presenter to relax and rejuvenate with a favorite hobby in off-hours, bringing new life to his or her show.

One newsman I know takes several weeks off, with the blessing of the radio station management, during hunting season. When he returns, his work always improves. Another example: An album rock music host who was also a serious mountain biker was allowed to change shifts in order to have more daytime hours to pursue his passion. He enjoyed the change so much that he went on to organize station cycling promotions, which have benefited the station and several charities.

It is also possible that someone is incorrectly cast not because he or she cannot do a job, but because he or she does not wish to do it. If you notice an employee speaking longingly of a position you never thought he or she would want, ask the employee why it appeals.

At stations around the world, and at the "Creating Powerful Radio" seminars, people ask how they can tell whether they are rightly cast. The shortest answer is: That which comes easily to you is probably what you do best. How much of that do you get to do? Do you have many perfect days at work? What is a perfect day at work for you? Is there an opportunity to do more of what appeals to you in your present position?

As a manager, you would do well to learn these things about your staff: What comes easily to them? When do you notice them having the most fun at work? Where do they struggle? These are areas that each host, manager, and programmer should look at from time to time.

Right Casting for Everybody

Just as many fine actors also produce and direct their own award-winning films, you can have natural ability in many areas. So the question becomes what do you like to do best? How do you determine which job at a radio station is right for you? How do you find which shoe "fits your foot"?

How do you know if you are rightly cast in your current role at a station?

- If you look at the clock all day long and find the minutes inching by, perhaps you are not rightly cast. If you are a manager, ask: Do you like to manage others? Do you get as much satisfaction from someone else's good work as you do from your own?

- If you are on air or producing but you find that directing and developing others is fun, perhaps moving from on air to management may be the right casting for you. There are no rules. Though you can be successful either as a performer or manager or both, it's often easier if you focus on and develop one area.

How do you know you are on the right track?

I cannot say this often enough: The skills that come easily to you are probably your strengths. But there is also a danger. Just as an opera fan who sings in the shower and joins the community choir may not have been blessed with a beautiful voice or perfect pitch, it is a sad but true fact that some gifted broadcasters waste years of their lives trying to make themselves something they are not. Sometimes the thing you love to do, or admire most in others, is not where your actual strength lies.

In her book *The Vein of Gold,* Julia Cameron explores this journey of discovering what you do best. Cameron quotes director Martin Ritt:

> All actors have a certain territory, a certain range, they were born to play, that is their "vein of gold." If you cast an actor within that vein, he or she will always give you a brilliant performance. Of course you can always cast an actor outside his vein of gold. If you do, the actor can use craft and technique to give you a very fine, a very credible performance, but never a performance as brilliant as when he or she is working in his or her vein of gold.

Here are some questions for broadcasters to consider, to help you decide if you are rightly cast in your current job.

Talent

When it comes to your show, are you more comfortable playing it safe than taking chances on the air? Do you worry about looking foolish?

Superstar performers take a few chances. If they spent a lot of time being anxious about their images, they would miss opportunities to be great. It takes bravery to risk looking silly in front of an audience, but your listeners appreciate courage even if you fail. If the thought of looking undignified petrifies you, perhaps you should try something safer.

Talent and Managers

When there is a mistake on the air, is it always someone else's fault?
Who is to blame for sloppy on-air presentation?

Successful talent take a lot of responsibility for their shows. If something goes wrong on the air, they do not throw up their hands, blame the equipment or the producer, and give up for the rest of the hour. They dump the boring guest, look up an expert's phone number, or carry the microphone down to the street. In short, they have courage to do whatever it takes to achieve a quality air product.

If the station has no budget for newspaper and magazine advertising, successful talent buy their own. If the station cannot afford a piece of equipment, motivated employees go out and find a sponsor who is willing to provide the product on trade. An executive producer I know once organized a collection among the staff to buy a much-needed piece of recording equipment. A manager went to the pharmacy and bought medicine for an ailing newscaster. A program director once told me, "I'd get down on my knees and shine (the host's) shoes if that would help him do a better show."

In a well-cast broadcasting scenario, if something goes wrong, each person involved, from the program director to the call screener, comes up with an idea of how he or she could help make it better the next time. If you are not willing to take responsibility for your product, ask yourself why you are doing this job.

How afraid are you of getting fired? Does that motivate you?

Everyone has a boss. If you live in fear to the extent that you are not willing to risk management's displeasure, you may be miscast. It is important that you feel strongly enough about your freedom to try new ideas on behalf of your station, your show, or your staff. You must be willing to incur a little fallout once in a while. Sometimes, the powers-that-be must be obliged, but there should be a little give and take here.

If you are immobilized by fear of losing your job, you should ask yourself the next question.

If you did lose your job, how easily do you think you could find another one?

If the answer is that you could not easily replace this job, then you may need to express your creativity in other ways. Technology has made it easier to do some of the work of our business outside of a radio station or broadcast facility. Many hosts, producers, and sales people have studios and offices in their own homes. That has cut down on some of the need to become a migrant worker for the sake of a broadcasting career. Still, if having to make sacrifices in the form of a move, pay cut, lifestyle change, etc., is something you are not willing to do, then seek out a job where you are more properly cast.

Managers

Are you willing to risk? Do you feel uneasy when you hear the format being broken?

If you know that nine times out of ten your format is going "out the window" for a good reason, then you are demonstrating the kind of flexibility that can come only when you have confidence in your air staff and are comfortable with your job.

Talent

Do you feel ruled and restricted by the station's format clock, or do you feel you have enough control and discretion to structure your show according to the needs of the moment?

If you are able to work within the confines of your format, yet have enough leeway to pursue the occasional "magic moment" or news emergency, you are probably working with supportive management in a role that fits you.

Talent/Producers/Management

Do you ever get ideas for somebody else's show or feature? If so, do you usually share them with the talent or keep them to yourself?

If you can pass material along or be of assistance, you are demonstrating courage, leadership, and a generous personality. You have a vision of the total health of the station. You are a team player. This attribute would serve you well either as a manager or as a member of a team show. You might do better working with a few other performers rather than flying solo.

Talent

Do you have total control of your show?

Almost nobody has that, unless you own the station. But, your goal should be to leave the studio each day feeling: "That was me. That was what I wanted to do on the air today." If you finish your show feeling as though you executed somebody else's agenda, with no personal stake in the outcome, you are probably miscast.

Managers

Do you feel you or your producers are constantly forcing ideas on the talent? Do you feel you must hold the reins tightly to ensure that he or she will do a particular type of show every day? Do you feel you are in a wrestling match with the talent for control of the show?

If so, you are controlling the show out of fear the talent is inept, or you are trying to put a square peg in a round hole and the talent is miscast, or you would prefer to do the show yourself.

Talent

Do you believe the work you do matters?

Having a microphone is not something one should take for granted. Because aspects of the job can become routine or mundane, it is easy to forget that listeners are giving you their most valuable resource—their time. There is a commitment on the part of the broadcaster to offer information, entertainment, inspiration, or whatever your station has promised to provide.

Talent/Managers

What is the best thing about your manager? What is the worst thing about your manager?

If you make an honest inventory of your manager's good and bad qualities, you may find that your job is better than you thought it was. What seems like an unsatisfied boss may actually be someone who is working very hard to bring you to the next level of performance. He or she may see potential where you see none. Although you might feel miscast in a certain job, you may be there to learn skills for the next position your supervisor has in mind for you.

However, you are probably miscast if you feel that your manager is the radio police, if he or she consistently makes you do things you don't want to do, or you work in fear of being caught making a mistake.

Managers

Are you proud to sell this product?

Would you be just as happy selling something more tangible or less contro-versial? While running a broadcasting operation gives you prestige, it also makes you a target. If you would be more comfortable managing a differ-ent type of company, give yourself permission to move on.

Managers/Talent

Finally, everyone should ask: Do any jobs at the station, other than the one you now have, seem interesting to you?

If they do, why not learn them? There are always vacations, emergencies, and fill-in opportunities. You may find another area of the business that is a better fit for you—one where you would be better cast.

If radio does not fulfill your need to be heard and to express yourself creatively, if it drains rather than energizes you to create something new on the air each day, if you find you are upset or tired of taking irate calls from a community leader or offended politician, there may be some other work that might be more suitable.

Most creative people have a lot of artistic abilities, and radio may not be the right creative venue for you.

Similar Goals

Part of right casting is making sure that your goals and the station's objec-tives work together. Broadcast consultant Andy Beaubien puts it this way:

> As much as personalities would like to think that their show is their own exclusive artistic responsibility, it is nevertheless part of the station's overall effort. It ultimately must satisfy the station's goals. If the personality's goals and the station's goals are out of sync, the result will be frustration and bitterness on both sides. In almost every case where there is a seri-ous problem between management and an air personality, the underlying cause is usually a conflict between goals or, to put it in the language of the trade publications, "philosophical differences."

Talent may also have philosophical differences with the audience. That is fine in many cases, and some talent build careers by flying in the face of convention, but it can be a tough road. Does this mean you should alter your true self to keep your job? Programming consultant Jaye Albright speaks from experience when she says: "Radio does reward the craftspeople who most accurately reflect the current cultural realities. If you can find it within yourself to respect the prevailing value system, while still being true to your own unique creative voice, you may be more successful."

Tips for Finding and Developing Talent

Radio can be taught, but talent is rare. If you find the real thing . . . MAKE THE HIRE!

1. Look for talent in nontraditional areas.
2. Make your choice and then stick by it.
3. Don't pull the plug if you don't see immediate results.
4. Have faith.
5. Motivate the talent with honest feedback and encouragement.

CHAPTER 3

Creating Powerful Radio
Generators and Reactors

"It's not what *you* say, it's what *they* hear."
— *Red Auerbach*

Putting Your Personalities in Power:
Are You a Generator or a Reactor?

Have you ever noticed that some on-air personalities, while they may be completely professional, are somewhat boring by themselves? But the minute someone else walks into the studio, they seem to come alive and get much better. Some personalities seem more talented when they are performing live in front of an audience. Others are funnier, sharper, and more creative by themselves. It turns out that talent usually falls into one of two categories, *generators* or *reactors*.

In order to coach talent effectively, it helps to identify the talent's strengths and natural abilities. Sometimes that can be achieved by clearly defining the talent's roles. Consultant Dan Vallie advises, "There must be an anchor or director, a creative chief, a producer, etc." But before you define the role, knowing the type of performers you are working with lets you guide them toward their maximum performance. The programmer is then able to design powerful radio by making the shoe fit the foot, instead of trying to do it the other way around.

What Is a Generator?

The natural skill of the generator means that he or she can easily work alone or as part of a team. A generative talent visualizes original ideas. A generator has a strong, independent imagination. The generator comes up with a myriad of topics, undaunted by the blank page.

What Is a Reactor?

Reactors are also creative individuals. A reactive talent takes existing ideas and comes up with numerous ways to make them better or more workable.

No less talented than a generator, the reactor nonetheless has a very different style. A reactor alone faces the blank page with terror. However, the moment a reactor comes in contact with a generator, he or she can instantly and very cleverly pick up on remarks, comments, or nuances and be very funny.

A reactor is usually the one who responds to just about any stimulus with an insightful or witty remark. Reactors can have a lot of fun talking back to their TV sets and radios. Reactors work best with other people in the room to spark their creative energy.

Both types of talent are valuable and good, but the right casting here is the key. Forcing a reactor to carry the show as a generator doesn't work, and forcing a strong generator into an equal or subordinate partnership with another generative talent can lead to an almost painful on-air clash. The trick is to identify each person's specific strengths and then to encourage the person to develop those strengths.

Putting two generators together as co-hosts or as a team can sometimes be a disaster. They tend to battle for the microphone, seldom listen to each other, and compete for attention. The show sounds like two kids fighting at the dinner table. It is hard to listen for very long.

Putting two reactors together is not much better. The audience hears them casting a net for ideas over and over again. The process is dull, and, if nothing swims into the net, the show becomes weak and boring.

Electric connection with the audience happens when you have a balance of both elements.

How Do You Tell the Difference between a Reactor and a Generator?

It is fairly simple. Generators have a lot of ideas and energy. They take huge risks and worry about it later. They have moments of brilliance. They sit alone in a room, and their minds overflow with ideas.

That is not to say that every idea a generator produces is a perfectly conceived show, but consistently they seem to be practically exploding with new material.

If you are looking at a reactive talent, you will notice that he or she is quick with a story, a memory, an imitation or a line for any topic you could give him or her. But you must lead the reactor by giving that first push, that suggestion, or a good opening. Leave the reactor alone in a room with no external catalyst for the show, and he or she is miserable. Reactors may do brilliant interviews, or pick things out of the newspaper that are unique, but they need some kind of initial stimulus to begin the process. You probably have a reactor on the air if he or she is dull until the news person shows up.

Generators are scarce. Most people are reactors. It is a little like being left- or right-handed. One is no better than the other. If absolutely necessary, right-handed people can adapt to use their left hands, and vice versa. You can certainly force people to improve in the area where they are weaker, but in most circumstances, it is best for the station to take advantage of their natural inclinations.

A Cast of Dozens

You might think it takes a generator to host a morning show. That is not always the case. One reactor, "Casey," found a cast of generators in his listening audience. "Rita" owned and operated a local beauty salon. She was also Casey's loyal fan and listener. Rita started calling in on a semi-regular basis to chat about hot movies and goings on around town. She was funny and charming and had unique views. Rita became a regular on the show. The listeners started calling in wanting to meet Rita. She participated at station events and appearances.

Next, Casey added another regular listener, a talkative cab driver. Then he found a local construction guy with fix-it tips, who also happened to be twenty-eight, dating regularly, and happy to talk about his adventures.

Casey continues to add appropriate players as they appear. He now has a winning show with lots of generators to show off his reactive talents. He assembled his own generator-reactor team.

As a manager or programmer, it is your job to identify each person's specific strengths and then to encourage each one to develop those strengths. Once you know who your generators and reactors are, you can get onto the business of creating powerful radio.

CHAPTER 4

Creating Powerful Radio
Performance and Formatics

"To escape criticism—do nothing, say nothing, be nothing."
— *William Teacher*

"If you bring forth what is within you, what you bring forth
will save you. If you do not bring forth what is within
you, what you do not bring forth will destroy you."
— *Jesus*

Performance

Now that you are on the air on a regular basis, you know what hard work it really is. When you listen to the radio, you notice people who sound spontaneous. They make their work look natural and easy. It seems these people never make a mistake on the air, or, if they do, you hardly notice, or the show takes an unexpected twist and gets even better.

Then there are broadcasters who seem pained and uncomfortable when things go astray. It can make you very nervous to listen to people reacting to a situation that way. How can you make sure you sound like one of the naturals?

The difference between accomplished professionals and talented neophytes is that the seasoned air talent always give you the feeling that they are in control, no matter what happens.

This skill can be learned. The people you admire on the air have mastered some basic techniques that carry them through the most difficult situations. Their experiences—successes as well as failures—are what make them so adept now. You cannot avoid some of the unpredictable aspects of this business, but you can learn reliable techniques to improve your show. You can escape certain traps by practicing a few elementary performance points, and there are things you can do to "self-correct" should the show begin to take a turn for the worse.

Performance Points

1. Pick Topics about Which You Really Care

A great talent or personality can make selecting a sofa interesting. Boring people, on the other hand, could ruin a conversation about the discovery of human life on Pluto. If you are interested, you will make it interesting.

2. Use a Strong Show Opening or Monologue

Be sure to do the following:

- Focus the topic.
- Engage the audience by forming a question.
- State your opinion or position on a talkable topic.
- Explain your view through example, experience, or storytelling.

Do not read entire prepared speeches. If you must read on air, do not *sound* like you are reading.

3. Never Be Boring!

Get rid of dull guests *immediately*. Remember, if you are bored, it is boring. If a guest starts out great, or was selected as an expert, but in fact turns out to be stiff, too nervous to think clearly, or is in any other way noncommunicative or inept as a storyteller, get rid of that guest.

How often have you checked your watch when a guest is talking, or have taken a mini-vacation in your head? If this is happening, try a few direct questions calculated to raise the energy level in the room. If that does not help, dismiss the guest.

If this is a problem for you, have a prearranged signal with your producer just as couples do at parties. News people can be sent in waving copy. Anything that allows you to shove a dullard out the door is fair. Make a transition, and immediately try doing something else.

Remember, you are probably more interesting than a boring guest. Be flexible and protect your air product. If the guest is great, keep him or her with you longer.

Why Is Getting Rid of a Boring Guest So Difficult?

It is surprisingly hard to speed the departure of a guest because we are trained from childhood to consider the feelings of others. As professionals in polite society, we do not wish to be rude. But it is ultimately better to be abrupt with one guest or caller than to be impolite to an entire listening audience, boring them because we feel uncomfortable cutting off the discussion. The audience is under no obligation to be polite to you, the host. They feel free to leave if things get dull.

What if the expert is in the room staring at you, expecting to go on the air for the full show?

With live radio, it is especially difficult to ask the tough, meaty questions or to cut off a boring guest if that person is in the room. Do it anyway. You should not have promised a guest more than a few minutes of airtime. Your producer can explain the show's "policy" on the matter.

It is easier for some hosts to exercise the "cutoff" switch if the guest is on the telephone rather than live in the studio. Try sacrificing a little sound quality by using a phone connection if this makes it easier for you to end an interview. One famous American host has created an environment designed to simulate the listener's experience. She places the guest in another studio, without eye contact, so that the conversation relies solely on listening and verbal communication. You may find there are some advantages to conducting an interview this way.

4. Don't Take Calls Just Because They're There

Program director Alan Eisenson has rules for guests and callers. He says, "Guests and calls are simply tools for the host to use to make a better show.

I would rather hear a strong air personality than boring callers or guests. It is up to the host to determine when a guest or call gets boring. Some guests could be great for three hours and others are only good for five minutes. Some callers could go on for five minutes, but are only worthy of five seconds. A good host and producer should be able to tell the difference and pace the show accordingly. Only use callers to enhance the show."

Talk personality Turi Ryder's theory is that many "callers will make their point, then begin to make it a second time if left unchecked. The trick as a talk host is to get them off the air when they finish their best material, before they say: 'just one more thing' and before they start to loop around again."

5. What If the Interview or Topic Goes Wrong?

Sometimes you ask a wrong question, or don't frame your talkable topic/ engaging question well. If you are not getting the desired response, perhaps it is time to change the story or example a little, or recompose the question to engage the audience differently. Do not be afraid to reset your topic going into or coming back from a break. But do not repeat your topic exactly. Add something new.

6. You Can Change Your Mind

Your opinion may change. As Alan Eisenson points out: "Views may change as an issue evolves over days or weeks. Do not be afraid to change your opinion as more facts become available or if a caller or guest per-suades you with a strong argument to change your mind. Do not stick to your guns if you find you are wrong. Remember, always tell the truth. And don't be afraid to admit you don't know something. You're not expected to have all the facts about every issue all the time."

7. Take a Risk on the Air

Sometimes you head into a danger zone with a comment, view, question, or decision you make about what goes on the air. Understand that not everything you say will be popular, even if you feel it is true.

A lot of what you can get away with depends on your relationship with management. Even more depends on your level of success. Proven personalities can get away with much more than an unproven talent or new arrival.

If you know you are heading into a controversial or "gray" area, some-times it is better to ask permission from your boss. A powerful show is not one where a host lives in fear of getting the axe. *Note to Managers:* If a talent calls you and lets you know he or she is about to move into a potentially dangerous topic, make a decision. If you need to take a moment to consult a lawyer, or another manager, do it quickly.

Is it better to beg for forgiveness than ask for permission? That depends. Trust your instinct or gut feelings, but try not to hold yourself back from potentially powerful moments. Do not be so afraid of failure or getting into trouble that you lose your spontaneity and sense of discovery, risk, or adventure on the air. Live radio is a live experience.

Radio executive Mel Karmazin always backs top multi-media performer Howard Stern. When they worked together at CBS radio, no matter what Stern said, if he "crossed the line" and got the network into trouble, Mel Karmazin paid the penalty fines. As a manager, Karmazin believed in Howard and liked the profits generated from the show. He understood that talent cannot be restricted. If you want the great moments, you must assume some risk.

At this point many stations have increased their "delay" time and have someone standing by with a finger over the "dump button." Since stations frequently make their on-air product available via alternate delivery systems, such as satellite or computer feeds, talent are less likely to get upset if a few seconds of their shows are deleted from over-the-air broadcasts once in awhile.

In America, there is often greater concern over offending special interest groups than over the occasional expletive that may slip out. Either way, great talent who have strong management backing them up will have a better chance of surviving and achieving success.

The best managers behave honorably. As a manager, if you tell your talent it is OK to do a certain type of show, you are honor bound to live by that commitment until you mutually agree to change it. Do not fire talent for your mistake. If you say, "Go ahead and speak your mind, create discussion, we do not mind controversy," then be prepared for the consequences. Your phone will ring constantly with angry listeners. Your mailbox will be filled with hate letters. Fifteen people may march in front of the station, threatening to boycott your biggest advertiser, and your spouse may be embarrassed to tell friends where you work. If you are not ready to live with that on a day-to-day basis, *then do not hire people who do those types of shows.*

Talent will occasionally do things you would rather they had not done. However, not all talent live on the cutting edge—most operate somewhere between the safe and the daring. But the more artistic and creative the talent, the greater the risks that artist is likely to take. The payoff can be enormous, but it may cost you your serenity and security.

In Chapter 22, Airchecking, you'll find various examples and methods of guiding talent to say what they want to say while generating less hostility or controversy. It is best to establish a line of communication where managers know what is happening and can choose what fights to support. Managers do not like unpleasant surprises.

8. Use Your "Off" Switch

From the wisdom of consultant Jaye Albright, "Master the use of the most difficult piece of equipment in the control room: the 'off' switch on your microphone. Practice moderation. Learn to recognize when a bit is over, and stop talking at that point."

9. The Day You Wished You'd Stayed in Bed

Not every show will be your best show. Even your favorite air personality has the occasional bad day. Sometimes you just can't hit the ball, no matter what you do. Your rhythm may be off, or you may not be feeling well.

When you had a show that did not work, it is important to do a quick analysis. Look for an easily identifiable reason why your show didn't work: Not enough sleep? Hungry? Inadequate show prep? A fight with your former spouse just before you went on the air? If it is fixable, fix it. Do it differently next time.

Perhaps you simply did a poor job of it. There are two things you can do: you can choose to pick it apart over and over and beat yourself with the aircheck, making yourself feel terrible, thereby ensuring you will do a worse job tomorrow, or you can let it go. Regular listeners who like you will forgive one bad show. Tomorrow someone will be listening who has never heard you before. That person will not know about today's bad show. Forgive yourself and move forward.

10. Treat the Staff You Work with Respectfully

Whether you know it or not, they have a lot of impact on your performance. The station's staff can help you or sabotage you in a million ways. A miserable team will cost you more than you think.

> "Art lives from constraints and dies from freedom."
> — *Leonardo da Vinci*

Formatics

Listeners like formatics. They provide structure, like the walls of a house. People want to know to whom and what they are listening, and they like to know what time it is. Jaye Albright says:

> For most of us in most situations, formatics are absolutely essential. They are like "the blocking and tackling" exercises of our sport. And, as in the NFL, where spring drills begin with the statement, "This is a football," before you dispense with formatics, you must execute them naturally, flawlessly. Formatics are all about memorability, habit, and familiarity. It is these things that make ratings, unless your content is constantly superior and compelling.

For a programmer, making sure the formatics are properly done is the easiest part of an aircheck session. The aircheck tells all. If anything is missing after a performance, follow it up in the session. Call attention to it and make it a goal for the next session. Sometimes new talent do not understand the importance of formatics to ratings results. Explain the necessity of getting this part right. As long as ratings are counted by recall, this is one element of success that is up to each host.

It makes sense to do everything we know to win. Repetition stimulates recall. It is that simple. Your station will be marketing itself to advertisers with hard data about website visits, store traffic, etc. Make sure you are doing your part by giving the information you are asked to communicate.

Overcoming Resistance

Programmers around the world share a common frustration and ask the same question of talent: "Why don't you simply do the formatics as you are told? How hard can this be? We have talked about this over and over again!"

Talent says: "You care more about call letters and time checks than you do about content! A monkey or a robot could do formatics. I am an individual. I got involved in what was happening at the moment."

Some managers take it too far and become obsessive about the number of call letter and dial position mentions. Although it is my belief that you can never say the name of a station enough times, New York City program director and personality Scott Shannon makes this important point: "Great stations are not built on hot clocks and contests, they are built on heart."

Why rebel with formatics or forget to do them? The reason is that many on-air personalities do not believe it is important. Because *they* already know who they are and where they work, it becomes boring to them to repeat their name and the station's dial position and call letters.

If the talent does not understand the absolute importance of formatics, they will not be a priority. Ask talent to imagine how they would feel if someone heard their show in a cab and wanted to listen again at home, but couldn't, because they couldn't remember the station's dial position and call letters. Not giving your call letters is like asking someone to find your house when you have no street sign or address out front. It is to everyone's benefit if talent understands how listeners listen. Make it clear that the audience has a short attention span and often uses radio as background. As a last resort, if a talent continually forgets to do formatics, try helping out with produced elements.If you have ever listened to a radio show and wondered, 'Who is this person and who is he talking to?' you understand the need for resetting and formatics.

Credit Where Credit Is Due

I once consulted a station with famous, historic call letters. Everyone associated with it was proud to work for this radio legend. They assumed that people were familiar with their station. Many were, but most of their actual listeners seldom heard the call letters or station name and had trouble remembering where they were tuned.

We increased that station's ratings 70% in one ratings period by saying the call letters and the name of the station every time we took a call, gave the time, started the news, opened the microphone. I would love to say we added 70% to our listening audience, but the truth of the matter is, we simply made it easier for people writing in their Arbitron diaries to remember where they were tuned. You can never say the call letters or the name of the station too many times.

Be responsible for eliminating what Arbitron terms "Phantom Cume"— i.e., those people who listen but can't exactly remember the dial position, Internet address, or name of the personality or of the station. Every fifteen minutes you are judged by what the diary keepers write down. That means *every fifteen minutes* hammer home:

- YOUR NAME
- NAME OF THE SHOW
- NAME OF THE STATION ("The Talk Station")
- CALL LETTERS AND DIAL POSITION

Repetition is the way we learn and memorize. Think of television's *Sesame Street.* Repeat and repeat and repeat until the audience learns it.

Talk-Radio Formatics

Each format in radio has a slightly different structure. They all have one thing in common: Your listener should never feel the pressure you feel to execute formatics correctly.

Never Let a Listener Feel the Format

Don't use "radiospeak." Try not to use those words and phrases you say only when you are in front of a microphone, e.g., "segment," "this program" or "forecast." Try to keep your formatics as natural-sounding as possible. Always answer the question, "Why should someone listen to this?" Only mention the "clock" if there is a benefit to the listener.

If you say: "Here's your traffic on the eights," it is helpful because the audience needs to know that you are keeping your promise to bring them traffic every ten minutes. You may also have a break at twenty minutes past the hour, but listeners should never feel your formatic restrictions. That's our problem, not their problem. They don't need to know when it's time for us to take a commercial break.

The structure of your show is there for a reason, mostly to market your station. But listeners care only whether it is interesting or relevant to them. Your audience should simply feel they are spending time with you.

For talk radio, the structure is more or less like the one Alan Eisenson uses:

- Open the hour with your name, the time, and the call letters.
- Do some short opening comments, if you have any that day which may or may not be your main topic.
- Launch into your monologue, i.e., engage the audience with your opinion/position and storytelling.
- Ask the question. This is your tightly focused topic.
- Give out the phone numbers.
- Take a break, using proper formatics: Use the term "up next" instead of "take a break."
- Open the flood gates (the phones) after your first break.
- Reset the topic by asking the question going in and out of each subsequent break (again, using proper formatics).

Resetting and Teasing

Radio Computing Service's Tom Zarecki spent years as a programming consultant. He says:

> Since new people keep tuning in, the host needs to frequently recap guests' names, what group they represent, and showing how the topic is interesting to a listener. Keep teasing upcoming show segments or features. Waiting five minutes in a drive-time interview to recap what's going on, or only teasing once or twice an hour, is simply not often enough.

Formatics do not have to be dry and boring. If you do them well, they can become a creative and exciting part of your show.

Formatics Tips from Consultant Tommy Kramer

Be sensitive to repetition. A good talent varies the way everything is done. The listener wants consistency but not predictability. Even if positioning phrases or branding should require that things be said in the same words all the time, the talent can still vary the inflection of the words. Repetition becomes boring quickly and is also an indicator of the deadly "automatic pilot" mentality that can bring down a talent or a station fast. Do your part. Keep the talent energized by pointing out good examples when they occur, or freshening things up that may have become tired sounding.

Here are more specific ways to use formatics to engage your audience from Tommy Kramer's *Coaching Handbook*.

Pull the listener into the radio with you

If you say "It's 72 degrees out there" you tell me, the listener, that I'm out there and you are not out there with me. You are somewhere else. In reality, I am in my car or at my desk and you are with me when I am listening. Why push me away? I've heard talent in Fort Worth [a suburb of Dallas, Texas] say "over in Fort Worth." Why? Just saying "in Fort Worth" will say it without distancing yourself from the Fort Worth listener. Avoid saying anything that pushes the listener away.

Sell the benefit

Always sell a benefit of the show or station. "Soft easy favorites" is not a reason for me to listen to you on my way home from work. What is the benefit to me? But "soft easy favorites to make your drive home easier" gives me a reason to listen.

Use real language

What is more effective? "For further information and details, call 456-1111" or "You want to know more? Give me a call." How about, "It's just about forty-five minutes after the hour of twelve o'clock." Would you ever say that if I asked you what time it was? Wouldn't you just glance at your watch and say 12:45? Talk on the air the way you talk in life.

Connect with the listener

Tell me—don't read to me. Let your language and manner pull the listener into the radio. Newsman Paul Harvey writes about a dozen key words on a card, and tells you the story.

The rule of one

Do one main thing per break. Obviously, you need to identify the station and/or music, give the time and whatever your station's "formatics" are, but do that stuff briefly and then do the one thought you set out to do this break.

Hit the target

Many stations find it helpful to draw up a specific profile of your listener, complete with a picture if possible. Post it in the on-air studio. Speak to that one target listener every time the mike opens. Say things that will appeal to and interest him or her. For instance, if it is a soft adult contemporary station, you might not want to dwell on the hockey scores. And keep it singular. Do not say, "If some of you listening would like to go…" Instead say, "If you want to go…" Always talk to one listener at a time and aim at the target.

Promote ahead

Promote anything of benefit coming up on your show. Be truthful. Instead of "I'll have tickets to give away in a few minutes," try "This hour, you will have a chance to win James Taylor tickets!"

If you tell me something is coming up in a few minutes and I only have twenty minutes until I get to work, I'll be mad at you if you don't get to it by the time I shut off the car radio. But if you tell me it's coming up within the next thirty minutes, and I only have twenty, I won't hold it against you. Never promote anything as, "coming up after the break." That is like saying, "I'm going away now."

Don't tell the listener what to think

It is irritating. "Here's one you'll really like" (How do you know? What if I don't?) or "You'll have a great time" (What if I have a lousy time?). Tell me that you like it and why (or why some people like it). Let me decide for myself. You may know the Chinese saying: "Tell me and I'll forget, show me and I may remember, but *involve me* and I'll understand." We do a lot of "telling" on air, which never seems to work as well as finding the way to "involve" your listener in your subject or topic.

Sell the dream first, before you give the information

In advertising, they say, "Sell the sizzle, not the steak." Seek an emotional link with the listener. Help me see why I want to win before I have to hear all the junk about how to do it. If you do not make me want what is being offered, there is no reason for me to care about all that technical information.

Have a road map

Know how you are starting. Have a destination in mind. Know how you are ending. Move on to the next element.

Often a talent takes way too long to get to the point. We have all heard breaks like: "WZXT 99 with Elton John and *Rocket Man* from 1973. You know, he's done a lot of great work over the years and this one is definitely one of the all-time favorites. Now let's go to the phones—Jennifer's on line three. Let's find out what her most embarrassing moment was. Jennifer, how are you this morning?" Tighten it up, cut to the chase! "WZXT 99 with Elton John. Jennifer is on the phone. Jennifer, what was your most embarrassing moment?"

How to edit phone calls

Keep the unnecessary parts of the calls off the air. "OK, Jane, thanks for calling in today" or "Thanks for having me on, taking my call," and other superfluous stuff does not need to be on the air. It is boring, slows momentum, and no one cares. Instead identify the station and keep to the point, "Jane you are on Sunny 98.5. What weird gift did you get on your birthday?"

Reset the stage

Adopt an egg-timer attitude, and every couple of minutes briefly reset the stage for anyone who may just be joining the show. (One talent coach I know actually leaves a fifteen-minute hourglass on the studio console.) If the listener cannot quickly get what is going on, he or she might choose another station. If I tune in and hear "Florida's winning coach Steve Smith on Sports Radio 540, The Team,"…this morning, I won't feel confused. Let the new listener know which voice belongs to which person and what that person's role is! "Celluloid Mike, our film critic is here. Mike, what should I take the kids to see this weekend?"

Break the habit of "taking a break"

Please do not use the word "break." It comes from TV, where they regularly *do* stop the action and break away from programming to do other things. But because everything on your radio station is a part of your total format, you are almost never "breaking away."

Do not "break now for the news." Each time you tell the audience there is a break, they think that they, too, can "break away." The whole show is yours. That includes sports, news, and anything else inside your show. Stations are rated not only on how many listeners show up, but also on how many listeners stick around. Try something along the lines of "Let's find out what else is going on. It's 6 o'clock and you are listening to WXXX. News is next." Do not throw away a single minute of your airtime, even if your station requests that you give a standard introduction to other elements. The mark of a professional is the ability to make every word his or her own.

Don't panic if you need a moment

Have you ever heard someone on the radio chattering aimlessly, verbally casting about for clarity of thought or direction? That talent has likely been taught to "keep the meter moving. Whatever else happens, keep talking."

However, that fear of "dead air" can provoke meaningless, manic episodes that will actually lose your audience. Do not be afraid of a moment of silence. The listeners will understand, and it beats the alternative. Do not panic. Take a pause if you need a few seconds to collect your thoughts.

Taking a moment of silence can also become a tool. Veteran New York radio host Bob Grant learned this trick and often paused for a few seconds after stating a powerful message to get the listener's attention. Grant, among others, learned that nothing can get the attention of the listeners more quickly than a second or two of "dead air."

Content Plus Formatics Equals Ratings

In addition to your content and style, here are some talk-radio basic formatics that can make a difference and get you ratings.

Before Each Break

- Remember to tease what is coming up or reset your talkable topic or engaging question.
- Involve your audience. Use a cliff-hanger to keep them coming back for more, staying through a break, or just listening longer.

After Each Break

Briefly reset your topic. A reset should include:

- Your name
- Dial position
- Topic: Ask your focused question or tease—preferably one that everyone listening to will have a burning desire to answer.
- Phone number
- Time check (if relevant)

    Example: "In case you've just joined us, it is 6:21, I am James Johnson and you are listening to WXYZ AM 690. Our guest is supermodel Christie Christensen, talking about her new book, *Sleep Your Way to the Top.* What do you think about using sex to get your job? Call us at 666-8255."

At first, working with formatics is a struggle. Aircheck yourself regularly. Keep practicing and you will notice improvement. When someone comes up to you in the hall and says, "You make it all sound so easy," you will know you have mastered formatics.

CHAPTER 5

Creating Powerful Radio
Morning Shows

*"An artist's working life is marked by intensive
application and intense discipline."*
— John F. Kennedy

Why Is the Morning Show Different from the Rest of the Day?

Morning drive is traditionally the most listened-to daypart in radio. It starts the day, commands the highest ad rates, and requires the most up-to-date information so the listener can get out the door and face the day. A solid morning show can set the foundation for a solid radio station. On music stations, morning drive is the last bastion of personality radio.

Most stations come up with the basics of traffic, weather, music, news, and sports scores, and other elements that drive a morning show. But what is unique to each show are the *hosts* and *personalities*. That is what the other stations cannot duplicate.

"Toothbrush Radio," or "I hate to get up in the morning"

A favorite research survey asked people in a Midwestern American city about their morning routines. The purpose was to look at listener needs, i.e., how each used his or her time in the morning, in order to improve programming during morning drive.

This survey showed listener habits. The list on the next page shows what that study found to be a "typical morning routine" for a "typical listener."

Of course, habits vary, and the list is a sample composite, but the research did show that people are creatures of habit and *rarely vary* from their personal morning routine. Based on my years of experience, here is an analysis of listener's morning habits:

Attitude

- People do not like to get up in the morning. They are tired, groggy, and do not feel like hopping out of bed on a dark, cold winter morning if they do not absolutely have to.

- People feel that from the moment the alarm rings to the moment they get to their jobs, they are on their boss's time, not their own. Many people do not love their jobs and there is resentment of the morning rush. Because of this, humor on the radio in the mornings is especially important. If you can make a bunch of grouchy, groggy people smile or laugh when they don't feel like moving, you can keep them listening!

Reality

- If the radio gets boring, there's more to choose from. Listeners tune out and turn on TV in the background. TV has gotten smarter, too. Those morning or "breakfast" shows now offer all the elements a radio show has—with the option of pictures.

- People want and *need* to know what time it is. Yes, they do have clocks in every room and some even wear watches. But it is easier if the radio tells you every couple of minutes what time it is so you know if you are on your morning schedule or running late.

The Routine

5:30 a.m. – the alarm clock rings

5:45 a.m. – the snooze alarm rings

5:50 a.m. – actually get up

5:51 a.m. – go to bathroom

5:55 a.m. – start coffee

6:00 a.m. – feed dog

6:02 a.m. – enter shower

6:08 a.m. – shave/brush teeth/blow dry hair

6:20 a.m. – drink first cup of coffee, look at newspaper headlines

6:21 a.m. – listen for weather report

6:32 a.m. – wake the kids

6:35 a.m. – get the kids in and out of bathroom/get dressed for the day

6:58 a.m. – feed the kids and eat breakfast

7:15 a.m. – pack lunches

7:25 a.m. – organize the kid's stuff for school and various other activities for today

7:30 a.m. – organize your own stuff for the day
Find kid's lost item

7:35 a.m. – final house check, grab jacket, check for wallet, cell phone, keys/lock door/out

7:40 a.m. – drive to work

What They Need

- When people wake up to face the day, they need to know basic information: What happened while I was asleep? Did anything explode? Are we fighting World War III? Can we drink the water? Is it safe to go out and pick up the newspaper? What will everyone be talking about today at work? If I don't have time to read the paper this morning, I still don't want to look like an uninformed fool. What can I hear on the radio that will put me a bit ahead of my colleagues?

- Give the time and weather a lot; listeners want to know: How cold is it out there? Where are my boots? Do I need a raincoat? Do I need an umbrella? How do I dress my kids? Will it take extra time to get to work?

More Reality

People are creatures of habit. Personally conservative, they do not like changes at any time, least of all in the morning, when they are tired and cranky.

Powerful Morning Radio

Up the pace, not the volume, for morning drive. Move it along. The people listening now are in a hurry and don't have the time to get deeply involved in long, in-depth interviews or ongoing sagas.

Understand your listeners; less is more in the mornings. But make what you do *count*.

Mornings are when show prep and planning your time on air matters the most. Your awareness of the brevity of the listener's attention span in this daypart is key.

Air personality Jonathon Brandmeier explains his method for a successful morning show: "I break my show down into hours. Every hour should be a different show. If you continue something you did from 6 to 7 all the way until 9 to 10, the guy from 9 to 10 just waking up doesn't know what you're talking about."

Small Packages

Consultant E. Karl wrote in his report *State of the Art*:

> In the morning, if you get your listeners listening for an average of fifteen minutes an hour, you're doing pretty well. So, look at each hour as a package that has four fifteen minute shows in it. . . . Each segment [should] contain all of the key elements you would have in any one whole hour of a morning show, e.g., entertainment, music, news, weather, and the other services.

Remember, it's important to

- Prepare

- Read everything

- Make it matter

- Have things to say

- Be real

- Have fun

It's Hard to Get Up in the Morning

Don't mention how tired you are. It's your job to get the listeners out the door with your morning show, to motivate and get them going. If it is already a drag to get up early and get out, the least you can do for people is give them some help in facing the day. Maybe they'll feel better about it because they heard your show. And don't get too wired on coffee. Frenetic energy makes people nervous.

What *Time Is It?*

Give the service elements a lot: time, weather, traffic updates and quick news headlines. Give people what they can use both now and during the day.

Morning drive radio is the place where music radio and talk radio most intersect. Here are some thoughts and ideas from those who know what it takes to create a powerful morning show.

Boston morning man and air personality Matt Siegel offers the following points, important in Creating Powerful Radio, no matter what your format or daypart:

What It Takes

- *Be Honest.* Praise what you like . . . rip up what you hate . . . don't lie for the sake of a joke. This is how the audience gets to know you.

- *Use your own life as a source of material.* It's amazing how the audience always seems to know what's real. If they don't get to know something about you, they won't be loyal.

- *Be funny.* Don't forget you are entertaining them. This is radio, not therapy.

- *Be specific.* Name names—your wife's name, your boss's name, your friends' names, etc. That's what makes it real, thus scary, thus interesting. (In my opinion it is better to use a pseudonym or leave out identifiable details. Be aware of the rules about slander and libel and the possible legal ramifications when naming specific people, companies, products, etc., in your show.)

- *Be vulnerable.* Say something that you think might be inappropriate or a little personal. Be a grown-up. You can play the latest teen band's hit song and you can talk about the artists, but if you act like you are 18 when you are 35, you sound like a jerk.

- *Don't put women down.* It's cheap and you are better than that.

- *Be nice.* No matter how far you want to go, no matter how wild your act is, let the audience see something in you they like or, eventually, you will start to annoy them.

- *Don't be a wimp.* If you think it's funny or important, say it. Stop looking over your shoulder.

Ross on Radio

Edison Research and Programming consultant Sean Ross has worked as a program director and record company executive. He writes a weekly column as well. Ross's thoughts on Creating Powerful Radio are valuable for programmers and morning shows of any stripe.

Sean Ross's Top Ten Tips for Powerful Radio

- *Program for yourself.* Despite all the dogma about thinking like a listener and not a radio programmer, if you don't enjoy the product yourself, how can anybody else?

- *Use your special gift.* If you are going to do something anybody else can do on the radio, why did they need to hire you?

- *Some of those old wives were pretty smart.* Do not reject the "old wives tales" of programming out of hand. A station will not live or die if there is a power record out of the stop-set, tempo at the top of the hour, etc. But it WILL sound better.

- *When you become the 800th person to defy a cliché, you're not defying a cliché.* If your taxi driver is really a natural, put him on. But if 799 others have already cluttered the airwaves with local politicians, punk rockers, and orthodontists, a good DJ will be just fine.

- *Hire writers.* Only somebody who can write is going to be able to sell the same record, the same contest, the same crossplug thirty-seven times and do it thirty-seven different ways.

- *Yes, talented people ARE supposed to be difficult.* But don't waste your time on anybody who abuses the privilege.

- *If you are lucky* enough to be working in live and local radio, use the station you now have to do great local radio that entertains or touches the listeners with every break.

- *You gotta believe.* The world is full of successful stations with no money, bad signals, etc. Clearly, nobody told them they had a problem.

- *Don't use the signal to hurt people.* There ARE listeners who will let their dog eat dog food out of their mouth to win concert tickets if you insist on searching them out. It's no big deal to them, because many folks with REAL jobs endure degrading existences anyway. But wouldn't you rather make people feel better than feel stupid? The latter takes a lot more talent, especially now.

- *Every generation's music will become an Oldies format someday.*

American music industry icon Dave Sholin is a legendary disc jockey, program director, executive, and editor. He has helped a lot of budding young talents become more powerful broadcasters. Sholin figured out early on that the secret to success in radio is to be yourself.

Dave Sholin on Creating Powerful Radio

- Always keep in mind the first eight letters of the word "personality": P-E-R-S-O-N-A-L. Whether one million listeners or one hundred, each one should feel that the conversation is being directed to them.

- Trendiness has a short shelf life. Reflecting trends is quite different from embracing the flavor-of-the-month approach.

- Origination always beats imitation. Allowing unique and likable qualities of your personality is the goal.

- Don't feel the need to be funny on every break. Forced humor often sounds that way.

- Try and avoid the echo technique, repeating what the caller just said.

  Example:
  "Hi, who's this?"
  "John."
  "Well John, where do you live?"
  "Hillview."
  "Oh, Hillview, etc. . . ."

- Don't be afraid to push the envelope and try different or improper techniques. Though batting a thousand is unlikely, play the percentages.

- Anyone in a music format needs to remember that the music is the star. Leave the negative personal opinions at the door. The songs must be great; otherwise, why play them?

- Become an expert on the varied interests of the local community. Get connected to those in the know. Before mentioning any well-known local figure or local town, make sure your pronunciation is correct.

- Less is more. The fewer the words, the greater the impact.

- So-called rules should be considered as guidelines. In some cases, they need to be twisted or broken.

Air personality Ross Brittain has been on stations around the country combining humor, heart, and reality with an edge. This list comes from his days of doing mornings on Z-100 in New York.

Ross Brittain's Tips for Jocks

- Over-prep the day before.

- Do the things your listeners do.

- Make things bigger than they really are. Use theater of the mind— produce BIG or overproduce.

- Structure your breaks BEFORE the mic opens. Use Post-it notes to remind yourself.

- Remember your audience composition when building in features.

- Don't get caught up in "information overload." DELEGATE!

- Cluster your commercials correctly and clean up your talk breaks to avoid clutter.

- Speak concisely. Edit copy or write down important items so you won't get lost. Remember to use your sense of forward motion to move, or not move, your show.

"That's not __my__ political opinion. That's just stuff I hear on the radio."

CHAPTER 6

Creating Powerful Radio
From Rock to Talk

"The great 'end' in life is not knowledge but action."
— *T. H. Huxley*

In the United States, it's been a long time since the truly "Full Service" radio station disappeared. Most in the United States have only heard of, but never actually heard, a station where music, interviews, news, sports, and personality call-in segments were equal parts of the programming day.

Not only that, even the highly formatted stations have narrowed their focus into subcategories of their genres. For example, in talk radio there are "Hot Talk" stations, "Lifestyle Talk" stations, "Truck Talk" stations, Political Talk stations (which includes its own sub-genre, some political station formats are geared toward either the left or the right wing), Sports stations, Religious stations, and Women's Talk stations, just to name a few. With the advent of high-definition, online, and satellite radio, formats now target audiences in ever greater detail, and the trend is likely to continue. If a "full-service" station appeared today, it would probably be researched and designed to fit that small subsector of the listening audience who have been determined to need nightclub music, political polling data, volleyball scores, and agriculture reports.

In music-based formats, personality elements tend to be restricted to morning drive, or have been done away with altogether. Morning shows tend to be filled with so many commitments—news, sports, commercials, business reports, traffic, weather, and promotions—that there is often little time for personalities to emerge.

One of the last bastions of personality radio seems to be in the talk formats. That is where people perceive an opportunity to be free to creatively express themselves. Consequently, we're seeing an influx of people who want to do talk radio, many of them smart, hardworking, and funny, but often having no experience in the format. And they all have one thing in common: They think it's going to be easy. After all, anyone can talk. It must be simple. Right? Wrong. As with any other demanding occupation, from pro football to ballet, the great ones make it look effortless, but if you've ever tried to toss that ball fifty yards or do a grand jete, you know that's not the case. This book can train you in powerful radio methodology, and the craft of broadcasting. You can improve your skills. But the one thing no one can teach you is talent. That is a gift you were born with. And even the most talented broadcasters work very hard if they're successful.

Talk show hosts as individuals are a diverse group, with a common element. They all tend to have strong opinions, they are funny or at least have a sense of humor, and they have original things to say. They stay topical, are interested in listeners' opinions, and enjoy interacting with people. These hosts connect with people in a real way. It is a real relationship, even though it often happens with one person in a small room with a microphone and the other in a kitchen, at a desk, or in a car.

It hit me years ago hosting overnights on talk station KOA/Denver. Taking late night calls from people in thirty-eight states all over America, I learned how people *needed* to be heard, how talk radio eased the collective loneliness of those glued to their radio dials all night long. How powerful radio could be. In his book *Radio Waves,* Jim Ladd writes about "sitting around the glow of the radio campfire, hungry for the sound of the tribal drum."

If you are working in a music format, you are ahead of the curve when it comes to launching a talk radio career. Many music radio air personalities turn out to be just the right people to handle talk radio. They have a range of interests and understand the time constraints of radio. They also have been schooled in the basics of formatics and why they are important.

Maintaining an audience requires great storytelling. In music radio, the songs are often the stories. When music hosts decide to become talk radio hosts, it is often a case of wanting to talk about the stories that are inspired by stories that songs are telling, or the stories behind the songs.

Music radio hosts are comfortable working with all the properties of sound. Most of the good ones know how to edit sound, use it to set an emotional tone, understand how sound affects thought and mood. Those skills are a great asset when making the transition to personality radio.

Among the better known of the "rock-to-talk" personalities is syndicated host Rush Limbaugh. His show advocates an agenda in much the same way music radio in years past picked up on politics, pop culture, and issues of the day. Rush adds excitement to his show by employing music radio production values, produced bits, jingles, and parody songs, all mixed in with a heavy dose of his conservative politics. A talk radio pioneer, Limbaugh took the format of "serious" or political talk radio, something that had been traditionally stodgy, and added the element of fun to a format previously unblemished by humor.

People ask me all the time, "What's Rush like?" When I worked with Rush at WABC in New York, the thing I remember best about him is that he was a pro and he worked hard. He'd be in the office hours before his show, going through dozens of newspapers looking for material and doing show prep. He didn't make life difficult for management, and he was a fun guy to have a cheeseburger with.

Limbaugh explains his success this way in his book *The Way Things Ought to Be*: "[On station KFBK in Sacramento, California] I was allowed to be myself." He says it was the first time in seventeen years on the radio he was allowed to be who he was on the air. Limbaugh warns, "You'll never be your best doing it someone else's way." He says his show has been so successful because he entertains audiences, not because of his right-wing politics.

One of the few other conservative political radio personalities with the same kind of following is venerable newsman and commentator Paul Harvey, and for almost the same reasons. Harvey is a master storyteller and is fun to listen to. You can see people parked in their cars, captivated, during the lunch hour listening to Paul Harvey.

The moral for success here: No matter your politics, be unique. Be yourself. Create your own style.

Play the calls like you play the hits

Another secret of Rush Limbaugh's success is that he "plays" callers like a DJ plays songs. Talk radio is not public service radio. Rush understood that you have to entertain listeners. Just because someone *calls* the show does not mean he has a God-given right to be heard on air. Rush says:

> The primary purpose of callers on my show is to make *me* look good, not allow a forum for the public to make speeches. I, after all, am the reason people listen.... Two minutes of a boring caller is the same as playing a record nobody likes. What do you do when a song you don't like is played? You go looking for a song you do like.

Despite a long-running emphasis on targeting a youthful demographic, it's a mistake to let age be a prominent factor when judging talent. It pays to remember: Whether a person is eighteen or eighty, if he or she captivates you with original thought and storytelling, can relate his or her own take on the truth, and communicate an interest in life, you'll have a winner!

What else does a rock jock bring to the talk table?

Talent can take you a long way, but it must be strengthened by experience. Good voices in talk radio are secondary. It's what you say that matters most.

Timing

A real advantage the rock-to-talkers have is timing. You can hear the polish and experience of a personality trained by years of short segment breaks on the air. They know how to hit the point, get to it fast, and get out of it.

Less is more

Former music jocks have learned when to end a bit. In listening to audition material, you can hear the difference between an experienced talent who has fought the clock and won and a talented beginner who doesn't quite get the timing. That training, which only comes from experience, is invaluable and shines through in talk radio, even without the tight restrictions of short songs and a format clock. The lesson here: Just because you get a couple of hours to play with, don't waste it!

How to Rock the Talk

Another DJ who made the transition is broadcast personality Phil Hendrie. After a successful twenty-year career in music radio, Hendrie was feeling cramped by the lack of freedom and formatic restrictions while doing morning drive at a Los Angeles rock station. When his station decided to make a change, Hendrie begged for a chance to try his hand at talk. A new L.A. talk station gave him an opportunity to host a weekend show.

Back then, Hendrie was a creative guy with huge potential. He spent years as a radio vagabond, honing his talk skills. Hendrie has become famous for his amazing talent of hosting a show where he plays his own callers, using dozens of voices who take on their own personalities. Callers become the "hits" of the show when they take the bait and phone in to argue with one of Hendrie's characters. Hendrie observes life, filters what he sees, adds his unique talent, and lets it roll. His career path has moved toward television and movies.

Phil Hendrie on CREATING POWERFUL RADIO

- *Get in there and flop.* Try everything. Powerful radio is experimentation. If the station you're now at doesn't appreciate it, sooner or later you'll find one that does.

- *Be a popular culture junkie, but not just TV and movies.* It means noticing dress, road signs, vending machines, faces, accents, window tinting, houseplants, snippets of conversations, drool, etc. Record all of it.

- *Forget callers.* Prep your show so that the material is interesting to *you* first, your *listeners* second, and your *callers* third.

- *Be absolutely clear and focused as to what your show is about.* Management tends to push around and overconsult talent that isn't. You'll be getting and taking a lot of bad advice.

- *Keep your show lean.* It's about you. If you don't need them, lose the sidekicks, the happy talk with the newsperson, the chronic callers.

- *Don't pre-record bits.* Do them live. So what if you screw up a sound effect or a line. Your chances of succeeding with a bit go up a hundred percent when you do it live. And don't overwrite. Keep your ad-libbing skills sharp.

- *Throw away the listener mail.* If they have something to say, they'll call. Listeners who write to talk show hosts are oddballs.

- *Listen to one aircheck a month maximum.* Listening to too many airchecks will only depress you as you nitpick every little thing. If you hit a home run on the air, you'll feel it.

Music Hosts

Are You Ready to Make the Move From Rock to Talk?

Do You...

- Listen to talk radio and like it better than music radio?

- Get really mad when things are clipped out of the newspapers or you can't find anything heavier than *USA Today* or *People* around the station?

- Have a home subscription to 10 or more magazines or newspapers?

- Find yourself calling talk shows?

- Resent your program director telling you to "shut up and read your liners"?

- Hate the "hits"?

- Check your watch a lot and feel mostly bored during your airshift?

- Enjoy taking calls on the air or do more phone bits than you're supposed to?

- Like doing interviews and wish you could do more?

- Long for more airtime to talk about things that matter—what's happening in the news, in town, etc.?

Trial by Fire Is Not for Everyone

Even if you get a chance for that on-air audition, it may not be the best way to strut your stuff. An audition is not the best of circumstances. Being on the hot seat is a nervous thing. It's been my experience that people who audition well are a bit like people who do well on tests at school. Those who "ace the tests" are good test takers, but they are not necessarily the smartest or best and brightest talents. Programmers can be fooled. They can hear a great demo or audition night, hire the person, and then be very sorry later when they are not as good as expected.

Ex-music jock Turi Ryder expresses it another way:

> Every person in the world is capable of three good talk shows. Each individual has a few things that he or she cares passionately about, at least for a few hours. After that, it gets much harder. Creative people constantly find new interests, new subjects they need to entertain themselves. That is how they come up with different shows every day.

Ryder was working as a disc jockey for a well-known music station when I met her. Her Top 40 DJ days included some of the best stations in America. She was bright, fun, loud, and lovable, but with a definite dark side. I thought she'd be perfect for talk radio. She has enjoyed a career as a major market talk host and a writer.

Tips from Rock-to-Talker Turi Ryder

- Audition as the entertainer you are, not as the host you think "they" want.
- Don't be afraid to say "I don't know" on the air. Audiences prefer honesty and ignorance to artifice and arrogance.
- A little silence can be a valuable thing.
- "Nice" is a luxury you can't always afford.
- Establish rules for your show, then play by them.
- You have 50,000 watts and a microphone, the callers have only a phone and a radio. Give them a break.
- Never make fun of a caller after he or she is gone. Exception: If he or she hung up on you.
- Changing the names of businesses and people lets you tell either more of the truth or bigger, better lies.
- Not everyone who has done something interesting IS interesting.
- EVERYTHING IS MATERIAL.

How Do I Break into Talk?

As a radio consultant who is constantly on the lookout for talent, while listening to airchecks is important, the best way to find tomorrow's stars are not necessarily airchecks. Airchecks can be heavily edited to sound great, especially since many people now have home editing software. But from a talent's perspective, all that home audio capability can be a great thing. You can use it to put together an "audition" show and post it on your Web site. Talk programmers are also giving audition opportunities to podcasters and bloggers in their quest to find new talent.

Whether you have a studio available, or some simple computer recording equipment, it's what's on your audition effort that counts.

I often ask the host to interview himself or herself and record it—by this I mean starting with a question, then moving to a descriptive monologue from the potential host's unique point of view. That's how most actual talk shows open every day, and you don't need callers to come up with an interesting fifteen-minute conversation.

I'm also listening for the likability factor. An air talent may be brilliant, but if you would not want to take a five-hour car trip with them, why would you put that person on the radio and ask your listeners to do exactly that?

Think of your audition as a spoken autobiography or narrative, where you are free to tell your favorite stories about yourself and your life. This not only showcases your storytelling ability—a very important part of talk radio—it lets people get to know you in a very personal and powerful way. Some of the best auditions tell of meaningful experiences that have changed or moved people, experiences that have made them the way they are. The more personal a story, the more universal it often is.

Another method for programmers who are considering an untested talent is to ask the host to do a hypothetical talk show. Ask, "What would you talk about if given a few hours on air?" Ask the host why he or she cares about those subjects—why would they be interesting? Ask the host to do an opening monologue for his or her "show" with opinions and personal stories or about some event of the day. You can offer a studio for recording this if you have one available.

I once had a client—a news anchor, author, and expert in finance—who had never before hosted a talk radio show and wanted to try it. She recorded a charming story of two little old ladies who came to her for financial help and discovered they were nearly millionaires as a result of their hobby of collecting antique dishes. A ten-minute recording got her the opportunity to audition and substitute-host on some of the top stations and networks in the country, without any actual talk radio experience.

Still, without an aircheck, it's definitely harder to find a program director who will risk putting you on the air. So how do you come up with some kind of presentation that will showcase your personality and potential as a talk host? How can you convince a programmer to put you on as a substitute host to "audition" on the air? Your best weapon in getting a shot at an audition shift on air will be a powerful demo.

How to Create a Powerful Demo

No one likes making a demo. Talent will take any excuse to hem and haw and procrastinate when a program director says, "Send me your stuff." The general feeling is "I don't know what to put on my demo. I am the worst judge of my own work. How will I know what is good and what is garbage? What really represents *me*?" I once waited five years for a talent to send me his aircheck! This is where having your own Web site can really help you. When you have your own site, you don't have to choose one particular type of show or talk format to submit, you can post several, with descriptions, and a program director can simply click on the topics and styles that seem to work best with his or her needs. You will have to sort through or create work that you feel represents you at your best. Even the most experienced talk hosts tend to avoid this task.

Here are some ideas and techniques to help hurry along those facing the excruciating dilemma of creating an audio demo.

1. The aircheck should always leave the listener wanting more. The worst thing you can do is offer too much. It's like overfeeding a fish until it dies. If you are sending a disc or posting audio files, be sure to segment them into tracks or subfiles. That way the PD can skip around more easily, or dip in and out of your show. If you leave your audience just a little bit hungry, it will pique their interest in you. Your goal is to get the PD to ask for more.

2. Don't get paralyzed deciding what to post or burn. If you have an hour showcasing your versatility, use that. If you have a great hour showcasing only one aspect of your personality, use that. Then let *me* ask you for more. Most PDs look for talent who are equally good with humor, substantive issues, interviews, and breaking news.

3. Show your heart. Show what you care about on your demo.

4. Show your stuff. Showcase your technique. News executive Bernard Gershon suggests: "If you are the person preparing that demo, put your best stuff up top—even a montage of some highlights—then more details. If you are weeding through audition audio tracks, listen for that spark—the edge that, with *your* guidance, will make that person a pro."

5. This is your self-portrait. This demo should be exactly as you want to be perceived by a potential employer. As air personality Turi Ryder advises, "Make your demo or audition not for the job you currently have but for the job you *want* to have or the show you *want* to do. Keep in mind, the people listening want to hear not only what you have done, but also what you can do for *them.*"

6. There is nothing worse than being told that "you were never as good as your demo." As Ryder puts it,

> It should be like a good, but not a rare, hour—one where you really do not want to edit anything out, but not as if a perfect human being with your voice was sitting in for you. I want whoever hires me from that demo to know what they are getting before I move my furniture.

On your Web site you can create a perfect self-portrait, but for your own good, make it an accurate one. Ryder warns music and talk hosts, "If in your typical day, a caller changes your mind or you must admit ignorance of which drug the murderer was on, or screw up the name of the Afghani foreign minister, then that is the show you do."

She points out that the exception is in the case of news. There, an error-free audition is preferable.

7. Showcase your most individual work. I like to hear shows that originate in people's lives. One example I use for coaching came from Swedish radio personality Jesse Wallin.

Jesse decided that he wasn't going to mix the formula for his new baby's bottle. He said it was easier to just spoon in the powder. That way, when the kid spit it up, all you'd need for cleaning would be a dust-buster or a vacuum. It takes a father who has cleaned up a lot of baby spit to think of that. I laughed, I was moved, and I cared about him.

8. Think like a program director. Imagine your disc arriving in the mail. Now it is in the player, with an attentive, hopeful, and open-minded program director beginning to hear your work. Then the phone rings. Ask yourself, would the PD stop listening and get the phone, or ignore it because he or she was too absorbed in hearing your work?

Looking for Talent

Make an audition that commands attention. Music radio consultant Guy Zapoleon puts it this way: "There is an 'X' factor. It is the feeling I get from listening to the talent." What do *I* listen to? Everything that comes in. As Bernard Gershon says, "You have to review demos, place ads, network, and listen to your competition in both smaller and larger markets. Try to find someone who you think 'gets it,' who has an original sound. If the person truly has potential, the rest can be learned." With most stations and satellite radio available via the computer, it's easier than ever to hear any host in any market in real time. Hosts should always remember, when designing their Web sites, to make it as easy as possible for a potential employer to connect to their stations during their airshifts.

What am I listening for? Anything that keeps me in a parked car in a dark garage with the groceries melting in the back seat, because I have to hear the rest of the show, is a keeper. If I cannot leave until I know what is going to happen next, you're in.

When listening to a personality music show, consultant Guy Zapoleon asks:

- Do they "connect" with the audience?

- Are there great phone calls where you get the feeling from the listener that they and the jock are truly friends?

- Are they creative at selling the radio station, using promotions, using liners?

- Do they still get excited by something that radio pros take for granted, but the listeners don't . . . the music?

Programming executive Denise McIntee sifted through New York City's radio applicants for years. Here is what she looks for in demo airchecks:

Do I laugh? First and foremost, I want to know if the host has a sense of humor. Do I want to keep on listening? Would I want this person as a friend? What did I learn from the host? Did I walk away from the show with a new perspective on a topic? Was the host able to persuade me to change my opinion? Is the host respectful to those who disagree? Can he or she "fight fairly" with a strong, intelligent caller?

The host should have talent walking in the door. That is a given. But, *developing* energy, communication, and humor is tough. If a host does not possess these important vital traits, you should re-examine your hire. Very few people have it all. That is why there is a shortage of "genius-level" talk-show hosts and entertainers. Most times, a leopard does not change his spots. If you start without the basics, you could end up stuck with a host you are constantly trying to change, rather than coach.

News executive Bernard Gershon has hired many news writers, anchors, and reporters. Most of what he wants in a candidate would be necessary qualities for anyone working on the air as well as for managers.

When searching for talent at any level, look for three primary qualities:

- Intelligence

- Desire

- Sense of humor

Intelligence does not just mean being book-smart or having a high IQ. Intelligence means the ability to solve problems; to complete complex tasks with resourcefulness, initiative, and resolve. A good job candidate also needs to be intuitive; to understand what is on listeners' minds, what will get them to tune in.

So, if you are interviewing potential talk-show hosts or newscasters, you need to find out what they are interested in, what stories push their buttons. Even if those story ideas sound boring to you, let *them* explain. They may win you over. That is what makes a talk host or newscaster great—the ability to communicate and excite.

An intelligent job candidate will also be looking for new challenges

If you are interviewing someone who has seen it all, done it all, knows it all—move on. Curiosity is key to intelligence.

Do not be fooled by a long resume with important-sounding titles and degrees

I look for job candidates who have traveled, and have taken an eclectic mix of courses in college. I hold nothing against history or economics majors, as long as they have the ability to communicate.

Look for a sense of humor

You are not looking for a wiseguy or a stand-up comic. But you are looking for someone who can roll with the punches, take criticism, and still take his or her job seriously. Someone who can relate well to fellow employees and diffuse difficult situations with humor and aplomb.

Getting a Job: The Demo Is Done, Now What?

You have made the perfect aircheck. It represents your best work. Your personality shines through. It is visual, informative, inspiring, funny, has tons of truth in it, and you know if you can just get the right person to hear it, it will get you a job.

You will now learn one of the most disheartening lessons in radio: getting someone to listen to your work is harder than you thought. Programmers, consultants, station group heads, and everyone else who can actually hire you are very busy men and women.

Jaye Albright explains, "It takes time to do justice to material people send. That is why I do not have time to do this sort of in-depth listening and thinking about more than one or two auditions per day."

Talent is very sensitive. If a talent calls a programmer, sends a demo, calls again to follow up but doesn't hear back, he or she is likely to get discouraged. My advice? Don't be.

Jock auditions tend to be three to five minutes long, and they arrive by the pound. Many of the people who send them have at least some experience, though not always. Talk airchecks are longer—around thirty minutes. It takes longer to listen to them. Whatever the format, there are always a lot of airchecks waiting to be heard, and the number of auditions I receive from complete amateurs is staggering.

Talk radio is an art, not a science. Finding those artists requires spending time sifting through the plethora of auditions that are e-mailed, mailed, handed out, or even dropped off at your door.

Here is how it happens for me: Typically, whenever I attend a talk-radio conference, I collect around fifty CDs or weblinks in less than six hours—all personally handed to me by hopeful talent. When I return to my office, there are dozens more waiting in my e-mail and regular mailbox, and my voice mail is filled with broadcasters asking, "Have you heard my show yet? I sent it a month ago!"

When I walk in the door after three weeks on the road, jet-lagged, hungry, and exhausted, that is *not* the time you want me to hear your work. Please cut consultants and PDs some slack. You want me to listen when I am "in the mood." And that mood is not on a reliable, methodical time-table. When I was an air talent, I never understood that things happened on *their* time, not mine.

Don't Rush Me

Programmers generally listen to new material when they are in the market for talent. It would be nice if stations' needs always coincided with hosts' availabilities. Unfortunately, it seldom works that way. Sometimes PDs miss their chance at a great hire.

I once did a talent search where I listened to dozens of shows I had stowed away, and found a young guy I really liked. I heard a lot of potential there. I called him in St. Louis, and he picked up the phone just as the moving van was arriving to pack up his stuff. He had accepted a job in Milwaukee two weeks before and was on his way. Although his work had come to my office four months earlier, I hadn't gotten around to hearing it—my loss.

Don't Develop "Attitude"

Unfortunately, when a programmer fails to respond promptly to an aircheck and resume, the talent can get really mad. Many lean toward the touchy side anyway. They take it personally. Some simply give up. If they are extremely annoyed at you, they could ruin great opportunities for themselves.

Talent may think: "I have called, written, e-mailed, and faxed. I put in a lot of work on that demo. My work is good, and I want somebody to hear it and find me a job. Hire me, or at least tell me 'no.' It has been two months." Or, "What a jerk this guy turned out to be. He [or she] never even acknowledged receiving my materials. They couldn't pay me enough to work there now!"

In truth, it is entirely possible that the programmer has been busy, has not gotten around to hearing your work, and does not want to call and say "no"—at least not yet. However, if you call fifty times, you may get a "no" from a programmer just to get you off the phone. You can be sure if you become a pest, your audition has very little chance of being heard at all. Most PDs would interpret an overeager host as someone who would be a pain to have around the station if he or she were actually hired. The goal is to be politely persistent, not obnoxious.

Sometimes It Pays to Be Aggressive

Decades ago I went after a job I wanted very much. I knew the PD had offered it to someone else, but I wanted him to hear me before he committed to the hire. I called him up and played my aircheck for him *over the phone*. It was too late to get that job, but my tenacity impressed the programmer enough that he recommended me for other positions.

When to Send Out Your Work

A logical time to start looking around is when you know people are hiring, unless you just want to make a connection for later. In the United States, it generally happens twice a year, like clockwork, just before the fall and the springtime Arbitron ratings periods. Although some stations do post openings, not all of them will. Be sure you have every e-mail subscription to every trade you can. If you can't afford some of the pricier newsletters, ask a trustworthy friend in the business to forward any leads to you.

Pay special attention to the Web sites that show the ratings for markets where you want to work. If you see a station on a downward path, chances are they may be open to making some changes. Do a little sleuthing when you're trying to contact station management. With a little ingenuity you should be able to figure out the e-mail addresses of anybody you want to find. Make sure you read online the newspapers from the cities where you hope to work, particularly their media columns. You can contact those writers directly through their Web sites, and they may have some good leads for you.

"Sorry, Your Show Is Garbage": A Programmer's Horror Story

When I programmed WABC in New York, I was fairly organized about the hundreds of applications that came in, especially because we had a well-publicized opening. It is my policy to listen to *everything*.

I had a system that included three big brown cardboard boxes. In the first box, which I kept on the floor by my desk, I had the "keeper shows." Next to it was the second box, where I kept the "possibles" or people from whom I wanted to hear more. I kept the third, the box of "unlikely" candidates, on top of my desk so that my assistant could write polite "no thank you" letters to them.

Late one night, a new cleanup crew, thinking that the two boxes on the floor were trash, threw them away. I came in on Monday morning and looked around for the "good" batch, but it was *gone*. Of course, the demos in which we were not interested were still there, right on top of my desk.

It was humiliating to have to put an item in the trades saying, "If you sent material and an application for our morning show, please resubmit it. The janitor threw it out." On the other hand, if you really want to hear all about certain individuals, by all means put their discs or business cards on top of your desk. It won't be long before you hear, "Oh I see you're talking to Brian . . . he's looking for work *again*?" Or "Is that Sue Smith's demo? Her auditions sound great. Too bad she can never do a show to match them!" And here is the best comment I heard from a staffer who noticed a package on her boss's desk: "Oh him . . . he's great on the air, but let me tell you about the time we had to bail him out of jail for drunk driving after he hit an old lady. Another time he showed up for work handcuffed to his date, and we had to hire a locksmith to get him out so he could do his shift."

Heed this warning: Unless you truly want feedback from the staff on potential candidates, and do not mind if they go ballistic reacting to what is on your desk, do not leave anything out for them to see.

If you are a talent who cannot risk having the world know you are looking to move on, use e-mail and a Web site, or, when you send your work, try saying, "I know some of your staffers. Whether or not you decide to hire me, I'd appreciate it if you kept my application under wraps." Most program directors will respect your confidentiality.

Finally, be sure to fully label everything you send with your contact information.

REMEMBER, materials get separated. WRITE YOUR DATA ON *EVERYTHING!*

CHAPTER 7

Creating Powerful Radio
Talk Shows

"A picture is nothing but a bridge between the soul
of the artist and that of the spectator."
— *Eugene Delacroix*

"Talkradio – Because all great minds *don't* think alike."
— *T-shirt slogan*

Talk radio in America evolved from full-service personality music radio. Here is how it happened: At first, a few music hosts began taking calls on-air between records, particularly on AM stations with strong personalities. Soon, there were fewer records and more listener phone calls. When it drew the listeners and advertisers, a few stations allowed the talk to stay, either in selected dayparts or, in rare cases, around the clock.

Talk Radio, When Talk Radio Wasn't Cool

When I entered the talk radio arena years ago, it was a format perceived by many as expensive, boring, and of no interest to younger demographics. Conventional wisdom held that talk radio was something your grandmother would listen to, and only dealt with events in her hometown.

Those of us doing talk knew this wasn't true. Our listeners were savvy, upscale, and worldly. Many were exceptionally well-read and well-informed. Generally, talk stations offering interesting programming produced healthy ratings, high revenues, and strong response for advertisers.

Even so, traditional talk radio stereotypes persisted until the early 1990s. That's when satellite program distribution and station economics helped to propel a talk radio revolution.

The "Rush" to AM Radio: The '90s News-Talk Explosion

One important catalyst was personality Rush Limbaugh, whose unique combination of politics and wit brought unprecedented success to the format. Rush proved that a lot of the stereotypes about talk radio were wrong. The seismic impact of Limbaugh's nationally syndicated talk show, which drew large daytime shares on hundreds of stations, many of which had been steadily losing listeners up to that point, collapsed the notion that talk had to be local. Content matters, addresses don't.

Previous talk offerings such as the radio incarnation of the *Larry King Live* show had applied this principle and succeeded by syndicating on large numbers of stations in nighttime hours. Limbaugh amplified it and shattered the network talk taboo in the lucrative daytime hours.

The critics of talk radio were wrong and the numbers proved it. Limbaugh's talk listeners were young, hip, and savvy. And, as station managers quickly noticed, there were lots of them.

When Limbaugh's syndicated show debuted in the late eighties, it was carried on fewer than 100 stations; by the mid-nineties, it was on more than 650 stations. Program suppliers rushed to meet the demand, offering station operators easy access to satellite-delivered talk programming at all hours.

The News-Talk format exploded. Once-dominant AM music stations, whose audiences had deserted them for FM, suddenly began doing talk. In the United States, markets that had one talk outlet suddenly found themselves with as many as five. News-Talk is now the second most popular format in the United States. Hundreds of stations have switched to the News-Talk format.

Talk saved many moribund stations from oblivion. But, prospering in an ocean of talk competition means providing a better product than one's competitors. Fortunately, like all good radio, talk radio doesn't have to be more expensive to be more powerful.

Curious People

Talk radio listeners are curious people. They want to know nearly everything: what is going on in their town, their country, their world. They tend to listen when they are by themselves, so the more personable the host is, the better it works.

Talk radio is intimate while being anonymous. It allows listeners and callers to interact without exposing themselves to the dangers that might arise in a real-life confrontation. It's a strange sort of freedom and can result in a deeply honest conversation. Maintain control, and remember: *You own the show*. When a personal truth is well articulated, it touches the caller, host, and listener. It has universal and mass appeal.

Who Will "Make It"?

It's difficult to predict who "has it" as a host and who does not. Talent does shine through, but talent must be combined with a skill for communicating, watching, and listening.

Some of the best, most talented, and original "talkers" are *lousy* communicators because they don't listen. For example, stand-up comedians are often hired on the assumption that because they are smart, funny, and observers of life, they will be naturals on the job, but unless they are also good listeners, they will fail miserably.

On the other hand, some of the most brilliant minds and greatest listeners are boring in a talk radio setting because they can't have a comfortable conversation in front of a microphone. The only way to know whether someone will make a good talk show host is to see how host and the audience respond to one another on the air.

Jack Swanson, program director of KGO-AM/San Francisco, one of the most successful talk stations in America, gives this sage and important warning, "Never be fooled into thinking that what *you* like is what your audience likes." An example is KGO's overnight personality. He gets huge ratings, but many sane and reasonable people find him hard to take for an extended period. However, he pulls in 25 shares, and you can't argue with that.

As a program director, you need to determine what you want from your talk show and what your listeners expect.

Listeners expect a talk show to present a point of view. Audiences also expect a talk show to expose them to new ideas so that they can learn new things. Famed CBS journalist Edward R. Murrow said of TV, but it is true for radio as well, *"This instrument can teach, it can illuminate and it can inspire."* A listener once commented in an Arbitron diary, "I didn't go to a college or university—*talk radio* is my college education."

NPR's Susan Stamberg writes in her book *Talk*:

Talk radio is a 'rear view mirror' [of our time]. The talk comes from rage, frustration, pain, pride, exhilaration. It's public talk absorbed in private. That private experience called radio. It's also talk between strangers, although it can sometimes sound like friends. The "unearned intimacy" [photographer Richard Avedon's phrase] of a call or interview on a radio show can make deep connections, two people who have never met—trying together in a brief period of time for clarity, understanding.

Listeners expect talk radio to both validate and challenge their beliefs. Most of all, they want it to be interesting and fun. They want this entire process to be entertaining and a little bigger than life. When these expectations have been met, you have created powerful talk radio!

The Formula

Broadcast consultant and program director John Mainelli says: "Entertain informatively and inform entertainingly."

The following sections describe how to select and handle topics on the air. This will make your approach both personal and powerful.

Set Powerful Bait

The talk show monologue, or "churn," sets the scene for the show. The monologue, like the first page of a great book, should capture the audience with an original approach to your subject. There is *no such thing* as a *boring* topic, just boring hosts, and dull, unimaginative approaches to the stories.

Much like a fisherman baiting his hook and then casting the fly, the host must first tempt the listener to engage and then think about the information, so that he or she wants to hear more. The churn must entice listeners.

It's up to you as the host to make everything you use work. Peel back each subject like an onion and find the most interesting ways to present your ideas. If the topic is truly interesting, it will also be genuinely interesting to you. And if it is interesting to you, you will find a way to make it interesting to the audience. Only use material you care about. If you can't make yourself care about it, don't use it.

Don't waste a minute of the listener's time on a list of boring stuff you feel you *must* discuss. The talk radio police will not be waiting outside to take you away should you forfeit discussing some big story of the day.

For instance, if your show starts at 10:00 p.m., and the TV news and the morning and afternoon papers have covered a story, CNN's been hammering it for 24 hours, and it's been on your station all day, do you really want to keep talking about it? Do you have a unique view of what has been happening? Anything else to add or to say?

Think of how your audience must feel. Think twice about using something of which you are already sick and tired. Don't be an "actor." *Real* always works. Keep it fresh for you. Tell the truth. Focus. Use effective storytelling techniques and your show will never be boring.

As in Life, on the Air: Picking Topics That Work

Ever hear that old expression, "God gave you two ears but just the one mouth"? The most effective and powerful talk show hosts talk less and listen more to the world around them. Start each and every day with this question: What are people doing—really doing—and what are they talking about—really talking about? What people are talking about off air will work as topics on the air.

You can also USE YOUR *OWN* LIFE as show prep. If you spent an hour waiting in a wrong line for a new driver's license, chances are other people have too. If you have something to say about it, use it. If your child is having trouble learning a new school curriculum, chances are you're not the only bleary-eyed parent.

In all radio, but especially in talk, the audience feels they know you personally. You and your views are the product here. You have your life to work from. You are the quarter-hour maintenance. Being *personal* works.

It doesn't take much to see how it works. A popular talk host had a baby. After a brief announcement on the air that she would be taking extra time off because her new baby girl had to undergo a complicated surgical procedure, she was flabbergasted to receive thousands of cards, letters, and gifts from listeners.

Most of the cards and letters began, "You don't know me, but I listen to your show every night and consider you a friend . . ." This host could not believe the level of support and, yes, even love, that came from total strangers who felt they knew her from listening to her talk show.

In addition to your personal life and experiences, you can, and should, scan the wires, newspapers, magazines, and the Internet for stories that outrage, sadden, amuse, or frustrate you. If it makes you laugh, cry, or bang your fist on the steering wheel, chances are it will have the same effect on your listeners and send them flying to the phones.

"It's always 'Get me a Godzilla type,' never 'Get me Godzilla!'"

Creating the Powerful Opening
Monologue or "Churn"

At Geller Media International's Creating Powerful Radio seminars or working individually, here is the method I work with:

Do:

- Find your focus. What is the issue or topic? What are you trying to say? Know your subject and know why you are talking about it.

- Engage the listeners. What do you want them to do with it? How do you want them to respond?

- Give an opinion. What is your position on this subject? What do you think about it? Why do you care?

- Tell the truth. Find your truth. It works every time.

- Personalize the opinion... with your own storytelling.

Do Not:

- Ramble.

- Appear aimless, scattered, or out of control.

- Talk about topics you don't care about (even if you feel you should care).

- Go too long before the punch.

- Be boring!

When Scott Borden managed public radio station WNYC in New York, he used the following techniques.

Scott Borden's "Creating Powerful Talk Radio" Tips

- Radio is totally personal. When I listen, I should feel like it's just me and the person on the other end of the radio.

- People listen to radio in groups of one. Never talk to a bigger group.

- Radio, especially talk radio, is part of the "information age." We have to define our unique information niche and work it like crazy.

- Every listener letter or e-mail represents exactly one listener. Every listener phone call represents exactly one listener.

- Talk show callers do not represent the talk show audience. They are NOT as important as the host, who is the thing that all the listeners have in common. Callers are only good if they help the host.

- The late American radio legend Rick Sklar pointed out that the problem with modern research is it asks people to tell you what they think and do. When asked, people often lie about these things. Actions speak louder than words.

- Good radio is like obscenity—you can't define it, but you know it when you hear it. Sometimes you have to trust your gut instincts.

- People treasure memories. And the things we remember are the things that go really right or really wrong. Make the most of these moments.

- It's radio, not brain surgery. Failure does not equal a dead body on the table. It has to be fun for us too!

- You have to have a great plan for every moment on the air. And you have to be prepared to scrap this plan entirely the first chance you get.

CHAPTER 8

Creating Powerful Radio
Integrating News and Talk

"*Art*—A means of communication by which mind reaches mind
across great gaps of space and time."
—*Francis Hoyland*

"Share, and share alike."
—*R. Edwards's "Damon and Pithias," 1556*

Research tells us that most audiences for news-talk radio perceive both the news and the talk elements as equally important. In America, due to tight budgets and restrictive formats, many full-time news-talk radio newsrooms consist of only two to four people, sometimes fewer, and not all of them are full time. It is not the ideal situation. Image is not reality. Of course, it would be better to have a bigger news staff. But if you have a couple of dedicated, talented news reporters and anchors, you can make it work.

It is possible to maintain a news image with very little actual news report-ing, because when talk hosts discuss news stories and current issues on their programs, the station conveys the impression of being "on top of the news."

News-talk stations short on people use a lot of smoke and mirrors. They may have any or all of the following: several network news services, special reports from the field, people with mobile phones calling in to report traffic tie-ups or as eyewitnesses to breaking news stories. Some stations use their talk hosts in live remote or outside broadcasts from places where news is happening. Savvy radio news people and talk hosts call on their friends and connections at newspapers, TV stations, and magazines to debrief them on the air about stories they may be covering.

Good reporters and news presenters work very, very hard. The fact that most stations now have smaller news staffs does not mean less work—it means more. Being number one is never an accident. Radio news is not for the lazy.

Break Down the Brick Wall

Have you ever noticed a psychological "brick wall" between the news and programming departments? It bears mentioning because news and talk should always work together, but often don't. News and talk presenters are often surprised to learn that audiences don't differentiate if they have heard a certain item on the news or in the talk shows. Somehow, the news department got separated from the rest of the programming. This is the old "Let's take a break for the news" routine. In the news-talk format, this is not a good thing. You must break down that brick wall, or at least put some holes in it.

Remember, your audience does not know there are two "camps" at work here; they only know that their radio is on, and if you are lucky, they know which station they are listening to. They want interesting, relevant talk. Listeners do not care whether they get their information from a guy wearing a news hat or a talk hat. Fight the war against the competition, not each other.

Failure to Communicate

Why don't we talk to each other? Because:

- Talk and programming says: *"The news writers, reporters and producers are always so busy, we don't want to bug them."*

- The news department says: *"The talk hosts are in their own world and don't bother to talk or listen to us."*

- Management says: *"Keep them separate because news is fact, talk is opinion and entertainment. Mixing them would damage our news credibility."*

On winning talk stations, however, news reporters, anchors, and hosts talk to each other both on and off the air.

They share resources, knowing their product is a marriage. In fact, the best news-talk radio happens during times of crisis. That is when the lines of demarcation blur, and everyone pitches in to do what they can to help each other get the full story on the air quickly.

News is the chronicling of events. Talk is the discussion, the "why" behind the events and how people feel about them. But, your audience will be well served if they hear the truth, no matter who tells it to them.

A perfect example of integrating news and talk is New York syndicated morning host Don Imus and his newsman Charles McCord, a credible "news personality." There are no brick walls here. Imus is at his best discussing the news of the day, and McCord is an integral part of the show. McCord retains total news credibility. One of the most important parts of the *Howard Stern Show* is when Robin Quivers does the "news," albeit in a nontraditional style. Long-time syndicated radio commentator Paul Harvey has blurred the lines between personality and newsman as well.

A word about the credibility factor: Audiences today are much more sophisticated. They know the difference between a newsperson being serious and one who is fooling around. Some newscasters even read commercials and manage to keep their credibility. Audiences know when they are seeing product placement, and they can spot a commercial, even if it is delivered by a newsperson, a mile away.

When a huge event affects the lives of listeners—a war, an earthquake, a flood, radioactive leaks—there is no fooling around. News anchors today have come to understand that much of the news is in place as an insurance policy. It is there in case you need it. Of course, when you need the news, it had better be there.

Look for Talkable Topics

Another way to build the relationship between the news and talk staffs is for the news people to keep a lookout for "discussable" news items. There is not much to say about a fire, flood, or breaking story other than giving the facts and information as they become available. After the facts are in about the massive car crash on the bridge, the talk show topic may actually be: "Why are citizens willing to endure life-threatening conditions to save ten minutes on their commute?"

A hard news story can generate a softer talk topic. Train your people to save the stories about Supreme Court decisions or any polls or items about which people are likely to have strong views. Peel the "onion" that is your story to find material for an in-depth, open-phone talk show.

The Crossover Talents

Opinion traditionally had no place in the news. On the other hand, talk has not been a forum for chronicling the facts. So, hybrid news-talkers such as Dave Ross are rare. Wearing both hats, they manage to bridge the gap. When Ross does a newscast, the listener can tell what he thinks; on the other hand, listeners know what an objective and conscientious newsman he is when hearing Ross's talk show. Ross hosts a daily talk show on KIRO/Seattle and presents news feature commentaries on the CBS Radio Network. Over the years, KIRO has sent Ross around the world to cover big news events such as the fall of the Berlin Wall. Dave Ross has found the equation to marry news to talk: keep a unique voice and retain credibility in both.

It is impossible to describe Dave Ross's creativity. Sometimes he sings his commentaries, often uses humor, and has a cynical "bright eye" on the world around him. If you have not heard his work, a sample script—archived from a CBS Radio commentary—is on the next page. It is an interesting twist on the health care cost issue in the United States.

Develop a Daily System

If you want to integrate your news-talk product, it takes extra effort. The list that follows is a system to develop news-talk integration:

- *Work together.* Meet with the producers, talk show hosts and the news assignment manager or news director every day. Compare what you know about the news and events of the day. If it cannot be done in person, do it for five minutes on the phone, instant messaging or e-mail.

- *Take today.* Go through the list of today's topics, discuss:
  - What will news do with the stories? What will talk do with the stories?
  - Any ideas that anyone else has.

DAVE ROSS CBS RADIO NETWORK SCRIPT
Health Care That's Always There

The simple solution to health care costs.

I'm Dave Ross on the CBS Radio Network.

It's an appealing motto, "Health care that's always there." The big unknown is, at what cost? The President says that the savings are obvious. You can cut paperwork to one claim form, encourage preventive care, and end the billions of dollars of unnecessary medical tests.

Well, I understand the paperwork, the insurance industry is ready to do that anyway. I understand preventive care, but how will you stop the testing? If a patient wants a test, does a doctor say "no" and risk a lawsuit? The key is to get the patient not to want the test. But how?

I was talking with Dr. Nancy Dickey with the American Medical Association, also a family physician in Texas, and she told me an interesting thing. Whenever she offers her patients a medical test, the first thing they ask is not, "How much will this cost?" since the cost is usually covered by insurance. What they ask is: "WILL THIS HURT?" That's what they want to know: "Will this hurt!" And I suddenly realized that's it!

We've been going about it all wrong. For years, doctors have been saying, "This won't hurt a bit." WRONG! The doctors should say, "Well, yeah, this is gonna hurt a little," and he kinda glances toward a big old four-inch-long needle sitting over by the sink.

That's why people didn't have as many tests thirty years ago, because those tests hurt! "Health care that's always there" is a great quote, but here's another one: "You bet that test is paid for, I'll just go and get the needle!"

I'm Dave Ross on the CBS Radio Network.

- *Prospect for gold.* Share the loot. Everyone should look through the wires, newspapers, and any other usual source materials. Talk about multi-version reports or anything that can be done in short-form news, then moved into a long-form talk.

- *Pick the right talent for the subject.* If a newsperson or host has an affinity for a specific topic, he or she will do a better job. Why not send your baseball fanatic out to do the baseball story? Utilize your talent's natural interests, background, and experiences. This means you will really need to get to know your talent. If you don't know, ask. "Is anyone interested in alternative medicine?" Again, interested is *interesting and powerful*.

- *Be flexible.* Things change quickly. You've got to be ready to change plans.

- *Listen to everyone's ideas.* If people are assigned stories or topics they do not like, ask them to give you better ideas. People always work better when the idea is theirs.

- *Communicate.* If things change news-wise or events happen throughout the day, talk to each other. This is a team effort, and the listeners are not necessarily aware that there is a brick wall between the newsroom and the talent area.

- *Listen to each other.* News departments, when they can, ought to be aware of the content of the various talk shows and whatever else is on air. Keep the radio on at the station. Talk hosts: *Listen to the news!*

- *Create a future file.* When notices arrive regarding future events, designate a person to file them in the computer in daily calendar form. Both news and talk should utilize these lists for topic and story ideas. Newspapers work these types of files as much as five years ahead.

- *Create a follow-up file.* On dull days when not much is going on, look back. Did the station cover any stories that need to be updated? An updated news story might ask:
  - "Where are they now?"
  - "Did the child in the custody fight live happily ever after?" "What happened to the neighborhood after the rapist was released?"

  Looking ahead is good, but you can also do mighty powerful radio when you look backward.

- *Do not fight over guests.* If there is a guest or an interview that a newsperson has set up and the talk host wants to interview him herself, work it out. Protect the on-air product, not your territory. Perhaps borrowing a clip, or piece, of that interview audio from the news department will be enough to get discussion going for a powerful talk show.

Conversely, if something noteworthy is said during one of the station's talk shows, use it in the news. You'll have an exclusive. Producers, endear your host to the news staff by getting that audio to the newsroom fast!

Be a Team. Be a Station. Be Number 1!

Work together. Cooperate. Powerful radio is a *collective* effort. William Shakespeare said, "The play is the thing." Put egos aside. Forget the players. Focus on the play.

Let the news people know what types of material you are seeking for your show. Ask them to save anything they come across. Talk hosts, do the same for your news team.

People are usually glad to help, and may have a lot of ideas and material that may not be appropriate for their own department or show but could work for you.

Break Format When News Breaks

This is when news-talk is at its best. During times of national or local catastrophe, go ahead and break format. Have a procedure (whom to call, commercials to move, etc.) in place in the event of an urgent news story. Get the information on air right now. Nobody cares about your "cover story" or "topic A" when all hell is breaking loose and lives and property are at stake.

Drop what you had planned and go with the breaking story. Debrief news reporters on the air. Ask them questions about the story. If it makes sense to do so, have them stay on the air and take calls. Talk hosts: Give the news department all the time it needs to get information on the air, even if it cuts heavily into your show.

Always Archive

Remember to keep audio files. If you have the archived audio accessible, you can easily re-purpose magic moments on air for promos or later for awards submissions.

Some of the most effective news-talk managers are those who have worked on the air themselves. Bob Christopher is one of those people. Christopher ran the Florida State Network, anchored at KTAR in Phoenix, Arizona, and was a manager at WWL radio in New Orleans, where one integrated newsroom served four stations.

Bob Christopher's Creating Powerful Radio Points

- Understand your listeners: where they live, where they shop, and what they want and need from you.

- Create an emotional bond with your audience.

- As often as possible, deliver more than you promise to listeners and advertisers.

- Surround yourself with people who want to win.

- Take time to talk to them and smile at them in the hall.

- Develop personalities your listeners will love.

- Focus on the positives in your corner of the world.

- Dream up fascinating promotions or special events.

- Remember, it's marketing!

- Know your competitors.

CHAPTER 9

Creating Powerful Radio Interviews

> "Men are born with two ears, but with just a single tongue, in order that they should hear twice as much as they say."
> — *Charles Caleb Colton*

Interviews are a necessary part of the information-gathering process for both news and talk. A powerful interview can rivet the audience to their radios; a boring one can make them disappear.

Remember, your guests—whether rock stars, artists, politicians, experts, specialists in their fields, or just "common" men or women with stories to tell—may be nervous when they show up at your radio station. You go on the air every day and it seems routine to open the microphone and talk to thousands of people. However, this experience can be terrifying to "civilians," who may be nervous or forget what they want to say. They can become unsure of where they're heading with a point and become boring—talking endlessly, and saying nothing.

The purpose of an interview is to get the interviewee to open up and tell you things of interest. You may even get the person to reveal things he or she does not ordinarily discuss in a public forum. You want your guest to share information, to *tell stories*.

A good interviewer knows that in order to get the most out of any interview, the person being interviewed must feel comfortable. Ideally, he or she should forget about the microphone. He should feel *heard*. If you catch your guest looking at her watch, there's a problem because during a good interview, time should fly.

It is up to you, as the interviewer, to maintain control. If the interview heads in a dull direction, grab it and steer the discussion elsewhere. For example: "I'm sure there are people listening now who fully understand the details of the photosynthesis process, but in layman's terms, could you explain why it's a bad idea to cut down the rain forests?" Your audience will appreciate it if you can keep your guests away from intricate and technical answers.

Often, you will be faced with an uncooperative interviewee, particularly in news situations. For example, politicians are notorious for not wanting to tell you anything substantive. They have their own agendas and want to use you and your airwaves to promote their ideas. Dealing with this tactic can be tricky.

Here is one method to get them to talk. It comes from Swedish newsman Stig-Arne Nordström. His technique is "getting it a little bit wrong."

Let's say you have a politician who is downplaying the significance of a proposed tax hike. You might say, "So your plan means no tax increases for anyone?" The politician will then feel frustrated and misunderstood. People in his profession can't stand that. He might come back with something like, "No, no, no, my plan would mean a uniform tax increase for almost everyone!" You've accomplished several things here. You got him to talk and explain it in a short form that is easily understood and you've landed the perfect radio interview sound statement. It is short, to the point, and cuts through the smoke and mirrors your interviewee was trying to use to hide his true agenda. Don't worry about the audience thinking that you are an idiot for "misunderstanding" your interviewee. If the interview is pre-recorded, you can cut out the "dumb" question and just air the tight, succinct answer.

CNN's Larry King is notorious for asking the "dumb question." He claims he doesn't read the books of the authors he's interviewing. He also doesn't admit to much in the way of show preparation. Larry King's key is to ask the questions members of his audience would ask as if they had the chance to sit down and interview the guest. His audience loves it.

This is how Larry King works, and while it's effective for him, it should not be construed as an argument against show prep, in which I strongly believe.

Here is another, somewhat controversial, trick for pre-recorded interviews. If a guest is nervous and the answers are too formal, stilted, long, and boring, try this: Wrap up your interview. Leave the recorder running (hopefully your guest won't notice). Then say, "Just to make *sure* I've got this right, could we go over it one more time?" The guest, now relaxed because the interview is "over," will often tell you, in a very conversational way, what the key points were. You can then "notice" that you left the recorder running and ask permission to use *that* interview, instead of the first, formal session. I don't believe this is an unethical technique. After all, your guest knew that he or she was talking to you for a broadcast interview, and this audio is often much better. Interview subjects are frequently grateful and will thank you for making them "sound so good."

The Art of the Interview: Powerful Listening

National Public Radio's Susan Stamberg got it right about interviews in her book *Talk*: "Talk always begins with a question. *Listening*. Listening for what's being said and for what is NOT said, listening for the silences, the cracks between the words, the hesitations, the contradictions, the glorious expositions."

Stamberg, like all good interviewers, understands that in an interview, the "star" is the topic or the guest, not the host. It helps if you, as the host, can sublimate your ego somewhat and focus completely on what your guest is trying to say. Listening is the key.

The interview will go much better if the topic is something you care about, as opposed to something you think will be of interest to your audience. Remember, "interested is interesting." If you are bored by the topic, odds are your audience will be, too. Listeners can tell the difference between affected and genuine curiosity.

Like a fisherman going for the catch, it is sometimes necessary to use a variety of baits and lures for different types of interviews. Your opening questions will depend on the circumstances. Sometimes it pays to be tough. Other times, kindness, empathy, or humor serves you best. There is no one right approach to getting a great interview. Part of the skill and art of the job is to gauge the method needed to get the interviewee to open up and talk. That "sense of approach" is a skill you develop by *listening*.

Uh, Uh, Uh... Nervous Guests?

Some stations actually hand out a list of helpful hints for guests to read before going on the air. If you would like to try this, here are some points to include.

Dear Interviewees...

- Please be available and flexible. If the interview time has to be changed, be gracious. The station may call you in an emergency, if another guest has canceled, or if the station is in need of your expertise right now. Be willing to appear. The host and station will appreciate and remember you.

- If you want to make sure you get a copy of the show, have someone record it for you off the air.

- If you're an author, PLEASE don't repeat the name of your new book over and over. Listeners will get annoyed. Your job is to be so fascinating that the listeners stay until the end of the interview because they want to hear the host repeat the title of your book. We will put your information on our station Web site if you give it to us in advance.

- Forget there is a larger audience. You will be much more effective if you speak to the host one-on-one, instead of addressing all those listeners "out there." The audience listens one at a time.

- Try to relax. Be yourself. Radio is personal and intimate. Listeners like to be spoken to that way.

- Watch your language. This is not a living room and certain expressions could slip out if you aren't careful!

- Keep to the point. If you don't have anything interesting to say, ask the host for another question.

- Do not bring in a lot of notes to the studio and read from them. Hosts hate this and it can be boring.

- Ask for what you need. Do you have your reading glasses? A pen or pencil? Tissues? A glass of water?

- Do you understand the process? You should feel in control as much as possible. Ask how to use the cough button, just in case.

- Can you stop anytime? Is this being recorded, or is it live, direct, and "anything goes"?

- By the way, have you eaten? There's nothing more embarrassing than a microphone picking up the growling of your hungry stomach.

- Do you need to use the bathroom? It's better to be comfortable than to be sitting there squirming around.

- Don't be rigid. As in normal conversation, the interview may take a turn that has nothing to do with your agenda. Be a good guest. The discussion may lead to even better things than you were originally prepared to talk about. A skilled interviewer does not stick to a script.

- Listen to the questions and answer them. If the host seems unprepared or unfamiliar with your topic, don't express anger or frustration. The audience is probably in the same boat. Just speak to the host as you would to a friendly, but uninformed, stranger you meet at a cocktail party or in the next seat on an airplane. If you can genuinely interest the host in your topic, you will also interest the audience, and will have a very good chance of being asked back.

Thoughts for Hosts and Interviewers

- Forget the long hello. Keep the introduction and greeting short and to the point.

- *Listening* is the key to successful interviews. Don't stick to a list. Often the best next question will come from the answer to the last one.

- Try not to ask "yes or no" questions. Ask the "how" or "why" questions. Ask how people feel, and have them explain things.

- If you didn't get enough of an answer, don't be afraid to ask again. This is especially important in recorded interviews when you are looking for that perfect sound bite.

- Curiosity counts. If you are genuinely curious about the topic, the interview will work.

- Ask "dumb" questions. Do not be embarrassed if you don't know all the answers, the audience probably doesn't either. That's why you are doing the interview.

- Get to the point. Don't clutter up the interview with lots of chit-chat. The audience cares about how what is being said affects their lives.

- *Control* the interview. Steer the subject in a better direction if the interview starts to get boring. Don't let slick-talking, verbally skilled guests get around you and not answer questions. Ask your questions again and again until you get answers, then move on.

- Focus on solutions, not just problems. Even if your guests have some pie-in-the-sky solutions or can offer nothing more than a phone number to call, that's better than ending an interview on some hopeless, downward note.

- Respect responses. Everyone is entitled to an opinion. If he or she is an idiot, that will come through loud and clear all by itself.

- End your interviews cleanly. Do a short good-bye. You don't need to recap points made during the interview. Trust that listeners got what was discussed and move on.

On Listening

Because listening is such a part of creating powerful radio, it's worth looking at separately. Years ago, at UCLA, a friend gave me a book called *On Listening* by psychologist Carl Faber. When I read the following passage, I was stunned. *On Listening* expressed what I felt in my heart about radio—about connecting and communicating.

On rough days, I still go back and read that book again. It always helps. Creating Powerful Radio is about creating powerful communication. That means powerful listening.

Dr. Carl Faber taught courses on relationships, myths, men, and women. His early UCLA lectures were broadcast on Pacifica Radio in Los Angeles. The following is an excerpt from Faber's book.

From Carl Faber, *On Listening*

Most people have never really been listened to. They live in a lonely silence—no one knowing what they feel, how they live or what they have done. They are prisoners of the eyes of others, of the stereotyped, limited, superficial and often distorted ways that others see them.

There are no words to adequately describe what it is to be free with another person. It is most often a sensing that someone will let us be all of what we are at that moment. We can talk about whatever we wish, express in any way whatever feelings are in our hearts. We can take as much time as we need. We can sit, stand, pace, yell, cry, pound the floor, dance or weep for joy. Whatever and however we are at the moment is accepted and respected....

This experience of freedom and communion helps us to feel that someone is for us. And it is this deep sensing of someone, somewhere, being for us that breaks into the silent loneliness of our lives and encourages us in the struggle to be human. It helps us to break the tyranny of the strangers' eyes and to give to our lives all that we are capable of giving. Because listening can bring about such powerful healing, it is one of the most beautiful gifts that people can give and receive.

CHAPTER 10

Creating Powerful Radio
Show Prep

"Creating is never given to us all by itself. It goes hand in hand with the gift of observation. A true creator may be recognized by his ability to find about him, to the commonest and humblest thing, items worthy of note."
— *Igor Stravinsky*

"All truly wise thoughts have been thought already thousands of times; but to make them truly ours, we must think them over again honestly, until they take root in our personal experience."
— *Goethe*

Why Is Prep Crucial?

A general would never go into battle without a plan. A surgeon would never go into the operating room without a preliminary work-up. Yet it is surprising how many air personalities show up for work and just wait to see what happens. Some days they might get lucky, but for winning over the long haul, show prep is essential. If a talent is prepared, it does not matter if he or she slides in a minute before airtime. The prepared host can still do a great show.

It is *never* an accident when a show is number one. It takes very hard work. The best personalities compile a stack of material from various sources: articles from magazines or newspapers, written ideas, and material collected from the Internet along with stories they have picked up from life or have observed or overheard.

Syndicated talk show host Rush Limbaugh is a master of show prep. He's disciplined. When I worked with him at WABC radio in New York, Rush would come in hours before each show. He didn't go on the air until he'd gone through dozens of newspapers, discussed ideas with his producer, and spent time on the phone talking with anyone from disc jockeys to political leaders.

Rush had concepts and stories, but no guests. He found things that interested him, collected them, and shared them with his audience. No one made him do this. Rush did it on his own, because he wanted his show to succeed. He realized the value of show prep.

Everyone has his or her own way of organizing show prep materials, but if a host sounds consistently disorganized on the air, try coming up with another system. If a host is prepared but cannot access an item during the on-air performance, all that prep is wasted and the show will wander.

Some talent are fortunate enough to have trustworthy people, usually producers, who do their show prep and planning for them. It then becomes the talent's job to creatively execute someone else's plan. Nevertheless, a plan still exists.

Creative talent are constantly doing show prep. Everything in their lives—what they read, eat, feel, experience, and even dream—all goes into their shows. Air personality Melissa McConnell-Wilson says, "Twenty-four hours a day, seven days a week—every conscious waking moment, I'm gathering information to recall later to use on my show."

How personal can it get? With some air personalities, the best you can hope for in terms of confidentiality is that your name stays out of it. Managers beware: your meetings or conversations with talent could become material.

There *is* a difference between personal and private. No one should be allowed to endanger others or personally harm them in any way. Not only can there be legal consequences to giving specific information about people's private lives, but there can be security issues as well. When in doubt, try asking: Will the story of the car with the Picasso in the back seat be as compelling if I don't give the car's make and model?

Oftentimes a little camouflage, using the essence of a true story, enables more creative and dramatic storytelling without risking someone's physical well-being or emotional embarrassment. What is your point? If entertaining your audience is the goal, then does it really matter if something happened to your wife or to "a woman I know…?"

Try television's *Dragnet* approach: "The story you are about to hear is true, but the names have been changed to protect the innocent."

Using Humor

Humor always attracts listeners. Some people are funny; others may not be funny but have great senses of humor. There are those who are hilarious in private but are not able to access those parts of their personalities on the air.

You can do show prep that improves your ability to be funny on the air. For example, you can learn to become a better storyteller. Consultant Jaye Albright offers this advice to those who would like to grow and develop in this area:

Read every book in the library about humor. If possible, attend improvisation workshops. These can be mind-expanding releases of creative expression. [When telling a story] memorize specific and colorful details. There is nothing funny about the abstract—comedy emerges from specifics. Make note of them and use them; allow the child who lives within you to emerge. Tell your truth.

"When you start to take this job seriously, you're in trouble."
— *Jimmy Buffet*

"Use everything in your life to create your art."
— *Stanislavsky*

Rules for Powerful Prep

Here are some ideas and questions to look at when doing show prep.

1. Go with the Moment

This is also known as the rule of "out the window." If something spontaneous happens on the air that is better than what you have prepared, go with it! You would happily take a "side trip" to see the Grand Canyon while traveling through Arizona. The magic moments on radio—a breaking news story or a fabulous caller—happen when you least expect them, and when they occur it is wonderful. Although there is no substitute for walking into the station thoroughly prepared, you must also be willing to throw that stack of stuff "out the window" when something irresistible turns up.

2. Always Ask Why—Avoid Slot Filling

Always have a specific reason for wanting a guest. Avoid "guest-o-mania." If a guest has been booked for you, know the reason. Ask the producer, "What has this person done? Why is he or she special?"

Ask: "Will we enjoy this guest even if we are not familiar with his or her latest book or area of expertise?" Is this someone you would want to talk to off the air? Think twice before you take the easy way out and book a guest to fill an hour of airtime. If you have always wanted to meet someone, and he or she lives in your town or is coming to your area, it is perfectly acceptable to invite that person to be a guest on your show, providing that the goal remains to entertain or inform your audience.

Never promise a guest an hour. Instead, just ask for a few minutes of his or her time. Make it clear that because this is live radio, it is always possible that a guest may be preempted by a breaking story. You have now protected yourself from the potentially embarrassing situation of having to dump a guest if he or she is boring or if a bigger opportunity arises.

I am frequently asked for a rule about how to use guests. Unless you are doing an interview-based show, I advise using guests as *spice*. Like great seasoning in a bland meal, guests can be wonderful. Good guests can make a show, but they must be gifted communicators with passion, offer new information or have something relevant to say. The best guests are people who have personal experience, with a story to tell, rather than being just experts in their fields.

A guest can also serve as an unwitting foil for savvy hosts with barbed tongues. "John and Ken" in Los Angeles are famous for finding "village idiots" and using them on the air for comedic purposes.

Warning to Managers

Many managers like to hear guests on the air. It demonstrates that the host and producer have done some work to book the show and justify their salaries. They like to see bodies at desks for eight hours a day. Sales reps are asked to turn in lists of people they have called on, called back, or visited. Managers feel comfortable seeing people working. It's that "all in their places with bright shiny faces" song we learned in elementary school. We are accustomed to believing what we see. Management has a hard time accepting that a talent reading a newspaper, getting a hair cut, or fighting with his or her auto mechanic is actually doing show prep, but it can be true.

Broadcasting is not school, or a factory job where we punch in our eight hours a day. Radio work is different, more like art than manufacturing. A gallery owner would not call an artist at 8:45 in the morning and ask, "Are you at your easel yet? How many brushes have you used?"

The only hard rule for powerful radio is: *Be prepared and on time* for your show. What listeners respond to is the *finished* product. Our product is what comes out of the speakers on the radio. Our preparation is real but often invisible.

Be Prepared

Carry a recording device or note pad at all times. Don't forget spare batteries for that device. If we were working as photographers, we would always have a camera ready. But we work in *radio* and our platform is *sound*. When was the last time you thought to yourself, "I wish I had a sound recorder right now?" They are small and light. Get one. Carry it. If you are not comfortable carrying one, at least keep paper and pen handy so that you can jot down a great idea before it is gone. Great ideas come in the shower; the car; wake you up at night. Write them down.

Make Friends Outside of the Business

Spend time with normal people. If you only associate with journalists and broadcasters, you limit your vision. Expand your horizons. Talk to everyone. Your inner circle should contain people who work outside of radio and have a variety of interests and experiences. Listen to them. Find out what they are thinking, worrying, and talking about. It will help your show tremendously. Read everything. Watch everything. Find mentors. As consultant Randy Lane says: "Hang out with creative people, and learn from them. Study creative performers outside of radio."

Know Your Target

Know your audience. Do the listeners have a different lifestyle than the program host? Probably so. Perhaps the host lives in a busy urban center, whereas the bulk of the station's listeners are suburbanites. You need to know what goes on where they live, too. Read the local press. Drive around to get a feeling for your area. Attend neighborhood functions. Meet people. Get to know your city.

This is not *Lifestyles of the Rich and Famous*. Even if you do not frequent your local Wal-Mart, Ikea, or Home Depot, you should at least know people who do. Eat where your listeners eat; shop where they shop. Stay curious, alive, and interested.

Take a Test Drive

Discuss show ideas with somebody else. Prep is much easier when you have the luxury of working with a talented producer. He or she can help you focus ideas to help form questions you will ask on-air and points you will make to engage your audience. Try bouncing the ideas off people around you: the call screener, the PD, the newsperson, or the station's security guard. It may help you focus on what is really interesting about the topic, or take it in a different direction.

Prep Warning

Do *not* do your show before the show. Testing out an idea should not be confused with rehearsing a monologue. Save your actual performance for the live microphone. It will never sound as good or as natural the second time around.

Pre-produce

Prepare the soundtrack for your show. Any bits, music, etc., that you think you might want to use should be close at hand. Inform your engineer or board operator well in advance if you will require any special technical assistance or equipment. Make sure your equipment is working.

Double-Check

Before you go on-air with a topic, ask: Is it relevant? Does it matter? Do you care? Do your listeners care? What will I do if this topic gets boring? Do I have a fall-back plan?

Be Generous

If you have found a topic that would be perfect for somebody else at your station, pass it along. Leave the article, book, note, etc., in that person's mailbox. E-mail him or give him a call. The success of your station depends on the efforts of all its creative members.

Experiment

Break rules if you can come up with a more successful method. Take what works for you, and leave the rest.

Tale of Total Show Prep

The following "tale of total show prep" comes from consultant Tommy Kramer's *Coaching Handbook*. It illustrates what can happen when you do not do your homework thoroughly.

A talent called with a problem: He had overslept on Tuesday, had no time for show prep, and just barely made it in time for his morning-drive show. Yet he and his partner had a great show that day. The next day, the talent did two hours of show prep and arrived on time, but the show was difficult and out of synch. His question for me was, "Do I really need show prep?"

This guy got lucky on Tuesday. His creative side bailed him out. But it won't and cannot every day. Wednesday he did tons of prep, but all the work was informational. He had lots of things on tap but had not thought about where to go with them.

The answer is, "Yes, you need to do your show prep. But look for balance and prep your creative as well as your informational side."

Prep and Topic Selection

Method acting teaches that the actor must convince himself before he convinces the audience. If the on-air personality is genuinely interested in the topic, it will work better. Broadcasters organize their show prep in different ways. There is no "right way," just the way that works for you.

Dig Deep for Talkable Topics or Engaging Questions

Remember to look beyond page one for stories. Take notes from conversations you've had or overheard. Try to come up with at least one story or observation from your own life for each show.

Andy Beaubien and Jeremy Millar's Prep Methods

Basic preparation techniques are similar for every format. The actual protocol works as well for music as it does for talk radio. International consultant and researcher Andy Beaubien programmed many of America's top-rated Album Rock music stations. Beaubien, along with Australian Radio Network's Jeremy Millar, outlined the following method for prepping and running a well-organized show: "Show prep is usually a team effort and not a task assigned to just one person. In most cases, the program producer becomes the official collector of show-prep material, since he or she is often more objective than the show's anchor."

Review

Ideally, show prep begins with a review (aircheck session) of the previous program. This is often accomplished at the daily meeting with the PD. Decide which segments worked and which did not.

Update

The producer updates the team on new material that has arrived. This may include items from publications, syndicated-radio services, press releases, the Internet, and so on. The update should include a briefing on the latest news items that may fit the show. The availability of in-studio (or phone) guests should also be reviewed and the producer should be prepared to provide background information on them. It is also good to look at upcoming major news, sports, and show-business events.

Sources

On the Internet and elsewhere, the local newspaper need play only a modest role in your show. If you find that you are depending on the newspaper for most of your topics, try a "newspaper-free" week.

Some teams hire writers who will generate exclusive material for their shows. You can often find talented freelance writers who will regularly deliver fully written, customized material for a surprisingly nominal fee.

Topics

Decide on a list of topics for the day's program, and assign a priority to each item. Gather additional information about items that have caught your attention. Often you may find that a topic which originally sounded interesting turns out to be a dead-end street. On the other hand, research may uncover amazing facts about a subject that had seemed limited.

If scriptwriting or prerecorded material is to be used, the producer can assign these tasks to others on the team. Most talents prefer an outline to a written script, so they can deliver material in their own style.

Production

Prerecorded material may include interviews with guests not available at airtime, on-the-street interviews, musical excerpts, sound effects, novelty voices, feature intros and outros, and highlights from previous programs.

Schedule

Schedule the program elements on paper. Make sure everyone involved gets a copy. Each program should be planned in quarter-hour segments (or smaller if necessary). Interview guests are also placed on the schedule at this time. The program schedule should be maintained on a daily and weekly basis. A good producer should always have a contingency plan, as last-minute guest cancellations are common.

Archives

An essential part of show prep is the maintenance of complete and accurate files. Include the following:

- A file of previous daily program schedules

- Copies of scripts and program ideas

- Background material by subject

- Audio files, including full-length recordings of previous programs and edited program excerpts

Accurate records allow the team to recycle successful program features. Great guests and new show topics are not always available. A good library will keep the show afloat through slow periods.

Tommy Kramer points out that another nearly effortless way a team show continues to prep outside the station is to "communicate with each other off the air. An advance phone call or e-mail can prepare your partner or producer for a bit you want to do tomorrow. It gives the other person time to turn it over to his or her subconscious and think of creative ways to contribute. Time spent going to lunch or a ball game together can teach you things about each other's speech patterns, outside interests, etc., that could otherwise take months to learn."

Be Selective

It is great when you have ten fabulous ideas for a show but only need four. But how do you know which topics should make it to the air? Is there a set criteria for topic selection? Consultant Jaye Albright says it very well:

> Do something that has something to do with me and my life. It can't be a cliche. It must be original and specific. If it is from your life, I hope that it becomes a metaphor for something about mine. Something that moves me emotionally, touches me personally, yet is delivered with spontaneity and the knowledge that my time is important. The less it has to do with me, the briefer or the more moving it must be.

WABC TV's assignment editor Howard Price chooses stories that air on top-rated *Eyewitness News* in New York City. Price knows how to spot popular issues and trends and, like many top producers, incorporates Frank

Magid and Associates research findings from years ago, which still hold true: three subject areas listeners and viewers always respond to are stories about "health, heart and pocketbook." He uses these criteria for topic selection:

- *You work for "WIFM"*—"What's in it for *Me?*"—and the "me" means your listeners.

- *Every day ask:* What are people really doing? What are they talking about right now at their desks or on the checkout line? How can my program engage in and advance the discussion? Explore problems *and* solutions. Unite your listeners with stories of personal crises or extreme viewpoints.

- *Have the vision and vigilance* to spot trends, take risks, and exploit opportunities. Do one thing, or a small collection of things, better, faster, and more reliably than any of your competitors. That is what builds your image in the minds of your listeners.

- *When selecting topics, ask:* Will people expect us to cover this? If your listeners know that you can be counted on for great coverage of sports, health, or politics, then they tune to you for those things.

- *People care about things that are close to them physically, emotionally, spiritually or intellectually.* They care about the security of their jobs, the education of their kids, the health of their parents, the cost of their homes, their favorite celebrities, etc. They care about the consequences of the decisions their leaders make. They want the answer to the question "What does this mean to *me?*"

- *Use radio's immediacy.* Radio can still get more places faster than TV. Do as much live as you can. If there is a current event where you can get a direct call through to the people involved, radio has the advantage while TV is still trying to push their camera in someone's front door. Pick that topic. Everyone has a telephone in the house, but hardly anyone has a satellite hookup in the living room.

- *Use the news.* Scan the wires, newspapers, magazines, newsletters, online services, and the Internet for stories that sadden, outrage, inform, enlighten, amuse, or frustrate.

- *Have a friend who has a friend.* Always get a phone number. Keep your database updated. Hang on to phone numbers of all sources.

Take advantage of all the sources that offer free directories: the government, universities, TV and radio stations, public relations firms, etc. Keep "hot lists" of relevant phone numbers. Today's guests may be tomorrow's sources. Ask them to call you when things are happening.

- *Get a life.* There really is more to life than news, weather, and sports. Explore a broad spectrum of interests. Become a dabbler who knows a little about a lot of things. Be as worldly as your guests and listeners!

- *People want more than just the facts.* They want to understand *why* something is happening.

There is also a basic philosophy behind hiring air talent who can spot a good subject for air. Programmer Alan Eisenson has the following ideas about choosing topics.

Topic Selection

The deepest I ever get into content is when I think a host is doing the same topic too often or if I think a host has missed a major top-of-mind issue. Beyond that, I stay out of it. I have found that it can harm true talent if you micro-manage them. Of course, I suggest topics all the time, but they are only suggestions.

When you first hire a talk talent, you should set the overall criteria for content on your radio station. My criteria is that the shows should hold up a mirror and reflect life.

Keeping the target demo in mind, topics should include a wide range of issues. News and politics (local, national, and international), should be there, also general life, pop culture, relationship issues, sports, etc. Hosts should also be able to cull material and stories from their personal lives and translate them into relatable talk shows. Self-disclosure is very important. Anything that affects your life should be covered on your talk show.

Do Not Stifle the Creative Process

My approach to content is that it is not the program director's role to take authority over topics. I never mandate a topic, and I never veto a topic. It is vitally important that the content of a show be solely up to the talk-show host. The host is the one who has to engage the audience, so the topics have to come from his or her gut. His or her opinions and passions cannot be dictated by a program director, general manager, client, or consultant. The host is the artist; the airtime is his or her canvas. Do not take the brush from the artist's hand.

Content Execution

I believe that, as a program director, you must hire talent you can count on to pick topics based on your criteria. You expect them to be creative, interesting, and original, have a sense of humor, and be relatable. They should be interested in a wide variety of things, have strong opinions, a deep knowledge base, be articulate, paint pictures with words, really live life, do incisive interviews, make people think, make people laugh, and act appropriately in a variety of prickly situations. If you do not have that trust from the outset, you have hired the wrong talk-show host.

If you truly demonstrate that you trust your talk talents with their own content and you do not interfere with their creative processes, the faster they will trust, respect, and respond to you when you direct and guide them in aircheck sessions.

Prep for the Dull Day

Radio is easy when there is a lot going on and plenty to talk about. The real challenge of creating powerful radio is making it work on those days when *nothing* is happening. Sometimes it's hard to find things to talk about that are meaningful, entertaining, relevant, and significant.

The last thing you should do on a dull Monday is to start scouring last Thursday's paper for material. The urge to do this is often overwhelming. Resist! Use your own life experience instead.

Look Inward

Try using stories you have heard from family members or friends. One host got on the air and told about his grandparents, both in their eighties and somewhat forgetful. They resolved to keep lists of things to do. One day, Grandma asked Grandpa to pick up some ice cream at the store.

"Do you need to write it down?" she inquired.

"No. Just the ice cream?" he asked.

"Yes," she replied.

"I'll remember," he said.

Grandpa came back with a dozen eggs, orange juice, a loaf of bread, and waffle mix.

"I told you to write it down," said his wife. "You forgot the bacon!"

This sort of thing goes on in every family, and the more personal the story, often the more universal it turns out to be.

When I was running a news department, one of our reporters went through a bad night, waiting for her boyfriend to come home. She was a mess at work the next morning. I suggested she make a story out of her jealousy and put it on the air. She came up with an award-winning series called "Can a Man Be Satisfied with Just One Woman?" The more personal you get, the deeper you go, and the more likely you are to strike a universal chord.

Big Ears and Eyes

Sometimes you may overhear usable material. A writer who was supposed to meet her husband at an appointed time showed up hours late. He was rather upset when she finally arrived, but she offered this explanation: "I'm so sorry, but I was riding the bus and when my stop came, the people sitting in front of me were right in the middle of a story, and I just had to hear how it ended. I couldn't get off the bus!"

Sparked by this story, she wrote a book that was then turned into a movie. She became fabulously famous and wealthy, all because she overheard a conversation on a bus that she could use as material.

If a story interests you, find a way to make it interesting on the air. Real-life stories are all around us. *Train* your ears and eyes to catch them.

Bring an Idea to Work

After you have used up everything in your own life, create powerful brainstorming sessions. Contrary to rumor, genius is sometimes a collective thing. Ideas can be built upon, and they can come from anywhere. A "bad" idea can quickly become a good one if a couple of heads get together on it. Some of the best ideas come from the least likely sources.

Imagine that the "price of admission" for every employee at your station each day is to bring in one idea. They wouldn't necessarily have to be good ideas, just something someone noticed, thought about, or even experienced in the past twenty-four hours. All the ideas would be written down and go into a fishbowl.

Get the creative group together, then look at the ideas. Not all of the ideas would be good ones. Some might be truly awful. But if one or two were usable, you would be ahead. This works for programming, sales, promotion, research—just about everything you do, on the air and off.

One example from San Francisco: Our news department had just completed a ten-part documentary program on the slump in the computer business in the Silicon Valley. My entire brilliant, creative staff sat around racking their brains over a name for it. Overhearing us, our front desk receptionist looked up and asked, "How about, 'When the chips are down?'"

There was silence, then applause. That informal brainstorm session led to a catchy title for our series. You never know . . . and that's part of the fun.

More ideas on brainstorming come from broadcast consultant Michael Haas, who programmed Munich, Germany's Antenne Bayern. He taught his staff that an effective "bit" on the radio includes:

- Statement (headline)

- Elaboration (details)

- Kicker (climax and punchline)

The seeds of an idea can be for any of those three.

Michael Haas's Brainstorming Rules

- During the brainstorm, there must be no judgment of ideas. No evaluation or criticism is allowed.

- Freewheeling is allowed and encouraged. The wilder and more outrageous the idea, the better.

- Look for quantity rather than quality. Try to end up with a long list of ideas. In brainstorming, quantity produces quality.

- Combine ideas. Make each idea better. In this case, only positive building is allowed.

- Every idea must be written down. If you choose not to write something down, you will have judged it, which violates the first rule.

- Every person taking part in the brainstorm is equal in rank. There are no bosses, no leaders, no hierarchy.

In order to come prepared to the brainstorming table, Haas reminds broadcasters to *get a life*. Listen to people and other stations. Read newspapers, books, and magazines. Watch TV. Notice billboards, commercials, and labels to get ideas. Use your life's experience, both private and professional, for material. Make friends outside the media world. Maintain your health with physical fitness and watch for stress. Bring some fantasy and idealism to the session. Have a positive attitude. Use empathy and people skills. Watch for trends. Keep in contact with listeners—drink at their bars, shop where they shop, etc.

Ideas

Do not underestimate the value of living in the world as a source of show prep. Consultant Jaye Albright embraces this idea as well:

> Communication is more about listening and observing your target listener than it is about talking. Live a life. Build off-air relationships. Learn to expose your true feelings. Be vulnerable. Explore your own beliefs. Listen to others talk about their values and beliefs. Open a window to the inner workings of varying points of view. Experiment with safely expressing these differing points of view and then listen to what happens.

Scott Shannon on Show Prep

One man who never seems to run out of show-prep ideas is New York City's WPLJ (95.5 FM) PD and morning man Scott Shannon. You feel you know him when you listen to his work. In an interview, Shannon explained his philosophy:

> There is no cookie cutter formula. You have to hit the listeners over the head with what you are doing . . . make your station sound different. I've always been able to figure out what people like, what's going to catch on and be popular . . . stay ahead of the curve. You could call me a "super-active consumer."

Scott Shannon's List for Creating Powerful Radio

- Carry a recording device at all times.

- Carry spare batteries for the recording device at all times.

- Read everything.

- Watch everything.

- Learn your computer and all your equipment.

- Answer your own telephones and talk to listeners.

- Hang out with normal people.

- Seize the moment.

- Create talk.

- Always remember these three words: *PREPARATION, CONCENTRATION, and MODERATION.*

CHAPTER 11

Creating Powerful Radio
Producers

> "The artist makes life more interesting or beautiful,
> more understandable or mysterious or in the
> best sense, more wonderful."
> — *George Bellows*

Producing is a tough gig. When the show goes well, the host gets the credit; when it fares poorly, often it is the producer who is blamed. Good producer jobs are difficult to get. Most demand long, stressful hours for little reward and low pay. Although many music DJs and presenters produce their own shows, in talk radio, particularly in major markets, a producer can add significantly to the success of the program.

Finding the Right Producer

I frequently get calls from station managers and talent looking for the "right" producer. I also get calls from producers who are looking to move on for a variety of reasons, but mostly because they hate their hosts. They want the equivalent of a "radio divorce" but don't necessarily want to leave their "child," meaning the show itself.

As with any good relationship, the producer and the host must listen to each other. Both should share the same goals for the show. Hosts and producers spend a lot of time together. One of my favorite hosts in talk radio once said, "It was easier to find my wife than the right producer." So how do you find the "right" producer?

When you are on the air, it's almost like being naked in public. You are exposed and vulnerable. It is just you, the phones, and that big microphone. You need a producer who is on your side, supportive when you feel alone on the air, a presence beyond the glass wall. A producer is someone who believes in your show and wants to make you and the product sound great.

That is not necessarily the same thing as agreeing with the host's point of view. Some great producers give their all for hosts who are not of their own political stripe. Professionals can work with just about anyone. Of course the producer does not have to like a host or presenter to produce a successful program, but there must be respect. If the host knows that he or she has the support of a sharp and talented producer, the show works better.

Grow Your Own

Great producers are not born, they are developed. Look for potential producers with their promise. *Ask:* Is this person bright? Good at handling pressure? Fearless? Can this producer pick up the phone and get the White House as easily as the local dogcatcher? Can he or she get along with the news department? Have ideas? Can this person say no? Does he or she like listening to talk radio *and* like listening to you?

Do not hire someone who wants to be on air. It usually does not work out. The job of producing is more "directing" than acting. Successful producers enjoy the behind-the-scenes aspect of making things happen. Hosts should not have to worry that their producers are coveting their jobs and secretly working toward that goal, instead of putting energy and skill into producing a great show.

Sometimes you get lucky and the right producer finds you. Often the best producers are listeners first, people who enjoy the show. One such listener and fan was Nuala McGovern, who became the senior producer for WNYC's Brian Lehrer program. She volunteered as an intern, learned the job, and then was hired to produce one of the most popular public radio shows in New York City.

Keep the Good Ones

Many American radio stations are sloppy about hiring and hanging on to good producers. They tend to promote secretaries, hire minimum wage students, or relatives. Good producers are often forced to go to TV or leave the industry if they want to be paid what they are worth. There is very little producer training or job security available. It is a trial by fire.

If you find a good producer, do whatever it takes to keep him or her. A good producer can contribute tremendously toward making your show powerful radio. A bad or angry one can damage you. Try not to upset them for no reason, and try to find it in your budget to pay them for the valuable work they do. When the right combination of host and producer comes together, it's a wonderful event. On that lucky day and forever after, the most important thing to remember about the host/producer relationship is this: Be patient. Be willing to work it out, not walk out.

Make your producer feel valued. Today's producers are tomorrow's program directors. When I am searching for program directors, I always take a serious look at who is behind the scenes screening and producing the best shows.

Share the Wealth

If you are a host, treat producers nicely. You get the glory, they're underpaid. You get the credit, they get yelled at. Share the perks, the books, the free tickets, and free meals. Take them to lunch or dinner. Give them honest feedback. If you blow up at them, apologize, and *don't* wait too long to do it. And if you get a ratings bonus, share some of that as well.

Thank Them Publicly

Lots of hosts take a few minutes at the end of every show to thank the producer, screener, writers, and the board operators by name. You should do this at the same time you thank your guests and listeners. Your producing team will feel appreciated, and that is worth it.

Don't Hire a Blind Date

Get to know your producer. Try him or her out before you make the final hire. Interns sometimes work out very well as producers after they get to know the ropes. Insist on having input into the hiring process. Again, get one who actually likes to listen to your show. Be open to working with someone who is not like you. Life-stage differences can be valuable. Let's say for example that you are an older male and your producer is a young female student. Now you have a couple of perspectives that can only help the show.

Hire Someone with Good Judgment

You should respect your producer but still be able to have an argument with him or her. Expecting not to have huge disagreements with your producer is unrealistic—as if expecting never to fight with your spouse. The producer–host relationship is intense. The disputes are never really fair because most of the time, the host wins. Conflict can be healthy. A host should be able to freely express himself with the producer. The producer should be able to do the same if the relationship is a fairly honest one. A "kiss up" trying to please you or agreeing with you all the time does not really help your show.

This Is Show Biz

Choose a producer who knows you are doing a radio show and knows that the show must be fun and entertaining, rather than a forum for long-winded guests. Again, your job is to keep the audience engaged. Your producer should never promise a guest more than a few minutes on the air. If guests are boring, have the producer dump them. Thank them and get rid of them. Great guests can always stay longer or finish out an hour. Make sure your host has enough material to talk about, whether or not you have guests or calls coming in.

Get a Flexible, Not a Rigid, Person

Make sure your producers understand that a great talk show does not always stick to one topic or move from point "A" to point "B." Sometimes, it meanders like a river. A spontaneous incident on the air or a wacky call can take the show in a whole new, and better, direction. But if you have hired someone who can only move on a set schedule, you could miss a great radio moment like this one:

> Three politicians were on-air discussing economic reform. A listener called in with a question. In the background dogs were barking so loudly, they could not be ignored. The host asked what size dog made such a racket. It turned out to be a rottweiler, and there were several, because the caller was in the rottweiler-breeding business. After some discussion of pets, another listener, this one a psychologist, rang through. He wanted to know what type of pets the politicians had. This psychologist had a theory about power and pet ownership. He reasoned that "cat people" need less control, because cats "do what they want." On the other hand, he felt control freaks would have dogs because dogs respond to commands. So what kind of pets did these politicians have? They all had dogs.

It's a good thing the screener-producer put through that psychologist, even though he was slightly off the point. It generated a magic moment.

Is There a Formula?

Although there is no crystal ball to see whether a host and a producer will take to one another, there are some personality traits that make for better matches.

Take a look at Chapter 3, "Generators and Reactors," in this book. A reactive host will work best with a generative producer. To do his or her best work, a generative host needs a reactive producer. A generative producer, even one that is not on the air, must still come up with original ideas and be responsible for feeding the host talkable topics that can be worked into a theme for the show. There isn't a formula for choosing show topics either, but experience has taught me a few things that definitely do and do not work.

Avoid the Manufactured Hour

The closer the show sounds to real life with genuine people having real conversations, the better it works. Try to avoid "easy" stories from headlines or from press releases—anything that sounds like: "And now another topic manufactured to fill another segment of radio…" Audiences prefer programs that sound as though the conversation could just as easily be taking place off the air.

Throw Out Stale Bread

Creating Powerful Radio means never being boring. If a subject or topic has been extensively covered and there is nothing new you can add to it, ask yourself whether this is really "powerful radio."

Resist the temptation to book celebrity guests or experts just because they are available to you. Never book a guest without a reason. Ask: "Why should the listener care?" Your job is to get and keep audiences. Theirs is to publicize or try to get the people in your listening audience to buy *their* latest movie, book, project, and so on.

Don't book a guest just because you think he or she will generate phone calls. Sometimes a great show has few or no calls, and a bad show can have a full board of calls. Psychics on the air will net a full board of calls. Mostly it's boring. The only person interested in hearing the program is the person talking to the psychic. Why would the rest of the audience care? Meanwhile, the scientist with information on how to avoid Armageddon may not get any calls, because the audience is simply listening. They are taking in the information. Book guests and pick topics as though you had no phone in your studio.

Know Your Source

It is fine to use the Internet, prep services, current events, and news stories for content, but producers should also bring their own original ideas for the program. Producers should read widely, listen to the competition, and generate ideas based on life.

A *cautionary* word about the Internet: The Net is not necessarily a reliable source of accurate information. The beauty of the Internet is that everyone has equal access. A lunatic in his garage can put up a Web site or create a blog that looks as convincing as a major university's. Some sites, such as those belonging to major newspapers, are more trustworthy than others. Sites with rumor, gossip, innuendo, and urban myth can still be useful, providing you acknowledge the provenance of the information and flag it accurately.

Do not undermine your credibility by presenting uncorroborated information as fact. There is room on radio and television for an entire range of sources and subject matter, from front page news to obscure phenomena, but be clear about what kind of a show you are doing.

In the Creating Powerful Radio Workshops, producers are asked to bring in three items to work into talkable topics for show prep. The following simple techniques should bring several topics to the host that no else will be able to cover in the same way.

1. One idea from your own life, something that has happened to you.

2. Something you've observed or overheard.

3. One item from the news that you would actually talk about with another person in real life, that is, if you did not have a radio show to produce.

In each case, find the "universal angle." A *universal angle* is a common thread or dynamic that affects everyone. Often the details of a story are interesting only to the participants and are no one else's business. While the personal is universal, the private can be boring.

Eavesdrop—Be a Snoop

Here's an idea where being a snoop paid off. On her way to work, Sara stopped for a take-out cup of coffee. Standing in line, she overheard a woman ahead of her in line on her cell phone, apparently breaking up with a boyfriend:

WOMAN: No. John, it's really over. No, please don't do this . . . A weekend at the lake house is not going to change my mind. We are through. John, this is the right thing to do. I am releasing you so that you can get on with your life and find the person who will be right for you.

The other customers were staring at their shoes, appalled and embarrassed. But it gave Sara, the producer, an idea for a question to engage an audience. She relayed the idea to her host and the show opened this way:

> What possesses you to think you are alone in your living room when you are talking on your mobile phone? Have you ever overheard one of those excruciating conversations? You know, the kind where you would like the earth to just open up and swallow you because it is so embarrassing to hear? What is the most awful conversation you've ever overheard in public when someone has been on their cell phone?

The first caller to the program was a man who had had an experience that morning. On his way to work he, along with everyone else on the bus, overheard a fellow passenger being fired. The guy answered his cell phone and said:

> MAN: What do you mean report to human resources? But what about the promotion? Jim got the job? But what about my PowerPoint presentation and the report? I have it ready to go here in my briefcase. Jim gave the report? Jim is in my office? I need to see Elaine in human resources?

It was a silent bus. Nobody could look at anyone else.

And that is how one producer's morning coffee stop led to a "universal angle" that created powerful radio—real people sharing real stories.

Use Your Life

Another producer helped his host get to the "universal angle" of a topic that came from the host's private life. "Bob," the host, had promised his wife he would paint their garage. But because Bob preferred to watch football on Sundays, they got into a huge fight. Bob and his producer decided that the paint, the garage, and the argument were Bob's private life...but there was a "universal angle."

Bob's question: "Why do women nag? Why is it a woman will ask you over and over again to do something when you've told her ten times you'd get to it...it's on your list, you intend to do it?" A female caller responded:

> WOMAN: Well, if you guys would just *DO* the things we asked you to do, we wouldn't have to turn into these nagging shrews!

Meanwhile, the producer found a psychologist who had just published a study on male–female relationships. It seemed most men didn't care whether a woman gained weight or was a lousy cook—what they hated was nagging. Why? Because their mothers nagged them. The topic went for two hours, with lots of humor. It took a talented producer to help find the "universal angle" and focus it for air.

Formatics Count

It is important to have a producer who understands the logic behind formatics. Lots of producers know the basics but are never told why they matter so much. Why is it crucial to mention the station's name or call letters before each call goes to air, and to reset the topic every few minutes— before and after commercial breaks?

As long as ratings are based on recall, what your listener remembers and reports to the ratings or research service will matter. Memory is not reliable. If people don't remember what they ate for breakfast, how can they remember what they were listening to at 7:17 last Thursday? How can they be expected to report accurately what they have heard to a monitoring service or market research interviewer? Of course they cannot.

Because of that, some radio listening, referred to as "phantom cume," is never counted in the ratings. Your staff needs to understand the importance of helping the listeners retain and write down your call letters by repeating them on air as often as possible.

DENNIS THE MENACE

"I LIKE THE WAY YOU DON'T EVER TAKE A BREAK FOR COMMERCIALS."

Geller Media International
Producer's Ten Commandments

1. Know your host/presenter, and his or her audience as well.

2. Do not covet your host's air shift, but be a faithful listener to it.

3. NEVER put a boring caller or guest on the air.

4. Have only ONE director or programming manager giving input.

5. Pay close attention to details so your host/presenter will not have to, and remember your address list or database and keep it and up to date.

6. Be organized, able to easily and quickly locate a contact, and find the things your host/presenter puts down and loses. Never throw away a phone number, e-mail address, or a good take-out menu.

7. Know the Internet world and the real world. Read about and live in both of them.

8. Have a life outside the radio station. It will serve you as show prep, twenty-four hours a day, every day, providing you with creative topics and angles nobody else is doing.

9. Study the station, and learn to do everything—the payoff will go to the producer who can run the board, edit and assemble audio, set up a remote, screen calls, make coffee, and plan events or travel.

10. Foster good relations between your host/show and the rest of the radio station, especially the news and sales departments.

CHAPTER 12

Creating Powerful Radio
Call Screening

> "Talent hits a target no one else can hit;
> Genius hits a target no one else can see."
> — *Arthur Schopenhauer*

The Art of Call Screening for Producers

If you take calls on your show, you already know that a great caller can make a show; a boring or bad call can be a show killer. You can almost feel the listeners tuning out. Like many tasks in life, screening appears to be easy. Answer the phone and put the call on the air? Not exactly. Screening involves being able to manage people. This job takes both art and skill.

Most producers have had the experience of putting what seemed to be a great call on the air and then watching it bomb. Sometimes a caller who seems like a long shot, slow-paced, slightly out of your demographic target, a little weird, will surprise you with his humor, passion, and a good story to tell.

How do you screen out bad or boring callers while attracting great ones? Are there methods to coach average or mediocre callers to become better and more powerful on air?

"That's not what you told my screener you wanted to talk about."

Contrary to popular belief, getting to speak on a talk show is *not* a given right in a free and democratic society. In order to qualify: You must have something to *say*. No matter what callers think or tell you, making it to air is not "their right." It is a privilege. Not everyone who demands to be on air is going to get on air, nor should they. Use your callers to the show's advantage, not the other way around. Do not put on a bad caller.

Hosts may panic when they see they have very few or no callers waiting to go on the air, but it is the producer's job to remind the host that less than one percent of the listening audience will ever call a talk show.

Sometimes a great show has very few or *no* calls. A bad show can have a full phone board for hours at a time. The number of blinking lights is a false indicator of how well a show is going. Unfortunately, hosts like to see a lot of calls or they get nervous. One solution is to cover the call lights so they cannot see who is waiting.

The job of the host is to focus the issue in such an engaging manner that interesting people with strong opinions and something to say actually want to call the show. But having no calls is not an indication that the station or show has no listeners. Sometimes a host can be so compelling, calls are not even needed.

Screening is a way to give power to a show by filtering out the elements that can hold it back and make it boring. It works best if the host does not make a big deal out of the screening process. Don't read off the computer screen.

Avoid ruining the fun for the listeners and for the host by telling them in advance what they will hear. Just give them a hint. There is no journey if the host gives the story away: "Mary on line three, my screen says you have a dog that found a million dollars in a garbage can?" That eliminates the surprise.

Keep a bit of the magic of radio. Work with and encourage hosts not to reveal what is happening behind the scenes. Try it this way: "Mary, tell us about your amazing dog." Or simply, "Mary, you are on WABC."

What Makes for a Good Caller?

You always know one when you hear the caller. A successful talk show may reject as many as *fifty percent* of the calls that come in. A good caller is relevant, interesting, funny, or poignant. This is a person who *adds* to the show and makes it better. Remember, normal people don't call talk shows. Sometimes so-called "normal people" aren't all that interesting. Often it's the weird ones, with the strange experiences and vision and stories to tell, who create those "magic moments" on air. A few tips:

- If you are bored screening the caller, how interesting will your audience find her?

- If you are discussing a human experience, it often works better to put on callers who have lived through that experience and have a story to tell rather than an academic or expert who is removed from the experience.

- Avoid multipart questions or a long, rambling preamble.

- Before you decide to put a caller on air, make sure the point the he or she wishes to get across is concise, clear, and focused.

- If you are targeting a young audience, then it makes sense to avoid "older"-sounding callers. However, those who are under eighteen must be extremely articulate to be "good."

- In the United States, callers who sound between twenty-five and fifty-four are optimal. But vital, passionate, interesting callers who have good questions, a sense of humor, are great storytellers, or have had a personal experience with what you are talking about will always work, no matter their age.

The Short Hello

Train your callers. Avoid "greeting cards" such as "Thank you for taking my call" or "We love your show." Avoid "How are you today?" The host is fine. The caller is fine. Everyone is fine. Congratulations or greetings are of *no* interest to the listener. Get to topic. Don't be afraid to say, "Get to the point." We are very happy you love the show. The long hello is boring. This is a radio show, *not* a phone conversation, even though it may feel that way to you because you are holding a phone.

Give the callers your rules. "No reading of prepared statements or articles. You'll need to ask your question or make your comment without a long preamble. No multipart questions."

The Host Will Hang Up on You

To avoid callers calling back after they've been on the air and complaining that the host rudely hung up on them, alert callers prior to going on air that when the host is done, he or she will abruptly disconnect the line, and while this may seem impolite, this is how it works.

The Pep Up

Before a caller is about to go on air, check back to be sure he or she is still waiting on the line and ready to go. You may need to remind the caller about the original point if they have been on hold for a while. Remind them again to turn their radios off.

Listen to the Show

Stay in communication with the host throughout the course of the program. Although you may be busy screening, do try to listen to the show and follow the thread of the program.

There Are Many Nice Ways to Say "No"

A screener needs a backbone. That does not mean being rude, but it does mean being firm. Get a screener who can tell people *"No."* Hire someone who can make a fast decision to get rid of a boring call. Ask: "Would this person keep a listener engaged?" If you think the caller or guest would be boring to a listener, do not put him or her on air.

Sample Script for Screening Calls

- Answer the phone with the station's name or the name of the show: "KFIX John Johnson Show, what is your comment or question?"

- If the caller does not immediately come across with a concise point or opinion, help them focus. Ask: "What is your opinion?" "Why is this important to you?" "Can you give me a brief summary of your point?"

- If the caller still does not meet your criteria, he or she should be rejected.

- Remind the caller to speak clearly into the phone!

You need to work quickly in order to have the next call up and ready to go. There should never be a time when the host cannot move on to the next call.

If the caller meets your criteria, summarize his or her point and opinion on the computer screen for the host. That allows the host to take calls in the order he or she prefers.

No one likes to say no, particularly if the caller is a sweet lonely old lady who lives by herself with no friends and this call to your show right now is the only adult conversation she's had all week. But you must protect your product. Serve thousands, not one. It's hard to do, but it is your job to take care of the show, not the caller. Politely say, "No, I am sorry, but I am not going to be able to take your call, not today. Perhaps another time. Thank you."

Other Polite Rejections

"We are running out of time this hour," "Thank you, I'll pass your comment along" or "We cannot use your call today, but we appreciate you taking the time to call." Do not give them time to respond—politely disconnect.

Be tough but professional. Should a rejected caller become angry or try to engage you in an argument, do not get upset or rattled. If there is time, hear the caller out, and then hang up. The management has hired you for your ability to judge what will make a winning show. Most reasonable management will support you in your decision to protect your show from boring callers.

Avoid speakerphones or bad cell lines. If the reception is poor, do not put the call on air. Avoid callers with heavy accents who can't be easily understood.

You certainly don't want a producer to anger your audience. But your audience is really the 99 percent of your listeners who will never phone.

A Rule about the "Regulars"

The only real rule about "regular callers" is this: Bad regular callers should not get on. Good regular callers should. In fact, we sometimes hire *hosts* who have been regular callers.

Your callers are your "active listeners." They are loyal, listen regularly, and are not too shy to call. One sharp producer made up a database of the "characters" or powerful callers to his show. He kept this list in the computer. Every now and then, when the board was slow and the night was long, he'd phone those people and ask them, by chance, if they were listening. If not, they'd tune in right away and usually come up with some good comments to move the show forward.

This producer also had a second use for his list of phone numbers and e-mail addresses. When the host was scheduled to make a public appearance or speech, he would e-mail an announcement to those listeners, who had asked to be included. Many enjoyed attending these events.

Sequencing Calls

To best determine the order of the calls, keep track of the show topic and be aware of the points of view of the host and each guest.

Conflict makes for interesting dialogue. If your host enjoys it, and it is appropriate for the program, move calls that do not agree with the host to the front of the line.

If the show has guests representing several points of view, then alternate the caller's points of view whenever possible. In reality, you may not get an equal division or balance of callers reflecting pro and con on any issue, but you can try, through the screening process, to eliminate clusters of similar callers and opinions. Push the interesting ones, the ones with passion, to the top.

The first call on the show should be the *best* available caller. That first call often sets the tempo for the rest of the hour.

Come out of each break with the strongest, most energetic and passionate caller you have waiting.

"She's Been Waiting for Forty-Eight Minutes . . . "

So what. The point is to make a powerful broadcast for the listeners. So if the host chooses to go with another topic or go long with a caller or guest, let them wait. Even if they get mad and yell at you, the first priority at all times is to protect the product on air and make sure it's powerful.

"He Sounded Fine When I Pre-interviewed Him . . . "

People get nervous when they actually go on air. Every call screener has had the experience of listening helplessly as a caller, who sounded so great before he or she hit the airwaves, flounders when the host takes the call.

Here's why: We are around live broadcasts all the time and forget that it can be a terrifying experience for someone who doesn't do this every day. Coach callers to take a breath, get right to the point, don't read from notes, be as you would in a normal conversation, forget the others listening, and don't worry about looking foolish.

Usually people lose the nervousness as soon as they get onto a familiar topic or subject about which they feel passionate. That is why we need to work with callers to help "get them there" as soon as possible in the call.

Put Yourself "On Hold"

If you as a producer or screener have not had the experience of calling a radio or television talk show, try calling somebody else's show. See how the process feels when *you* get screened. When the shoe is on the other foot, you will be amazed. When you understand what it feels like to be on hold, then it's your turn ... and *you* are on air with a question for a host or guest, it will add another perspective and allow you to be more effective as a screener.

Messaging and E-mail

Hosts like to use interactive media, but the criteria for including e-mails and instant messages is: "Is the content relevant?" During the business day, some people cannot use their phones to call a talk show, so you may be able to get more opinions on the air using e-mail or messaging.

Be aware that reading messages on the air is not as interesting as having the actual person delivering his or her thoughts in his or her own voice. Reading messages should be a second choice if you have a good call waiting.

If you do use text on the air, read it with drama and introduce the sender this way: "Carol, you say in your message that you have been watching shoplifters at your neighborhood market ... " Using a "you" to address the sender makes the message sound more like a conversation with a caller.

Go to Our Web Site for More

Stations that run edited interviews or performances on the air are allowing listeners to access the long form or complete versions from their Web sites. Your Web site should also be used to move detailed content, such as a guest author's mailing address, a recipe, contest rules, etc., out of your broadcast and make it available to the audience at their convenience.

As a producer, if your host promises listeners they will find a piece of information on your station's Web site, it is your job to make sure it gets there. If you don't, you make your host and your station look bad.

Tips for Talk Show Producers and Screeners

Here are some methods and ideas that have emerged from the Geller Media International Producer's Workshops over the years:

- Focus on your audience, not the one percent of the listeners who call in.

- Make sure your host has material to talk about if there are no calls coming in. Plan your show as if there will be no calls.

- Don't let all your lines jam. Screen out weak calls and keep some lines open so better calls can come in.

- If you don't understand a caller, nobody else will either. Get rid of the call!

- Get your callers relaxed and talking, but don't promise them that they will be on the air.

- Build a database of sources that you can use during shows for alternate/opposing opinions, or for emergency guests if the planned guest cancels. Cross-reference by areas of expertise, affiliations, etc.

- Build a database of great callers. On a quiet day, a savvy producer can use the list to find one to go on the air.

- Be sure to give guests specific instructions on how to get to the studio and phone contact information. What if the station door is locked?

- Guests should fax or e-mail background materials ahead of time for the host to study. Guests should understand who their audience will be.

- Make sure guests *know* that the host will take care of any promotion for their book, their seminar, and so forth. There's nothing worse than a guest doing an awkward job of self-promotion.

- Develop a good relationship with your news department.

- If something major occurs, don't be afraid to cancel a guest! Radio's greatest asset is immediacy. Go with what's happening now and reschedule.

Caller Criteria

1. Can he or she offer an interesting personal experience pertaining to this topic?

2. Do you or the audience care about this person? Does this person sound like a distinctive "character?" *(Hint: If you can "see" this person in your mind's eye, it's a good character!)*

3. Is he or she a good storyteller?

4. Does he or she have a sense of humor?

5. Does this caller have strong passionate opinions on the subject?

6. Is this a person you would find fascinating or enjoy talking with *off* air?

7. Can this caller take the audience on a journey they cannot get to on their own?

8. Does he or she have something interesting, or of value, to say?

9. Can he or she offer new information about a story or subject or add specific knowledge or special expertise?

10. Is he or she entertaining?

CHAPTER 13

Creating Powerful Radio
High-Ego Talent

"Creativity takes courage."
— *Henri Matisse*

Perhaps you have had the experience of knowing people in the business who were great on the air, always got big ratings, but never kept a job for any substantial length of time? Many of these people "station-hopped" because they had demanding personalities and were tough to deal with *off* the air.

Often, great radio personalities have large egos and are not the easiest or most tranquil people to be around. But allowing your station's professional atmosphere to be blighted by tantrums is ultimately damaging. While managers need the skills to deal with touchy talent, no one can save a truly self-destructive host. Remember this when considering hiring a personality who has a "reputation."

One day, I was taking a break in the lunchroom of a client station. In between bites of sandwiches, staffers were talking about one of the station's most talented and successful broadcasters. Actually, he was one of the station's most talented *former* broadcasters, because he had just been fired.

"But he was so good on the air. I just don't get it," lamented the newest member of the staff. "I listened to him all the time. What happened?"

The room went silent. Had this guy done something truly terrible or maybe even illegal? Then one of the producers said, "Well he was kind of hard to work with . . . "

Another staffer chimed in, "Yeah, he could really get on your nerves. He complained all the time about everything."

A quiet young woman who had been working as an assistant producer to the ousted personality added: "If you weren't a big shot, he'd ignore you. He treated me like I was dirt, instead of a professional there to help him with his show. He made me feel like his personal slave. He'd order me to move his car or run outside to put money in the parking meter. He'd never ask or say please, just 'do it!' "

Having worked herself into a righteous frenzy, the young producer continued: "Whenever something went wrong on the show, like missing a network join, or a spot, or losing a guest on the phone, it was never his fault. He made a huge stink about it and blamed other people. He went through six producers in a year and a half."

"But the audience loved him!" argued the new guy.

"We didn't," said the PD, who walked into the lunchroom at that point, ending the discussion.

It has always been my belief that if people are difficult but truly talented artists, then it is worth some extra effort to put up with their nonsense, to a point. Talent is special, and artists are different. Gifts in this life are not distributed evenly. A person with abundant talent may have an equal lack of social skills. In her song about singer-songwriter Bob Dylan, Joan Baez wrote, *"A savior's a nuisance to live with at home."* And she's mostly right. True artists can be challenging to be around day to day. We love and respond to their originality, creativity, and art, but we have little use for their anger, insecurity, need for attention and approval, and lack of respect for authority.

The PD at the aforementioned station admitted that his former staffer had made him so anxious that he shut his door quickly or picked up the phone when he saw the "problem" air talent walking down the hall. Even so, he felt the dismissal was a loss both to the talent and to the radio station. It was a bad situation. However, I'm just the consultant and only looking at what went on the air. The rest of the staff had to put up with this guy every day. The station succumbed to the temptation of hiring a lesser talent because he was easier to live with.

How can managers effectively handle this type of personality? The answer is, *very carefully*. The first thing is to recognize that while the performer in question is an adult, legally speaking, that 40-year-old body may hide the emotions of a six-year-old. Don't be fooled by the long legs and beard. You can learn a lot about managing difficult talent by hanging around kids. Like children, they may be very insecure.

I walked in a day too late to save that situation. Had I had the chance to sit down and work with this talent and his manager before the situation blew up, here are a few of the points I would have communicated:

- Don't be a talkaholic. People are busy. Don't distract them. Let them go about their work.

- Do it yourself. If you need special equipment and the station doesn't have it, consider buying your own headphones, microphone, etc.

- Be selective, don't fight every battle. Save your energies for the important issues.

- Don't question authority until you've given the matter proper consideration.

- Have a little patience. Don't overreact.

- Your boss is not a mind reader. Tell your manager when you need attention. Set a time. It can't always be now.

- Don't ignore or mistreat those "below" you.

- Be a human being. Have a heart. Be sensitive to others.

- Save your show for on air, not in the hall!

One of the challenges for overworked GMs and PDs is coping with the air personalities. Top radio talent can be sensitive, volatile, ego-driven, self-absorbed, insecure, and infantile. In other words, they are difficult to manage. They need a lot of time, attention, and positive feedback. These same "pains in the neck" can also be likable, charming, and tremendously talented. They perform and connect with the audience, and can potentially bring in huge numbers of listeners. It may be up to you to decide to make the effort to manage them.

It's worth developing people. If you can afford it, financially and emotionally, try it. When it doesn't work, remember right-casting: Someone who is not right in this job may be very successful in another situation. Even the failures can teach you something. Don't dismiss it, or worse, give up, just because it is the more challenging, risky route.

Talent vs. Management: Two Worlds

For a group of professional communicators, we often don't do a very good job of it amongst ourselves. Here is a typical unspoken dialogue between a manager and an on-air talent.

TALENT		MANAGEMENT
I want you to listen to my show and respond everyday.	vs.	Your listeners love you, what more do you want?
I'm important. Make me feel that way, NOW!	vs.	I have ten other things to do right now.
I'm a creative person, I don't like anyone telling me what to do.	vs.	We talked about this: I'm not changing my mind.
Pay attention to me! You never make enough time for me!	vs.	You leave me emotionally exhausted. I have a radio station to run and you're only one part of it.
I need positive feedback; nobody appreciates me!	vs.	Why can't you just do your job and be happy with your big paycheck?
I want to make a difference. I want to be great!	vs.	I can't deal with this right now. I just spent a half an hour on the phone with an angry listener.
I want input, look at me! Listen to me! I want to count!	vs.	I get this from my three-year-old at home. I do not need it from you at work.

CHAPTER 14

Creating Powerful Radio News

"The essence of entertainment will not change. What has always counted is the story and the skill with which it is told."
—*Michael Eisner, former CEO, The Walt Disney Company*

"Storytelling is a basic part of every human culture—people have always had the need to participate emotionally in stories."
—*Marlon Brando*

News broadcasting is really two separate jobs. The first is covering the Big Story, an event of such magnitude that it affects the lives, well-being, or safety of your audience. The other is covering everything else.

On those "big news" days, it is not so important to worry about being creative. On those days, just gather the facts and get them on the air quickly. Give your listeners what they need to know. On those other days, the slower news days (that is most of the time), the news is like an insurance policy. Your newscast is in place, covering the day-to-day events of life, so that people know where they can find the information and where to go on the big news day. And those big news days are often the days that journalists live for, when the adrenalin is pumping and the stories just seem to write themselves.

But it's important *every* day to choose stories that are interesting and affect your audience in some way. Every day, the stories you choose should be interesting and affect your audience in some way. Pick items that connect listeners to what is happening in the community, what is new, interesting, or absurd. Give audiences talkable topics and entertain them with information.

Radio news can be much more exciting than many people realize. By doing what radio does best—getting on the air from a scene quickly, and describing an event so listeners can visualize what is happening—we are using the most powerful tools we possess: immediacy and imagery.

Building a Great News Team

Network News Executive Bernard Gershon looks for these traits in a newsperson:

Desire or hunger is crucial

The best employees always want to improve their performances. They display this by asking for additional assignments, wanting to learn different parts of the business, asking to be sent to training seminars. They also understand that getting better requires hard work and long hours. Look for people who are aggressive when it comes to getting interviews, going after callers, going 'prime time.'

What we look for

An effective newsperson is a storyteller who exudes "energy," someone who can generate enthusiasm and excitement from listeners and is interested in the topic, the caller, the *job*. My definition of dull? Demos of newscasters who sound like they are reading. Those can be identified in about 30 seconds—out they go. Yes, it is a cruel business, but everyone is busy.

Warning: I have seen far too many job candidates who expect to become radio or TV stars—or both—overnight. These people are usually too egotistical to understand that they have to work as a team, pay their dues, and gain a reputation. My suggestion…pass!

If a newscaster tells the truth in an interesting and, when appropriate, entertaining way, he or she can keep the attention of the listeners. A good reporter can cover a fire so descriptively that the listeners should almost be able to taste the smoke in the backs of their throats. When you create "word pictures," your news story is almost like a movie. It should be great storytelling. Then it will never be boring.

There is concern within news organizations, especially in Europe, about keeping the news very serious and credible. While the journalists have been trained to report accurately and credibly, there has been little emphasis on teaching journalists to attract or keep the attention of audiences. Their focus has been entirely on keeping journalistic integrity. This is admirable, but it does no good to be serious and credible if the results are so dull that listeners tune out.

Imagine being presented with a 14-course meal of totally bland cuisine. Nobody wants to eat it. What is the point of doing all the work of assembling a half-hour newscast that is so dry or arcane that most people cannot pay attention to it? Sure, there will always be somebody who can make it through to the bitter end, but most of your potential listeners will have given up and gone elsewhere. By making it interesting, powerful radio, you can have both credibility and interest.

Don't Be Interchangeable, Be an Individual

Information is available everywhere: over the Internet, in the paper, and on TV. So why should a listener come to you for information? Because that listener cannot hear *you*, the storyteller, anywhere else. Storytelling is the power you have to make the listener experience an event or take in information in a unique way. Be creative. Put yourself into it, keep your opinion out of it, and get your facts right—but find the way to make the story yours.

Here is an example from a Creating Powerful Radio news seminar that took place in Nairobi, Kenya. In this exercise, we gave the facts of one story to a dozen reporters. Here is the story we used:

A young woman had been arrested, tried, and jailed with a life sentence for murdering her father. She became pregnant while in prison, and gave birth to a baby girl. The question now was, "What will happen to that baby?" Should the authorities let the mother keep her baby in the jail? Or should they take away the child and give her to another family to raise? The woman's family wants nothing to do with this innocent baby. After all, the woman killed her own father. Her mother, who was his wife, had not forgiven the murdering daughter. Perhaps the people who run the jail ought to allow the baby to stay for a little while until she reaches school age, then make a decision?

And who is the father? No one knows, and the woman won't say. This was a new situation for the jail. Everyone had an opinion as to what should happen.

Several journalists got to work, with this assignment: "Take these facts and report the story, but find your own unique and creative way to tell it. Use your voice, your personality, in the storytelling."

The result: One reporter, writing in Swahili, introduced the story this way: "The last immaculate conception happened two thousand years ago. The latest was yesterday, at the Nairobi jail.... "

Another reporter, a woman in her early twenties, wrote the story from the imagined perspective of the baby: "I do not know my father. I will never know my grandfather because my mother has killed him, and I may never see the light of day, for I am born in Nairobi jail.... "

The Sound of the Story

The power and glory of a story often lies in its sound. Whenever possible, record and use natural sound. If you are covering a parade, festival, or demonstration, this is obvious. Use the sound of the event underneath your report to give listeners the feel of "being on the scene." Less obvious, and less frequently heard, are the sounds of more routine events. Think creatively. Use sound to help you tell your story. If you are doing a story on day-care centers, it makes sense to record children at play and run that underneath your report.

Here's a story everybody does twice a year, done two ways:

"Daylight saving time is over. Don't forget to turn your clock back an hour at 2 a.m."

But when a reporter went to a clock store and recorded the clocks at noon, the story came alive with the sound of chimes, bells, and cuckoo clocks under the lead:

"This is the sound of time. Remember to turn your clock back an hour tonight."

That's more powerful. The sound makes it work better, even for a story that happens twice a year like clockwork. Don't settle. It doesn't have to be boring.

Television has pictures, but in radio we have something even more powerful in our arsenal. We have imagination. By using sound and describing events and people in detail, we can stimulate imagination in a way television simply cannot.

One example comes from my former newsroom in San Francisco. A young reporter had spent all night covering a fire and was now at the station recording his reports for the morning newscasts. While the fire he'd covered was exciting, his reports were rather dull. I chalked it up to inexperience, and made a note to talk with him about it later. His story sounded like this:

> The fire burned throughout the night at the intersection of Powell and Main. The home was completely destroyed. No one was injured. It took two fire companies to extinguish the flames. The damage is estimated at four hundred thousand dollars. No one knows what started the fire.

When the reporter was done recording his story, he picked up the newsroom phone and called his girlfriend. Since he had been out all night, he needed to explain his whereabouts:

> You should have seen the fire! It was incredible! There was a full moon and you could see the black smoke billowing for miles around! All these people were out in their bathrobes and underwear watching it burn, with kids and dogs running around wild. They needed two fire companies to put out the flames because the first company couldn't get their hoses to work. So they lost the house and everyone had to wait for backup firefighters to show up. At one point, they thought there was a cat in the house, so all these firemen went in with oxygen masks to find the cat, but she was hiding under a car a block away! You could hardly breathe because the smoke was so thick and the wind kept changing, and they still don't know what started it. And that house! It's completely destroyed—nothing but ashes. They say it was worth four hundred thousand dollars! Can you imagine, even in that neighborhood, prices are up that high?

I impolitely grabbed the phone from the reporter's hand and asked why he couldn't put all that good stuff in his reports, instead of saving it for his girlfriend.

That reporter learned a lesson. Now he works for two national networks and has a wall covered with awards for making powerful radio.

Trying to convince a group of journalists that news does not have to be boring can be tough. They assume that some "important" details of a story have to be included, even if those details are not interesting. If such details do not interest you at the human level, it's likely that those details won't interest your listeners and they will probably tune out, leaving you and your "important" details behind.

If you feel you have not done your duty to your community unless you make every fact available, stash the minutia on your Web site, where those who are interested can find and peruse them.

Again, if news is presented in a boring manner, listeners tune out or "zone out." Once, at a workshop in Finland with a group of radio journalists, I played them 10 minutes of their newscast from the previous day. The group was sitting quietly and appeared to be listening intently. When it was over, I asked them, "What was the first story?"

Dead silence hung over the room. Not one journalist could remember. By the way, these were the same people who, the day before, had written, produced, and presented this newscast.

"What about the second story?" Silence. "How about the third?" No one said a word. Even though the group had just heard the newscast, the stories were so boring nobody remembered them. They had mentally tuned out.

Finally, I asked, "Does anyone remember anything from this newscast?" The only story anyone remembered concerned a church that was urging people to cremate their dead because it was cheaper than burial and the cemeteries were filled to capacity. The only story they could recall was a weird, interesting piece about cremation. Lesson: If you don't make the news interesting, listeners may "hear" the stories, but they won't sink in.

One broadcast reporter who is *never* boring is Mike Sugerman. At KCBS in San Francisco, he has been known for taking the dullest stories and bringing them to life. Because he is creative, Sugerman's work is equally good on the hard news and lighter features. For example, take a "perennial" story like America's Academy Awards. Every year, reporters cover that story the *same* way: celebrity interviews, clips of the movies, and lists of nominees. Sugerman adds a dimension by doing his own "Oscar Poll." He asks guys named "Oscar" who ought to win. Nobody else does that.

When Sugerman does a story on the homeless, he gets into their world; he lives among them, gains their trust, and gets unique perspectives. Once he did a story about garbage by accompanying an apple core to the dump. He uses sound and humor. He retains his humanity and is never above the audience. Sugarman uses imagination and is a master storyteller. He advises reporters to take risks:

> First, learn the rules of traditional journalism. Then break them. After you learn what you are supposed to do, you can cover a story and figure out what all the other reporters will be doing. Then do something different. Often, the resulting story will generate comments such as, "What the hell was that?" But eventually the comments turn into, "Hey, that was good. How did you think of that?" Occasionally, you'll still hear, "What the hell was that?" But, if you don't make mistakes now and then, you aren't pushing the envelope far enough.

Mike Sugerman has only *one warning*: "Avoid making mistakes with *actual facts*. If you are factually challenged too often, you'll lose credibility, which is all a reporter owns."

Another amazingly creative reporter is Warren Levinson, head of the Associated Press Bureau in New York City. Levinson is a master of taking seemingly boring stories and making then fascinating. Because of his credibility and expertise as a newsman, Levinson has managed to do some of the best work on the Associated Press.

Warren Levinson has some great tricks to make even an older story new without compromising any of the facts, like the time a water main burst in the city of New York had left some neighborhoods without water. Several streets and subways had been flooded for days. Because the problem was ongoing, people in New York were sick of hearing about it even though their city was still a mess. Warren gave them what they needed to know in the following poetry-style report. Try reading it aloud.

Warren Levinson's AP Poetry-Style Report

(Opens with sound of jackhammers, running water, construction noise.)

There are time bombs under New York,
aged a century or more.
The one that went off Thursday was put in in nineteen-four.
The water mains under Forty-Second Street gave way…

[Gaynor] 'Some of our older mains, that's safe to say'

Dick Gaynor is a deputy of H-2-0 supply.
Half gainer is the sort of thing that you or he or I
might have been tempted to attempt instead of catch the train,
since what subway tracks were under equaled forty weeks of rain.
And subway riders feeling more than usually harassed
sought detours. Were they mad?

[Martinez] 'No, New Yorkers are adaptable, they adjust fast'

Manuel Martinez got them round the crippled four and five train
while road and track were closed to anything that has a drive train.
We don't whitewater raft here, but you could bob like a cork,
as you whoosh down Forty-Second, Warren Levinson, New York.

(Close with the sound of more running water, jack hammers, construction noises.)

The story has all the required news information—who, what, where, why, when—and it is fun to listen to, even if you've heard it all day or all week!

Levinson says, "Newsmakers in their own words and their own voices are vital to good radio, but never forget that you are the storyteller. I have seen any number of reporters do verbal backflips just to work in a piece of audio better left on the cutting room floor. If you think that your voice cannot carry a story by itself, look to improve your writing or delivery."

Levinson emphasizes the importance of ambient sound. "Don't overlook the sound that does not come in quotes: the street sounds of a fire rescue story, the special acoustics of an art gallery or museum." Levinson advises, "Don't use background sound for its own sake, but ask yourself, 'Are there sounds that can tell an aspect of this story more concisely than I can do in words?'"

Sometimes it works very well when a reporter expresses genuine feelings about a story. It would have been almost shocking to American viewers and listeners if reporters had managed to seem emotion-free during the events of September 11, 2001, or Hurricane Katrina. Stay *objective* with the facts, but if you can personalize the story in some way, the audience will be more likely to remember your work.

Wherever there is a personal connection to a story on the part of the reporter, there is the potential for more powerful radio. One example comes from Sweden's Radio Jämtland. There had been a "mobbing" in a local school. A child had been forced down and beaten, then nearly drowned when his head was held in a toilet. The reporter remembered mobbing attacks from when she was a schoolgirl and how scary they had been. As it turned out, her daughter attended the school where the incident occurred. Like any decent mother, she was afraid for her child. She reported the story, but also told the audience she had special concerns about the safety of her own child. She brought her own life experience to the job. Any parent could relate to this story.

The Art of the Interview

The interview is the heart of the news story. When a reporter comes armed with a list of questions for an expert, spokesperson, or victim, it's easy to forget the most important thing—listening. The reporter is so eager to get to the next item on his list, the real story might be missed.

How many times have you heard an interview like this?

NEWSPERSON: So Dr. Thompson, I understand you have discovered a new species of snake?

DR. THOMPSON: Yes, its venom can be used to cure certain kinds of cancer, and the coating on its skin seems to protect it from radiation as well as heat.

NEWSPERSON: Interesting. Are you scared of snakes?

While this is a slightly exaggerated example, the failure to listen is not unusual. Your most important interviewing tools are your listening skills and natural curiosity.

Often, if you dispose of your list and simply hear what your interviewee has to say, you'll ask better questions, get much better answers, and present a better story. Ask simpler questions to generate simpler answers.

When interviewing experts, there is a tendency to let them get away with giving long, drawn out, complex, and incomprehensible answers. The problem is that journalists don't like to admit that they don't know something or don't understand a complicated answer. But if you, a broadcast professional, don't "get it," what are the odds your audience will?

Nobody likes to feel or to look foolish, but it is your job to make sure that you get straightforward answers to your questions. Better to admit you don't understand something and try again for a simple answer than to leave your audience in the dark. After all, even your expert wants to be heard and understood.

If you present the news in an interesting, topical and relevant way, the audience will consider it a reason to tune in, not tune out. Listeners will feel that they can't go a day without finding out what's going on, as explained through your newscast.

Top Tips from Reporters

Reporters from various newsrooms share their most important lessons:

- Talk to one listener at a time.
- Use silence, it's powerful.
- Avoid clichés.
- Get new ideas from calling on old story sources.
- "Off the record" means off the record. Don't "burn" your sources.
- Is collecting audio actuality or doing an interview worth the effort? Can you better use what little time you've got on another story?
- *Localize.* Know your city and use familiar terms for things.
- Keep a tease a *tease*. Make them want more later.
- Don't use the same lead that the reporter uses. It's lazy and boring and makes you look stupid.

- *REWRITE* all source material and use multiple versions. Don't use the eight o'clock copy at nine o'clock.

- Use one thought per sentence, one thought per actuality.

- Write to be *heard*. Maintain a sense of speech rhythm in your writing and read it out loud before you read it on air.

- Avoid statistics if you can. Listeners don't usually remember them.

- No one knows what is in your recorder but you. Only use the best and most powerful sounds.

- Save time by listening to recorded audio on the way back to your studio. Mentally have your multi-versions ready to go before you start editing.

- *Make* decisions. You will never get every detail into the story. Decide what goes in and what to leave out of each story version.

Valerie Geller's Top 10 Tips
for Creating Powerful Radio News

1. In the case of an urgent news story, get your facts first, and then worry about your presentation.

2. Describe things visually—paint word pictures.

3. Write shorter! Use fewer words but make them count. When in doubt, leave it out.

4. Use effective storytelling techniques; tell stories the way you would tell them to friends.

5. Use natural sound.

6. Stay *objective!* Keep your opinion out of the story, but put your humanity into it.

7. Really listen when you are interviewing. Ask simpler questions. Know when to ask a "what" and a "how" question versus a "yes" or a "no" question.

8. Understand your story well enough that if the copy blew away, you could continue the report.

9. Make the news *part* of your station's programming, not an interruption. Tease upcoming news between newscasts.

10. Present a solution for every problem, if possible.

More great ideas come from veteran newsman Ed Walsh. Walsh has worked with top stations and networks in Boston, Phoenix, and New York:

- Know when to file! In the United States, radio news deadlines are rarely more than an hour away, and the appetite of the news monster is insatiable. Better to give it something accurate to chew on while you're collecting more information for a follow-up report.

- Wearing comfortable shoes cannot be overemphasized.

- The value of most press releases received through the mail or e-mail rarely exceeds the price of the postage.

- In real estate, the top three attributes of a property are "location, location, location." In radio news, it's "local, local, local." That often means developing local angles to national or international stories.

- No verb in news writing is more overused than "say," as in, "Officials say…" Put some life into your copy! They don't "say": They "insist," "maintain," "claim," and so on.

- Avoid overattribution. The name of the press flack for an agency is, in the vast majority of stories, not necessary to report. Officer Smith, in his capacity as spokesman, is "the police."

- Never lapse into nonconversational transitional phrases such as "closer to home" or "in other news." If you can't develop a clear, declarative lead, pose an interrogatory: "Have you ever…" It makes a much more plausible transition between stories.

- Establish presence by pre-filing when you won't be able to phone in, radio in, or send an audio file at the time of an event. If a reporter is to be at the airport for the Pope's 11:00 arrival, he can't file at 11:00; pre-file "The Pope is expected here shortly…"

- Remember, we're doing news, not history. Use the present tense wherever possible. Don't refer to "yesterday" unless chronology is crucial.

- Tell me a story—a true one, but a story.

- Never pass up a chance to go to the bathroom. Ever staked out a story in the early morning after having had too much coffee?

- Always say, "Yes!" when they offer you free food and drink.

Another experienced reporter with a lot of useful ideas is Sharon Katchen. Sharon, works with Los Angeles's KFWB, the 24-hour-a-day all-news format, designed in 22-minute segments. Their slogan is, "Give us 22 minutes and we'll give you the world." Katchen has picked up several Golden Mike awards for running the Los Angeles Marathon while broadcasting live.

Sharon Katchen's Creating Powerful Radio News Tips

- Quality never goes out of style.

- Don't run with rumors.

- Keep your views out of the news.

- Take notes; sound recording devices can fail.

- Accuracy; accuracy; accuracy.

- Report fully and fairly. Omitting major facts or viewpoints is bad reporting.

- It's not news to barge into a disaster or crime scene and ask a victim, "How do you feel?"

- Listen. The best questions come from answers.

- Good reporting and good sound make good radio.

- If it is not clear to you, it's not clear to the listeners.

Newsman Mark Howell also has good ideas to share. His career has taken him from reporting in San Francisco to directing the award-winning news department at KCWR/KUZZ in Bakersfield.

Mark Howell's Creating Powerful Radio News Tips

- Grab 'em with the lead. If you don't get their attention with the first sentence of a story, you've lost them.

- Don't pull punches. Reject euphemisms. Speak the language of the common people, but clean up the grammar.

- Do not trust the police or the politicians.

- Natural sound is often better than interviews in helping you tell a story.

- A good newscast has a subtle, almost subliminal rhythm created by phrasing and proper placement of sound.

- When interviewing, concentrate more on what your interviewee says than on what you are going to say next. Use each answer to lead to another question. The only stupid question is the one you did not ask.

- Read out-of-town and alternative papers. Surf the Internet. Listen to shortwave radio. You'll find story ideas that haven't been done in your town. Keep them in a file and pull them out on slow news days.

- Don't waste time pursuing a story the local newspaper or TV has already done unless you can genuinely advance it, not just repeat it with a sound bite. Spend your time on stories they have not done.

- Get professional voice training if you need it; it is worth the cost.

- Understand the technical basics of sound reproduction and develop an ear for high fidelity. Then, don't accept bad audio in your own work. Make sure you know how to use equipment, and be very meticulous about maintenance.

Denise Jimenez-Adams has worked in both TV and radio as a reporter and anchor, at WBBM in Chicago, WCBS in New York, and others.

Denise Jimenez-Adams's Words of Advice

- Work as hard at communicating with your bosses and co-workers as you do with your audience. Communication is not an art well-practiced in the broadcast business.

- Know your boundaries—and those of the station.

- Practice, practice, practice ad-libbing factually so that your spontaneity with the news doesn't tarnish your station's reputation or your own.

- Words can be swords. Choose them carefully for an impact that enhances understanding of the story, not of you.

- Wire services are important resources, but not always an appropriate style to emulate.

- Read, read, read, for content and style, for emulation, and for information. Be a sponge forever.

- Don't assume:

  a) That you know more than your audience.
  b) That your audience knows more than you.
  c) That your opinion is welcome or important.

- Create your *own* style in writing and delivery.

- Experience what your audience experiences so you can ask the questions that matter. Communicate the facts that are needed and tailor the emotion to the situation.

- FEEL…and they will feel with you.

Award-winning broadcast journalist, personality, and author Lynn Jimenez has worked at top stations, including KCBS and KGO in San Francisco.

Lynn Jimenez's Creating Powerful Radio News Tips

- Take a breath.

- Pace yourself.

- Learn how to fix any equipment you use.

- Never throw away any phone number—EVER.

- The news crew is not your family, no matter what management says.

- Be comfortable with change. Versatility means survival.

- Have a conversation; don't lecture.

- You are a human being. You are worthwhile and so is everyone else.

- Remember that broadcasting is a small world.

- Have fun.

CHAPTER 15

Creating Powerful Radio
Traffic and Weather Together

> "The ability to communicate color, content, and drama
> in thirty seconds is rare and glorious."
> —*Doug Harris*

Traffic and weather "together" are important. Traffic and weather are often the reasons people tune in regularly to news and news-talk radio. Traffic and weather reports should be accurate and delivered consistently during key drive times. Some stations provide this service twenty-four hours a day.

Since most traffic and weather information can be instantly obtained from a variety of sources, the advantage radio has is in the personalities who deliver the data. It is useful to know that there has been a four-car collision on the road ahead of you caused by a sudden hailstorm, but it *feels better* to know that the person giving you the information understands what it is like to have your new car hit by a piece of ice the size of a golf ball.

Another Hot One

Listeners respond to and seek accurate information. While many radio stations or networks may choose to have a relationship with a TV meteorologist

153

or an accredited weather service to provide forecasts, trained meteorologists may not be the most scintillating personalities.

It is best if your station can have weather reports given by someone who sounds likeable and conversational. If possible, help train your weather presenters. Make sure they talk as if they are speaking to only one person, and not "all you folks out there."

A lot of explicit data about high-pressure systems or other technical information may be very interesting to the meteorologist and his or her colleagues, but unless the forecast concerns something extreme, such as a tornado, flooding, snowstorm, stick to the basics.

What would most people say if someone asked them, "Is it going to rain?" "How hot is it going to be today?" or "What's it like outside?" The answer is what should be in your report. Listeners need to know what to wear, how to dress their kids. or whether to bring an umbrella. Toward the end of the week, people begin to plan their weekends. Tell them what they can expect, in plain language.

Non-meteorologists often do a great job with the weather because they are *not* experts. One Los Angeles announcer consistently engages his listeners with creative brief weather updates, such as: "Aren't you glad you got that haircut? Another hot one today. Sunshine, high of 83."

Traffic: Bad for Commuters, Great for Radio

If you have ever been stuck in a traffic jam, you know how vital the information can be. Even satellite radio networks offer local traffic updates. Stations have found ratings and financial benefits by promoting and delivering frequent reports at specific times. Audiences will tune in at the exact minute they have been trained to expect the latest traffic report.

Since so much of the information that radio provides can be found elsewhere, once again, it is the presenters who can make a big difference here. Personalities make your information not simply accurate, but genuinely powerful radio. Personality Caroline Feraday was the "Flying Eye" over London, first for Capital Radio, then for BBC Radio's Five Live.

> Your listeners are counting on you to make them feel better. If they are stuck in a jam, they need you to validate their frustration, anger, or annoyance with that delay.

I know this sounds obvious, but it is easy to be blasé about a traffic jam that will really mess up someone's day. Every single person that is in their car is there for a reason. Maybe it's because they have to be somewhere on time? Perhaps they have to pick the kids up? Or that they want to make a good impression at a job interview or a first date? Maybe their favorite TV show starts soon.

Whatever the reason, listeners want to know if they are going to be late and they want to know why. It makes them feel better. Maybe they can call ahead? Perhaps leave extra time for the journey or travel a different route? Maybe they can do nothing but wait, but either way, that mention of their problem works psychologically.

Credibility Matters

Be on time, get it right. Never say, "There are *no* stalls or accidents." You are tempting fate. Instead try "No *reports* of any stalls or accidents." If you declare, "It's all clear," the situation may immediately change and you'll lose credibility. What you said moments ago may no longer be correct.

On the other hand, some facts do not need to be repeated day in, day out. Caroline Feraday says this:

> A gripe of mine is telling a bunch of commuters the stuff that they can work out for themselves. Don't waste their time. If there is always a half a mile back up at the Blackwall Tunnel, then do you need to tell them every bulletin? At the very max—remind them sometimes, "Usual jam at the Blackwall Tunnel. How do you put up with that every day?"

One frequent listener complaint is: "I tune in to find out what is happening on the roads, but they almost never report on the mess *I'm* stuck in, or they'll report an accident that doesn't exist. While I'm hearing that, I'm sailing through that area. They just don't get it right."

To counter that complaint, if you report traffic, make sure to check periodically to find out if accidents you have reported have been cleared or not.

Keep your listeners from becoming bored during traffic reports. Each person should be able to "see" what it is you are talking about. Caroline Feraday stresses the importance of making a movie in the listener's mind:

> Try to talk in pictures, and say what you see. If you can't see the crash but you can see smoke, then tell the listener that. If you can see the ambulance coming along the hard shoulder, then tell them. Make it visual.

Very rarely will a story change as rapidly whilst you are on the air, nor will it matter to people as much as the travel news does. How we are all addicted to watching those car chase tapes on the television! Have you watched how the traffic slows down to see a crash? We're naturally voyeuristic.

Very few of your listeners will actually be stuck in a traffic jam at the moment you mention it, so for the rest of them—make it interesting.

I once did a travel bulletin for BBC Radio Five Live in which I mentioned that a church roof had blown off in high winds. A famous film director, visiting the studio remarked, 'What an amazing vignette of life.' It was true—you can say so much about life in those 60 seconds. That church roof was now blocking the main road through a sleepy Devon Village.

"Where" Before "What"

Give the *location* of the traffic holdup before you detail *what* happened. People first want to know, "Is this near *me*?" Caroline Feraday puts it this way:

Travel the listeners' journey with them. If there's a queue, or backup, on the motorway, it's no good saying, there's an accident on the M25, causing it to back up. As a driver, you'll hit the back of the mess first. 'You're going to come to a halt at around Leatherhead. I know it's miles up, but I can see that the traffic doesn't really start moving again until you've passed the accident the other side of the Staines turning!' Oh, and people don't know the numbers of the junctions, so tell them exactly where they are. On what road is it? Where on that road? In which direction? Also, listeners hate a mispronunciation. Plus if there's a colloquial name for a junction, or landmark, learn it.

By the way, if you know the roads where the problems are, then I've found it helps to be able to picture it in my head. If you can do that, then you'll barely use your script. "Heading around the M25—you know the stretch where it goes down to two lanes just before the A10? Well, I know you get stuck there most days, but actually, it's going to take you about twenty minutes more today because some poor guy has broken down in the inside lane."

What Is Your Source?

Traffic presenters, make sure you know where your information comes from and how old each item is. Cultivate a healthy relationship with the police department or highway patrol. Can you easily contact them to obtain the fresh, updated information? Does your newsroom monitor police and highway patrol scanners or Web sites and check press releases from the state about highway construction projects?

Maintain an accurate phone and contact list with twenty-four-hour emergency numbers and keep it where anyone who might need it can find it in the event of a big problem during off hours. Your list should include not only highway patrol contacts but fire department, power and gas, and airport and railroad contacts, since these are all areas where an unusual incident can affect traffic and you may need to gather relevant information quickly.

Calling on the Cars

Does your station use "traffic spotters," listeners who call from their mobile phones to report on various traffic jams? If so, credit your valuable resource, the caller: "NEWS 105 traffic spotter Ben in Hampton says he's looking at the big rig truck that lost its load of chickens on Highway 5, Ben tells us he's watching the police try to round up the birds. It sounds like it may take a little while to get everything back to normal since the chickens are outrunning the cops." To keep current, ask the spotters to call you back or find out if it is all right to phone them back, to see if there is new information.

There is a place for personality and humor in traffic and travel reports. Obviously you never fool around with a serious situation when lives are at stake, but there is a lot of room in the mix for having fun and playing off the show personalities and presenters.

I once heard a traffic report about an accident involving an overturned truck carrying condoms. Not only did the spill cause a twenty-minute backup, it generated lots of comedy in the studio and for listeners stuck behind the "road full of rubbers" as well. The traffic story also became a news report.

Career On-Ramp

Traffic announcing and reporting can also be a great "entry" into broadcasting. Many have found, if you start out reporting traffic and do a professional job, that it may open doors to other parts of the business for you.

Caroline Feraday moved from reporting travel conditions in the United Kingdom to more prominent on-air roles. She offers some lessons she has learned.

If you want to be part of a team, you simply have to play. Any anchor wants to be sure that you will make their show sound good. If you sound good when they ask you a question, then they will do it again and again until that is part of your role. If they feel nervous that you won't spark when asked to deviate from your script, then they will definitely try it less. It is worth trying, and you will soon get a feel for how much or how little you should say in a segment. Don't feel you have to show off or be wacky for the sake of it. The listeners simply want you to be good company.

What about that script then? I reckon the fewer words you have on it, the better you'll be. It's not a memory test, though, so keep any facts you need at hand. If you can keep the information in front of you down to the basics and chat around it, then you're more likely to speak like a normal human being.

Lots of on-air personalities have worked as traffic reporters. It is a good way either to start your broadcasting career or take it in a new direction. Many traffic services also offer newscasts to their client stations. If you work for a traffic service, you may have a chance to add news writing and anchoring to your list of skills. This area of the business tends to provide a little more job security than other parts of broadcasting. As long as there are people in cars, there will be a need for traffic reporting.

CHAPTER 16

Creating Powerful Radio
Newswriting

"Write to express, not to impress."
—*Mervin Block,* Writing Broadcast News

The Long and Short of It

Anyone who writes knows it's harder to write shorter, but less is often more effective. Newspapers specialize in detail. Radio cannot compete for sheer tonnage of information. Radio's job, and yours, is to get information out *quickly* and *succinctly*. When you hear it on the radio, it's news. When you read it in the paper, it's history. Put in the big stuff, the important things that you would tell friends. Give enough information so listeners can think about a story and discuss it at their dinner tables.

Author George Orwell was deeply concerned with the effect of words, especially those that cause confusion. In his essay "Politics and the English Language," Orwell set down the following writing rules that will probably serve you well, regardless of which language you are using.

Never use a metaphor, simile, or other figure of speech you are used to seeing in print. Never use a long word where a short one will do. If it is possible to cut a word out, always cut it out. Never use a passive phrase where you can use the active. Never use a foreign phrase, a scientific word, or a jargon word if you can think of an everyday English equivalent. Break any of these rules sooner than say anything outright barbarous.

Mervin Block is America's newswriting guru. He wrote the news for CBS television for years. Many generations of American news journalists have read his books or attended his television newswriting workshops at Columbia University in New York. He has written several books. What follows is from Block's *Writing Broadcast News*:

Bad News

- ***Don't label news as good or bad.*** What may be bad for some listeners is good for others. Heavy rain may be bad for pedestrians, motorists, and sunbathers, but it can be good for farmers, taxi drivers, and umbrella vendors.

  "Good news" abounds on broadcasts when the prime rate drops, but for listeners, a drop in the prime can be either positive or negative. Anyone who takes out a home improvement loan will benefit from lower prime rates and could save on adjustable rate home mortgages and similar borrowings.

  However, for other listeners, lower rates are "bad news." Many consumers *like* high interest rates because they are able to earn strong returns on investments like money market funds or U.S. government securities.

- ***Don't tell your audience that a story is distressing, interesting, or amusing.*** The best policy is to stick to the facts, tell the news, and let the listeners decide.

  If the "good news" or "bad news" is tied to a specific person or group, characterizing the news may be valid. For example: "Mayor Murphy received good news today from his doctor," or, "The IRS has bad news for taxpayers."

Lead-Ins, Lead-Outs

There are some definite do's and many don'ts for writing into and out of correspondents' reports and actualities. In *Writing Broadcast News*, Mervin Block advises:

- ***Don't use the same key words the reporter uses,*** and don't introduce him or any speaker with the very words he starts with. Violation of this rule produces "the echo-chamber effect." It sounds—and resounds like this: "Good evening. Governor Goober warned today he's fed up with state employees who loaf on the job." Instantly, we hear Goober say: "I'm fed up with state employees who loaf on the job." Listener: "Haven't I heard that somewhere before?"

- ***Don't steal the reporter's thunder.*** Although the lead-in for a hard news story should hit a few highlights, the anchor shouldn't skim off all the reporter's best material. Otherwise, the reporter's account will seem anticlimactic and will seem as though the reporter got his news from the anchor.

- ***Don't write a soft lead-in for a hard news story.*** A soft lead-in may work for a feature story, but a hard news story calls for a hard lead-in. A lead-in is something like a store's display window. A dime store doesn't dress a window with diamonds, and a diamond merchant doesn't display dimes. Hard news, like diamonds, deserves an appropriate showcase.

- ***Don't write a lead-in that conflicts with the reporter's script.*** This may seem basic, but every once in a while we hear a reporter say something that contradicts what the anchor's lead-in has said. That's a mislead-in.

- ***Don't overstate or oversell.*** The lead-in should not promise or suggest more than the reporter is going to deliver. It should adhere to standards of journalism, not hucksterism or showmanship.

- ***Don't be vague.*** Sometimes, because of the way newscasts are put together, we don't know precisely what the reporter in the field is going to be saying, or which segment of a speech is going to be used. We have to write "blind" (i.e., without saying anything specific). We put down only enough words to allow the report to start: "The chairman of the city transit agency, Lionel Train, spoke out today on the agency's problems…" Writing "blind," like flying "blind," can be risky. Wherever you can, say something substantive: "The chairman of the city transit agency, Lionel Train, said today he'll clean up the agency's problems within six months…"

- ***Don't use a faulty "throw line" at the end of the lead-in to introduce a reporter.*** If the next voice we're going to hear is not that of the reporter but of a woman taking an oath of office, you'd confuse a listener by saying, "Jerry Jarvis has the story." One way to handle that "throw line" is to say, "Jerry Jarvis looked on as Mary Barton took the oath…"

Most lead-ins run less than twenty seconds, and a few run barely five seconds. No matter what it takes to do the job, no matter what the length, every word matters. The shorter the lead-in, the greater the need for every word to carry its weight.

Words Count

Everybody complains about bad writing. Broadcast journalism trainer Deborah Potter worked for years as a news reporter on CNN and CBS-TV and radio. Potter maintains:

> Your staff won't learn if no one teaches them. Much of what we hear on the air is badly written. Good writing is not magic. It is a craft. It can be learned and it can be improved, but first everyone has to know that it matters.

Potter adds it is important to offer regular feedback about writing. "Words count. If you want listeners to tune in and believe what they hear, you need to care about what is being said. Praise good writing and you will get more of it."

Deborah Potter's "Write Stuff"

1. Take time at the front end to understand the story. Candy Crowley of CNN puts it this way: "The less time you have to write, the more time you should take to think about it." Try telling someone in six words or less what your story is about. If you can't, you will have trouble writing it.

2. Choose information that will tell the story best. Avoid the cramming impulse. Select specific details—the brand of beer, the make of the car—that will bring the story to life. Leave the rest out.

3. Organize your information in a logical way. If it helps, make an outline. Keep related facts together. Answer questions as they come up. Know where you are going before you start.

4. Tell it, don't report it. Imagine that every story you write begins, "Hey Mom, guess what I just found out!" Or, "Honey, you won't believe what happened today!"

5. Rewrite. Revise what you have written by looking at it backwards. Look closely at the end of every sentence, paragraph, and story. That is where you want the strongest words, because that is where they have the strongest impact. Crisp endings are one simple way to sharpen your writing.

6. Put your writing on a diet, and think of adjectives as empty calories. Particularly the adjectives so overused in broadcast news: *senseless, horrible, tragic, ironic,* and the like.

7. Do use active verbs that add energy to your writing. The right verbs do more than convey information. You build understanding and make the audience care. It's the difference between a story saying that a bus was involved in an accident and a story that tells how the bus skidded down an embankment, rammed into a guardrail, and flipped into a ravine. Active verbs in the active voice are the hallmark of writing that communicates clearly. The active voice tells you *who.* Then leave out all the words you do not need.

See It on Your Radio

People do not think of radio as a visual medium. But a talented storyteller who writes with dazzling detail can tap into all of the imagery and emotion stored in the listener's brain and make him feel that he really is "seeing" the story. While telling a story in just a few words is key in writing powerful news copy, the visual element is important to keep listeners engaged. Many songwriters have mastered this in their lyrics. Take for example, Bob Dylan's "Mr. Tambourine Man." When you hear the line "To dance beneath a diamond sky with one hand waving free," you can see it. And that makes it more powerful.

In 2004, I was in Australia during the Athens Summer Olympics. Part of my job was to listen to some of the Australian Broadcasting Corporation's coverage of the events. I didn't have much enthusiasm for an item that began, "Up next, it's the women's archery competition..." until I heard the reporter tell the story.

REPORTER: This young woman picked up a bow and arrow when she was just a child. Her parents are right here beside me. Now here's what she's got to do: Hit a black target the size of a grapefruit, across three football fields.

Two minutes ago, I could not have cared less about the women's archery competition. Now I was paying attention and fully engaged in the story being told. If you can get a listener to "see it" or "feel it," then they will care and pay attention.

Visual descriptions are especially important to men. Brain research shows that men are more stimulated by visual details, and language that describes events with accurate visual elements tends to make them pay closer attention to a story.

Sports announcers are the best in the business at visual description. They are mostly men, talking to men, in a way that men understand. If you have ever attended a baseball or football game, you will notice men listening to radios while they watch the game with their own eyes. The play-by-play announcers enhance the visual experience for these men.

Women, on the other hand, are emotive. If a woman can "feel" an emotional connection to a story, she is more likely to listen closely and take in the information. For a story to appeal to both men and women, it should deliver information using both visual and emotional language.

Here's an example from England. A reporter, working from a camera phone video taken by a bystander, paints the visual and emotional scene of a pit bull attack on a small child. He uses both kinds of language to make men and women see and feel what happened in this story:

> The boy and the pit bull were about the same size. The dog had its jaws embedded in the little boy's neck. The child screamed in terror and pain. Within moments you couldn't tell the difference between the red-and-white pattern in the child's shirt from the blood. And can you imagine how his mother felt, standing by helplessly as the vicious beast attacked her child?

You can improve your visual writing and learn to speak more visually by imagining you are talking to a blind person. Start by seasoning your everyday off-air conversations with descriptive details. Use all the colors in your verbal paint box. Make observations of little things in life a part of your normal speech.

Get out to places where you will have a lot of interesting things to see. Find new places where you will experience things to talk and write about.

Build and stockpile files of mental imagery. Describe events so loaded with sensory information that the audience actually feels transported.

Where Have All the Writers Gone?

Newswriting expert Mackie Morris is an advocate and teacher of effective broadcast newswriting. In an article for Radio-Television News Directors Association's *Communicator,* Morris warned managers that it is up to them to encourage good broadcast news writing: "The best writers are those who have something meaningful to say. Unless our newscasts begin to communicate…with clear and effective writing, we may not have any audience left. Our audience will have gone elsewhere for information and inspiration."

Mackie Morris offers three suggestions to managers who are training their staffs to write better news copy:

1. Require your people to read.

2. Challenge them to think, and reward them when they write well.

3. Establish a standard of good writing that applies to everyone in the newsroom.

Mackie Morris first put out the "Good Writer's Dazzlin' Dozen" during his teaching years at the University of Missouri–Columbia School of Journalism. The "Dozen" is a list of what to look for and how to do both radio newscasts and news reports right (see next page). Even if you broadcast in a language other than English, there is much usable wisdom here.

What Listeners Want

The essence of news is the well-told story. If informative, entertaining, and up-to-the-moment, the story will always work. Most listeners turn on the news and want to know: Is my world safe? Did a nuclear bomb land somewhere or can I go about my business and lead my life today?

After that, audiences want to hear about the world they live in, their community, and what is happening. They want "talkable topics," weather, sports scores, and updated traffic reports. Breaking news aside, research

Mackie Morris's Dazzlin' Dozen

1. **Write factually and accurately.** The best technique and the finest form mean nothing if the copy is wrong.

2. **Write in the active voice.** Your copy will be tighter, complete, easier to listen to, and more interesting. Do whatever you must to avoid the passive voice or past tense (examples: "He says" instead of "He said"; "tells" instead of "was told")

3. **Write in the present or present-perfect tenses.** They make your copy more immediate—and immediacy is more interesting

4. **Keep your writing simple.** Write one thought to a sentence. Do not search for synonyms, since repetition is not a sin. Do not search for complicated intellectual language. Give the audience a better chance to understand the story.

5. **Be complete.** Make sure your quest for brevity and conciseness does not cause you to omit necessary information.

6. **Be creative.** Stick to the rules, but develop your own style. Try to say the same old thing in a new way. Make use of the "rule of threes" ("Lions and tigers and bears, oh my!" or "Life, liberty, and the pursuit of happiness") and other effective writing devices that cause copy to be more interesting.

7. **Write to be heard.** Maintain a sense of rhythm in your writing. All life has rhythm, and rhythmic writing is easier to hear. Be careful of confusing homonyms. Always, always test your broadcast copy by reading it aloud.

8. **Avoid interruptives.** Do not force the listener to make difficult mental connections. Put modifiers next to what they modify. Do not split verb phrases.

9. **Avoid commas.** A comma demands a hitch in your reading and the result is a jerkiness that frustrates the listener. Avoiding commas also will eliminate awkward subordinate clauses. Such clauses kill the impact of copy, especially if they come at the top of a story or sentence. Put a comma only where you intend to pause.

10. **Avoid numbers.** The listener has trouble remembering them. Instead of "48 percent of a population consisting of nearly nine-hundred and eighty-seven thousand people," try, "About half the population of nearly a million..." It is easier to "see" and remember.

11. **Avoid pronouns.** If you must use a pronoun, make sure it agrees with its antecedent.

12. **Create word pictures** so the audience can "see it." Use the medium of imagination.

shows that listeners shut off news, talk, or information broadcasts for the following two reasons:

1. "It's too depressing."

2. "It's boring."

Using the Powerful Radio methods takes care of the problem of being boring. The other challenge is to work to keep audiences who find the news depressing, who say, "I just can't take any more. There is nothing I can do to fix this problem."

A steady stream of stories detailing human suffering, environmental destruction, homelessness, war, and natural disasters can overwhelm people. Audiences become uneasy, then shut down or tune out.

Find a Solution

You can do something to prevent the listener fatigue that results in listener tune out. Each time you report a "problem story," try to find and present some sort of solution. That will lift the audience and be more effective in keeping your listeners.

One example of this was the American coverage of hurricane Katrina in New Orleans in 2005. The first images of flooding and human suffering were followed by details of the disastrous official response. After days and weeks of watching and listening to the suffering of the newly homeless, many turned away. They simply couldn't stand hearing any more.

But one reporter found a few uplifting stories in the midst of misery. First came hopeful stories of animal rescues. Then the story of a 9-year-old boy who had been living in New Orleans with his unemployed, drug-addicted mother. Malnourished and barely able to read due to sporadic school attendance, he had few friends. He told the reporter that in his old neighborhood, the other kids had regularly beat him up.

But now everything was changed. The boy had reached an emergency relocation center in Houston where his mother was given medical care. He was attending school and had made some friends. His new teacher asked him to stand up and tell the class what it was like to survive a major hurricane. With a donated backpack filled with books, this child was now in an individualized reading program and eating a hot nutritious lunch in the cafeteria every day.

Hurricane Katrina gave this boy a new chance. That little bit of good news uplifted the audience, giving them a small but much needed break from the horror they had been witnessing for weeks. Presented with a "solution" story, people could listen longer.

CHAPTER 17

Creating Powerful Radio
News Anchoring

> "Stories are as essential as the air we breathe and the
> water we drink. They captivate our imaginations,
> enchant our minds and empower our spirit."
> —*Matthew Kelly*

> "May you live in interesting times."
> —*Chinese saying*

If you anchor or present the news, whether you or someone else on your staff did the actual writing, it's you that the audience connects to. Yours is the name the public knows and yours is the voice they hear. If the job is well done, listeners stick around, ratings result, and management applauds. If you do not communicate powerfully, listeners leave.

Zen Rules of News Anchoring

KOA and KTLK Denver managing news editor Jerry Bell could paper the walls of a mansion with the awards he has won for news excellence. The following are Jerry Bell's "Zen Rules of News Anchoring."

Background, Not Foreground

It is shocking for some talent to realize that the listeners do not sit with their hands cupped to their ears to make sure they are hearing everything you say on the radio. A good newscast demands attention and must cut through the clutter of everyday life. Imagine your newscast as it is being heard on the car radio. Mom and Dad are driving their three screaming kids to school. At least three different conversations are going while the radio is on. What is going to come out of that speaker that will silence the crowd for even a few seconds? That is your challenge. *Guess what? Your audience is not hanging on your every word!*

To Err Is Human

Get your facts right, but cast off the nasty baggage that it is unacceptable to flub now and then in your on-air delivery. What is more important is taking risks and being able to put yourself out there without fear. The beauty of radio is that mistakes travel quickly to the void of outer space and are soon forgotten. So you make a goof—no big deal. It is not the end of the world.

Radio Is a One-on-One Medium

Use the word *"You"* in a newscast. You are storytelling to *one* person at a time. If your news copy is written in a detached way and you speak *at* and not *to* your listener, you miss the essence of the medium. Radio is portable and personal. It travels with people. Aim your newscast at the individual, not the collective group.

What, Why, and How before Who, When, and Where (Most of the Time)

As mentioned, good radio leads are not good newspaper leads. The newspaper gives you the old who, what, where, when, why, and how. In newspapers, the most important part of the story is where and when it happened, and who was interviewed. But in radio news, the more compelling radio leads usually deal with the effect the story has on the listener. Quite simply: (1) How will the story affect you? (2) What is the reason for it? (3) Why is a change taking place?

Here is a good radio lead: "Your taxes are about to go up."

That works better than: "Legislators at the State House voted last night to raise the property tax levy..."

Be a Person, Not a Newsperson

Read this lead:

> Police are beginning a probe into a probable homicide at 361 Elm Street. A 35-year-old woman was found slain. The suspected murder weapon, a Colt 45 revolver, was found next to the woman's corpse. Homicide detectives say the slaying reported has similarities to five other homicides in the neighborhood this year.

What is wrong with this lead? Everything. You have words no one ever uses in normal speech and it sounds so pompous as to be almost silly. Instead, try this lead:

> A murder on Elm Street—and the cops say the killer left his gun at the scene. Police are investigating the death of a thirty-five-year-old woman and think it may be the work of a serial killer. Five other murders in the neighborhood have the same M.O.

Sound Paints a Picture and Creates Energy

A good radio story should have sound that imprints pictures in the mind of a listener. You could read a story about a flood and get all the facts. But if you add the sound of the flowing water, a cry for help, or the motor on a boat going down what used to be a highway, then you use our medium best.

Sound is not just sound effects. Most stories you hear on the radio have an audio segment somewhere in the middle. That is predictable and very dull. Clever news anchors will lead with sound or even use multiple sound bites to tell a story.

A Pause Refreshes

The small nuances of announcing separate the men from the boys and the women from the girls. Use a fraction-of-a-second pause for emphasis. The ever-so-slight elongation of a word will stress its importance. These are techniques used for centuries by the best orators in the world.

Take the "I Have a Dream" speech of Dr. Martin Luther King, and imagine how it would have sounded being read by a dull monotone news reader. The beauty of this speech is in the power of its words, the ups and downs. The elongation of key words and the changes in volume and pace give the speech motion and emotion.

These speech techniques, toned down a bit, can make your newscast come alive.

Fight Your Fears

Jerry Bell adds:

> Everyone wants to do the perfect, flawless newscast. That is a good goal, but a fear of making mistakes may end up being just the thing that keeps you from being a good news anchor. How? If you fear making a mistake, you will never take a risk with your voice. You will be so uptight that you will constrict your voice and cut off all the power and fullness that can come when you use your full vocal instrument. If you read every word individually, while being oh-so-careful, you will sound like a robot instead of a human being. You will be boring and lifeless on the air.

If It Were So Easy, There Would Be Tons of Great News Anchors

The sad fact is that most news anchors sound exactly the same: dull and predictable. Here is why:

- Fear to go beyond the acceptable to reach the exceptional
- Lack of hard work
- Lack of coaching or airchecking

Final Zen Notes

If you are learning this trade:

- Make airchecks of your work, constantly.
- Send your work to people you know and trust. Ask for and accept their harshest critiques.

- Acquire mentors who can coach you to greatness.

- Make daily airchecks, and listen back to your own work. Be your own worst critic.

- Becoming a good news anchor does not just happen. You have to work at it to make it happen.

Mystery List

I picked up the following list years ago. When I found it, tucked inside an old journalism reference book at a public library, it had already been well used. It was covered in coffee stains and torn at the corners. I never knew who wrote it, but I carried it in my wallet, copied it for fellow broadcast journalists and friends, and used it all the years I worked in broadcast news.

- **Create radio news with "ear appeal."** Open your news with a sounder or great story to grab attention and set it apart from the other entertainment on the station.

- **Use the station name or call letters** at the:
  - opening of the newscast
  - close of the newscast
  - going into the commercial
  - coming out of the commercial
  - in the sports segment
  - in the weather segment
  - within at least one story ("Mayor Grover tells KIOI News...")

- **Ditch all wire service copy.** Rewrite every story in your own words. *Tell* the story—do not *read* the story. Rewrite multiple versions for ongoing stories.

- **Put "what" before "who."** Never start a story with a source. Phrases like "Police say...," "Senator Joe Jones says...," or "The Red Cross reports..." make weak openers because these guys say things all the time. Most of the time it is *what* they say, *what* is in it for listeners, and *what* happened that is important, not who is saying it.

- **Open with action words.** Use powerful verbs that clearly tell immediately what the whole story is about.

- **Keep actualities and sound bites short and colorful.** Avoid using sound just for the sake of using audio. Remember, a good movie director leaves a lot of film on the cutting-room floor. Try to put only the great stuff on the radio. A rule of thumb is "one thought per actuality."

- **NEVER put on a dull spokesperson.** If you can say it better and quicker than a boring expert, do it yourself.

- **Commercial radio is a headline service.** No matter what a newswriter thinks, a story becomes bulky and hard to digest after about three lines unless it is an ultra-hot breaking event. Research indicates listeners feel most satisfied when hearing a lot of items, rather than a lot of details on a few items. In your newscast, try fitting in more short stories instead of a few longer ones.

- **Promote your newscast about ten minutes before it airs.** Bring on the newscaster to deliver a couple of quick teases. In talk radio these can provide many magic moments. The best two stories to tease are usually the top story and the kicker.

- **Don't sweat it.** How long should it take to write a story? Not long. If you understand your story, it should take about as long to write as it does to tell. Read it out loud as you write to make sure it sounds conversational.

Basics

Use a checklist when training new broadcast news anchors, reporters, and producers. Just as a pilot does his or her checklist before taking off in an airplane, double-check the "list" before you go on air. Avoid the "disaster" of incomplete stories or items without purpose or focus that are boring.

Make sure all your news stories contain *all* of the following: who, what, where, why, when, and how (how it happened, how it affects people, how much it costs, how it can be solved). And ask a final 'how': How would you tell this story to a friend?

Checklist: Powerful News

- What is the subject?

- Is this new information?

- Who cares? How will this matter to your audience?

- Would you have a conversation with someone about this story off air?

- Does this story affect health or safety, human emotions, money, or other concerns of our listeners? How?

- Who are the "characters" or people involved in this story? Do you care about them? Will the audience care?

- Is it visual? Can a listener "see" this story in his or her "mind's eye"?

- Is the writing clearly understandable? Do you understand this story? Could you tell the story on air without reading it?

- *Go global:* How big can the story be? Can a huge national or international story be told with a local angle? If so, how? *Think local:*

    Example: "One hundred million dollars is the amount that Best Oil Company will have to pay for cleanup of the largest toxic spill ever to hit the American Southwest. But right here in Franklyn, the Environmental Protection Agency reports some dangerous pesticides leaking into our own groundwater. The cost of cleaning that up will be high."

- If there are several angles to the story, can multiple versions be made? Does this story have a second-day angle or potential for Monday morning? Can it be used on a slow news day?

- Double-check your work before it goes on air. When you are pressured or in a hurry, it is easy to leave out one or more important elements. Make sure the story contains everything important.

CHAPTER 18

Creating Powerful Radio
Multi-version News

"One theme with endless variations, like life itself."
— *Photographer Alfred Stieglitz*

Multi-*what*?

It is a given that good newsrooms update stories as new information becomes available. The multi-version method is different.

Multiple-version or multi-version reporting is the evolution of a news or feature story over time; or the retelling of a single news story in a variety of different ways by using a different mix of writing and sound in each version. The story takes on new forms, angles, and voices each time it is presented to the audience. This replaces the former technique of simply recycling and repeating the identical story in full detail for hours at a time.

Any one version of a story written in this manner will leave out some details and include others. In this way, each multi-version piece should be able to exist alone, containing who, what, why, when, where, and how. However, if listeners hear all the parts of a multi-version story, they should have a deeper and more complete comprehension than one could get from any single part.

In America, multi-version reporting is fairly standard. It is not uncommon for a news reporter on his or her way out to a story to ask the assignment manager these two questions:

"When do you need it?"

"How many do you want?"

Why Multi-version?

Multi-version became popular in America in the 1980s. For years, news had been the venue through which most stations fulfilled the majority of their federally mandated public service requirements. When the Federal Communications Commission deregulated, many of these long-standing rules disappeared.

Because news was expensive, many stations immediately cut their news staffs down to the bone. Thousands of FM stations were left with just one morning news reader. It became clear that if news was going to be part of commercial radio at all, it would have to earn its keep by generating both audience and revenue, just like any other element of a station's programming. Public radio has also adopted multi-version. They want to attract listeners too.

Why did they put the news back if they didn't have to have it? Some stations discovered, after shaving their news departments down to nearly nothing, that people in the audience wanted their radio news back. They preferred radio as their source of news and information. When news happened and no one was around to cover it for radio, stations lost listeners and credibility. It is no accident that the top-rated stations in the top fifty American markets are news-talk. Talk programmers and hosts are grateful for the interested and informed audience that a successful multi-version newscast can bring.

The Theory of Evolution: Adapt or Die

The result is that American news is now packaged better than it was before deregulation. People want news, and they know how to get it. They can pick up a newspaper, go online, turn on CNN, or they can use their radios. Your station is competing with these and many other news sources. Your presentation must be shorter, sharper, faster paced, and very interesting.

Let Them Know

In any market, it's not uncommon to find a station proudly proclaiming—on buses, billboards, and, if the station can afford it, TV—"If it's happening, you'll hear it here on Z-97." Since for many stations the five-minute segment has been cut to three, two, or even one minute of news every half-hour or hour, that news better be darn good radio. If your station has a news commitment, work hard to promote it.

What Can Multi-version Do for Me?

There is a lot of European interest in American-style multi-version reporting. Why? News broadcasting in Europe was historically dominated by public service radio. With the success of commercial stations, there is competition to earn listeners with news.

The multi-version method gives a report variety. It breaks the story up into pieces to keep people listening longer. A good multi-version report is powerful radio; it prevents the audience from being bored and tuning out.

Multi-version can serve as an audience teaser enticing the listeners to stay tuned or come back later. For example: "Coming up in the news at five, more of our report on man-eating alligators loose in city parks. How did they get out?" Who would want to miss that?

Builds Local on National

Here is another way multi-version can work for you. Your local newsroom can now build on what national network news is sending. For example, if there is a big trial involving a violent gang, your local newsroom might add the hometown angle of that story in a multi-version format. You can promote that hometown angle and save some feature pieces for the next day's morning news: "Our neighborhood schools, overrun by gangs. Join us tomorrow morning for part four of 'Your Kids and Crime' after the news at seven."

Multi-version can also be your secret weapon against Monday morning "no-news" doldrums. Leaving a multi-version feature in progress guarantees a few minutes of interesting material on a day when there may not be much happening.

Multi-version can be applied another way. When a story is going to be part of your news all day long, you don't want the audience to get tired of it, even if the basic information isn't changing. By rewriting lead-ins and changing the actualities, you can make it sound different enough to hold the audience's interest.

The Method

Everyone figures out his or her own way to do multi-version. I actually take four sets of notes, on paper, one for each version, before putting them into the computer. I like to have four versions when I begin, instead of going back four times to write the different versions. I plug in all the facts about the story on each page, and then assign each page a different angle and its own sound bite covering a different part of the interview. No two pieces should be the same. If a listener hears only one version of your report, he or she should feel "satisfied," but if listeners hear all of the parts, they should feel "full." Taken all together, the collective minutes of your multi-version reports should resemble an in-depth documentary piece.

In the case of a feature story, you can think of multi-version reporting as a miniature soap opera. Build your audience through the morning and leave them with a "cliff-hanger" to bring them back tomorrow. Multi-version is ideal for features that can be held.

For example, "Now that we've told you about the shocking death of the baby monkey, be listening tomorrow at eight as the drama of animal abuse at the city zoo continues to unfold."

A caution: If you bring your audience back for a second helping, there must be something new and substantial in your next feature segment. Don't just rearrange a few words.

Lee Harris is the morning anchor on all-news 1010 WINS in New York City. His job requires a constant updating of news stories. Harris offers his tips on the multi-version method as applied to breaking news:

> While covering a news conference or other event, start writing the story in your head while the information is conveyed. Listen for usable cuts. Mark them. When you have five or six of them, presumably the most exciting of the bunch, you have the ingredients you need to produce multiple versions of your story.
>
> Here's how you can crank out three or four versions of the same simple news story in a hurry: Use a lead-in, then an actuality (prerecorded interview statements). In the next story, paraphrase that actuality, then use

a new actuality. Work your way through your best audio in this fashion, creating as many versions as you need, or until the story changes.

Advanced Techniques

Sometimes on a "charge and reaction" story, you can create several versions by focusing alternately on the charge, then the denial. Let us say an attractive, successful fashion model has mysteriously disappeared. Police are investigating the photographer of her last known assignment.

Story one could be an interview with the police investigator talking about why evidence points to the photographer. At the end of the story, you would mention that the photographer has hired an attorney and denies all charges.

Your second piece could feature an interview with the suspect's attorney talking about what an insult it is that his client is under suspicion. At the close of version two, mention that the police continue to investigate the photographer as their prime suspect.

In both stories, the information conveyed is essentially the same, but the stories will sound different because the narrators are so diverse in their voices and views.

Another multi-version technique that can give your reporting depth and set it apart is to briefly give the meat of your story, then focus on an interesting element. For example, a building with many housing code violations bursts into flame. One of the firefighters working on the blaze is killed. Sad as the story is, it doesn't take long to give the hard facts. You have a sound bite of a resident who is sobbing that the building was a deathtrap.

Using that audio adds depth to your story without detracting from the necessary information that must be conveyed. With this technique, the entire story can be colorfully told in several different ways, each less than a minute long. Multiple versions might include sound of the reactions of the firefighters, eyewitnesses, the arson investigator, and housing officials, along with a spokesperson for the Red Cross describing emergency services available to those displaced.

If time permits, you can let the news anchor handle the hard news story and select one of the angles with or without an accompanying actuality. The anchor will then hand the story off to a reporter, who can add yet another angle with or without audio.

By mixing the angles and assigned introductions, still other multi-versions of a story can be created. If there's not much time, the anchor can handle the hard facts, and the sidebar multi-versions can be done by the reporter in the field. Again, this works best if the anchor can handle the basics of the story in his or her lead. Remember, the key to multi-version is alternation.

Example: "A seven-year fire department veteran is dead. Twenty-six-year-old John Jones was killed while fighting a fire in a downtown apartment building this morning. The building had multiple housing code violations and the fire is considered suspicious." Now that the anchor has given the basics, the reporter is free to do multiple versions of follow-up.

The following pages contain a few multi-versions of a single story about a blizzard in New York City that aired on 1010 WINS. The station had already broadcast reports on the traffic tie-ups, interviewed storm experts and city officials, and reported on electrical outages. In short, all the "hard news" on the blizzard had been reported, yet the snow still came down. Harris's assignment was to get the "human angle."

Harris went underground to one of the more central subway stations in Manhattan, where people were sheltering from the storm. He filed these four reports, which work well with all the parts together, and equally well with the individual pieces alone, the hallmark of a good multi-version.

New York Blizzard Multi-version One

This first version does not use an actuality. It just describes the scene.

The Columbus Circle Station is a pretty strong argument for placing the rest of the city underground and having New Yorkers evolve into a race of mole people. I mean it's dirty and you can't understand the announcements, but at least there's no slipping and sliding down here, because there's no snow down here. About the only hint of the weather above is that a lot of folks are dressed in clothing usually associated with Arctic exploration. But nobody looks any more testy or miserable than they usually do.

Lee Harris, 1010 WINS, at the Columbus Circle Station.

New York Blizzard Multi-version Two

Lee uses a quote here, but the woman is difficult to understand, so he repeats her statement and leaves it in the report.

Well, there's no snow down here in the Columbus Circle Station. In fact, there's very little indication of the situation topside at all, other than the arctic-explorer look favored by many of the commuters this morning, and the above-average number of homeless people who came down to get out of the storm. This 35-year-old woman says she actually likes this kind of weather because it tends to make people more generous, and she needs the help:

WOMAN: I'm off the streets and I'm eight months pregnant. Welfare's finding me a place pretty soon.

HARRIS: You are eight months pregnant and you slept on the street last night?

WOMAN: I sleep on the street, that's right.

HARRIS: And she says she slept on the street the last time she was pregnant.

Lee Harris, 1010 WINS, at the Columbus Circle Station.

New York Blizzard Multi-version Three

Well, on top of everything else, the weather is apparently making a bad impression on some of our foreign visitors. This businessman from Hong Kong just doesn't see the charm in having his flight delayed thirty-six hours, and waiting almost that long to get a cab.

MAN: Well, it's interesting. But it's not…very impressive.

HARRIS: Oh, uh, I suppose the weather is better in Hong Kong?

MAN: Well we are having a tropical climate over in Hong Kong. So hot, wet, wintertime you are up to like 50 to 60 degrees!

HARRIS: That's OK if you like being comfortable. And that sort of thing.

Lee Harris, 1010 WINS, at the cab line at the Sheraton, New York.

New York Blizzard Multi-version Four

We're back at the subway station with the woman who's pregnant and homeless.

One of the reasons the subway was put below ground was to make it impervious to days like today. And below ground it looks like just another day. Including the usual contingent of people who call the subway home night after night. This woman says she's been homeless for eight years, but weather like this has its advantages.

WOMAN: Even though it's colder, street people have a tendency to be more friendlier—if it's snowing, if you're homeless. And they do help you out more than when the weather's nicer.

HARRIS: By the way, that woman claims to be, and appears to be, eight months pregnant.

WOMAN: With my last kid, I slept on the street also.

Lee Harris, 1010 WINS, in the Columbus Circle Station.

Fitting It All In

Most news professionals have found individual ways to make their news fascinating and brief, yet thorough. If you have written news for broadcast, you know how much harder it is to write short.

An expert at the craft is CBS News Anchor Jim Chenevey. Chenevey's talent is understanding that you cannot explain every detail of a story. He wrote and anchored eight newscasts per morning. Each averaged five or six stories, a kicker of some type, plus a piece of sound, *all in one minute*. His advice to newswriters and anchors: "Cut out extra words, write the piece, then go back and CUT." Chenevey is a master of the six-word story: "Guess who turns eighty? Hugh Hefner."

Jim uses the culture for material. His style is conversational. He varies the audio and rotates the good stories, just as is done with the music in music formats.

Chenevey includes "A," "B," and "C" stories in each cast, varying the rest. He adds the new, breaking stories into the mix but uses multi-versions of the ones that will run all morning. The best way to illustrate this is to actually show you his scripts that he read over the course of one morning.

The newscasts on the following pages aired years ago. While the copy is dated, you can still pick up the basics of multi-version methodology from the Chenevey news scripts.

CBS Spectrum
Chenevey Newscast

6:00 AM

Good morning. This is a CBS Newsbrief.

The Toronto Blue Jays have won the American League pennant...

'... It was a tough year and they came through for us...'

One of the ecstatic Toronto fans. The Jays will play either Philly or Atlanta in the World Series beginning Saturday night.

Bell Atlantic has scheduled a news conference this morning, reportedly to announce it's agreed to buy Tele-Communications Incorporated, the nation's largest cable TV outlet. This would create a mega-media company, number six on the Fortune 500.

President Clinton has cleared 65 million dollars in emergency funds to help fight public health problems resulting from the flooding in the Midwest.

In Sydney, Australia, a twin-engine cargo plane crashed after hitting two kangaroos on the runway. No one was hurt.

In Concord, California, voters will cast ballots for or against a school voucher program. But one group plans to cast spells. A coven of witches wants to open a pagan school under the voucher program and hopes to whip up some votes with a little black magic.

From CBS News, I'm Jim Chenevey.

CBS Spectrum
Chenevey Newscast

6:30 AM

Good morning. Here's a CBS Newsbrief.

Two more Americans are Nobel Prize winners. Russell Hulse and Joseph Taylor of Princeton have won the prize for their studies of gravity. Doctor Taylor I presume?

'…It certainly is a great honor and it's a very humbling one.'

Bell Atlantic reportedly wants to buy Tele-Communications Incorporated, the nation's biggest cable company. The deal would create a sixty-billion-dollar media giant.

Toronto has won the American League pennant, beating Chicago last night six to three to take that series four games to two.

Several students at Oakland University in suburban Detroit are being tested for HIV. They were not informed that a lab they were using was also being used for AIDS research, utilizing a live virus. So far, none has tested positive.

Police in Schenectady, New York, are looking for a few good "Johns"—men who would be willing to hit the streets looking for sex, as part of an undercover prostitution investigation.

From CBS News, I'm Jim Chenevey.

CBS Spectrum
Chenevey Newscast

7:00 AM

Good morning. Here's a CBS Newsbrief.

A "monster merger" is in the works. It could be the biggest ever:

'...Bell Atlantic Corporation, Tele-Communications Incorporated, and Liberty Media Corporation today announced that they have signed a letter of intent to merge.'

She's with Bell Atlantic. If approved, the deal would create a sixty-billion-dollar multimedia giant. Number six in the Fortune 500.

American scientists Russell Hulse and Joseph Taylor of Princeton University have won the Nobel Prize in physics. This for their work on the study of pulsars and Einstein's theories. Relatively speaking...

Toronto has won the American League pennant, beating Chicago last night to win the series in six games.

Fire officials in Austin, Texas, say three recent fires were set by kids who say they got the idea from MTV's "Beavis and Butt-head" cartoon.

The mayor of New Haven, Connecticut, says it felt like a bee sting, but it was a bullet that hit him in the leg. Police say it went through two steel doors and a wall before it bounced off Mayor Losure's leg. He's OK.

From CBS News, I'm Jim Chenevey.

CBS Spectrum
Chenevey Newscast

7:30 AM

Good morning. Here's a CBS Newsbrief.

Bell Atlantic has announced a major merger. It plans to buy cable giant Tele-Communications Incorporated and its Liberty Media subsidiary.

Russell Hulse and Joseph Taylor, both of Princeton University, have won the 1993 Nobel Physics prize for their studies on Einstein's theories.

Some students at Oakland University in suburban Detroit are upset about not being informed that a lab they were using was also home to AIDS research using a live virus...

'...We have absolutely no indication that any of these students were exposed, however we are discussing this matter with the students to alleviate their concerns.'

The school's David Dissen.

Rats are nothing new to ships, but this ship is the space shuttle Columbia. Forty-eight rats are now on board the orbiter, preparing for tomorrow's scheduled launch.

Deputies in Citrus County, Florida, were chasing Daniel Benock, wanted on a probation violation, when Benock jumped into a lake and tried to swim to freedom—That was until he saw a seven-foot alligator floating nearby. He's now in jail. Glad to be there.

From CBS News, I'm Jim Chenevey.

CBS Spectrum
Chenevey Newscast

8:00 AM

Good morning. Here's a CBS Newsbrief.

Somali warlord Mohammed Farah Adid has today vowed to release captured U.S. pilot Michael Durant and a Nigerian peace-keeper. Adid says the two hostages will be released today or tomorrow.

The Philadelphia Phillies will take on Toronto's Blue Jays in the World Series beginning Saturday night. The Phillies beating the Braves six to three last night to win the National League pennant. Phillies manager Jim Fregosi:

'...I guess we're going to be the underdogs again. It's not a bad way to go.'

The space shuttle's fueled, and so far all systems are go for the launch later this morning.

The Rite-Aid and Revco drugstore chains are expected to announce today they're suing several drug makers for alleged price-fixing.

Quite a scene during a radio debate featuring Nylo Yuri, a candidate for mayor of Hialeah, Florida, and suspended incumbent mayor Raul Martinet. Yuri claims that during the debate, Martinet stood up and spat at him. Martinet says he was just blowing. A third candidate, Salvatore De Angelos, says it was all very embarrassing.

From CBS News, I'm Jim Chenevey.

CHAPTER 19

Creating Powerful Radio
Integrating Radio and TV News

"The business of every art is to bring something into existence."
— *Aristotle*

Every TV news director I work with says the same thing: "Our best people come from radio." That's because radio people know how to communicate, tell stories, and spontaneously improvise.

Smart broadcasters use TV for what it does best, presenting pictures to show events as they happen. Radio is great training if you want to make the move to television. Many broadcasters have found they enjoy doing both, and a lot of TV people look back wistfully, remembering their days in radio as their happiest, when they did their best work.

Radio broadcasters are often curious about working with pictures and would like to give television a try. I'm seeing more and more TV and radio newsrooms around the world moving toward combining their efforts into an integrated product. In Europe, they call it "bi-media." Bi-media, or combined newsrooms, started as a cost-cutting measure, but it can be beneficial overall. When a TV and radio station are under the same roof, or even on the same floor, it makes little sense to send two sets of reporters to the same press conferences, the same fire stories, and to interview the same local figures or celebrities.

"A Face for Radio?"

Talented radio people can and do make it on television. Radio broadcasters should take it upon themselves to do as much as possible not to discourage television stations from utilizing them. If your radio station is often a source for TV footage, always be ready to make an appearance. The audience no longer expects their TV news to be delivered by people who look like movie stars. A small amount of coaching, grooming, and effort may be all it takes to convert a successful radio talent into a shining television personality.

Producing the Pink Elephant

A lot of TV interview, discussion, or "talking head" programs are really just talk radio shows with cameras pointed at them. Managers can enhance the level of creativity for personalities doing these types of shows by allowing them to work in both media. Talented TV people can be taught to speak "visually" for radio reports.

Radio people can be taught to leave space in their writing for pictures. A good assignment manager for either TV or radio can decide which stories fit best with either medium. There's another great benefit in using reporters who work in both media: TV and radio can promote each other, increasing visibility and audience.

CNN (Cable News Network) was first to try the all-news radio format on TV. CNN hired a lot of radio reporters. They worked cheaper, and they had the necessary skills. CNN realized that the basics for both radio and television are the same: You must tell an interesting story in a fascinating way. Each medium has assets and drawbacks. On radio, if you want to talk about a pink elephant, all you need to do is describe one and people "see" it. On television, if you want to talk about a pink elephant, you must actually produce one.

In the early days of television, reporters and hosts alike had backgrounds in either print or radio. Where is it written that broadcasters cannot be great at both TV *and* radio? Here are some techniques that we use at Geller Media International to help make the transition from TV news to radio news easier.

From TV to Radio

1. When on radio, speak visually. Paint word pictures. Don't refer to pictures—the audience can't see them. Use details, small things that you notice.

2. If you are stuck for a way to begin a report, pretend the anchor has just asked you a question or write the question into your report: "Why are six hundred nursing mothers converging on a small theater in suburban San Francisco? To get into the *Guinness Book of World Records*—it's the Third Annual Nurse-in."

3. Use TV to promote radio and radio to promote TV. On morning or "breakfast" TV shows, try saying, "When you get in your car on your way to work this morning, don't miss the interview coming up on Z-97. The mayor, his mistress, his wife, and his mother will all be on live with host Jim Smiley."

4. It's OK to promote your TV news coming up on the radio. Most people now in their cars will be checking out the pictures tonight on the TV news anyway. Why not send them to your channel?

5. Whether on radio or TV, *promote within your programming.* Let your audience know what is coming up next. Tease them with exciting tidbits about upcoming stories so they stay with you.

6. Use TV anchors and special reporters as regulars on radio shows. They get a chance to express themselves as people instead of sticking to a tight script. Conversely, television viewers are often curious to see what their favorite radio personalities look like. At many stations, the meteorologist, the sports guys, and the traffic reporter all do both radio and TV. If you have talent, that is all that matters. If someone has talent, he or she can make it on radio or on TV.

7. Even though you can hear most radio stations over the Internet, people are often busy at their computers doing other work. Make sure there is a radio monitor that comes in clearly in your television newsroom so the reporters can actually hear themselves on the air.

8. *Use multi-version.* We've covered this for radio (see Chapter 18), but it's an important tool in television as well. Remember, you may need

extra footage and additional comments. Use details and small things you notice.

9. Remind the audience how the story affects them, whenever possible. Try to present a solution to every problem when you can.

10. Remember to make it matter. Ask yourself: "*Why* is it important?" Make sure your story explains.

From Radio to TV

Consultant John Catchings's background includes both radio and television. He managed newsrooms at KGO-TV and KPIX-TV in San Francisco. Catchings is a brilliant problem solver, never taking "it can't be done" for an answer. I asked him to contribute some of his ideas to help radio people create powerful television news:

- Play to the *visual*. You witnessed it, but the photographer missed it! Never assume that because you saw it with your own eyes, the picture was taken. Look at what the camera is capturing. Do this while you are on a story. Do not wait until you are back at the studio editing to realize you do not have the right shots. It is better to make your photographer mad at you than your news director—or worse, not do your best for the story.

- Start with the *best video*. Be the director of your piece and use your best pictures. Avoid the temptation to start the story with a stand-up shot.

- Put *movement* into each shot. Do not be a human mic stand! Be involved in your shot. Choreograph the shot, be engaged, demonstrate your points. Keep it moving forward. Walk around, move, point.

- Let the *pictures* tell the story, but let the story breathe. Do not allow it to become boring. Watch for length.

- Make good use of *natural* sound.

- Do *not* overwrite.

- Use graphics, charts, and your own imagination to *jazz up* less interesting stories.

- When you edit, do not hang on too long to the good shots. It's tempting, but keep it moving. *Be creative.*

- *The essence is storytelling.* Never forget that. Do what it takes to tell the story.

Grab the Spotlight

Money can't buy happiness, but it can buy TV exposure. If you can afford it, purchase commercials to advertise your radio station on TV. A TV ad campaign is expensive, but if it draws in new listeners and brings higher ratings, it is worth it.

Still the most time honored use by American radio of American television is and has always been the free "plug" or mention on the air. Get all the free TV publicity you can! Do things on your radio station that are newsworthy and attention-getting, and the TV stations will come knocking on your studio door. When they come in, make sure they see your call letters. American radio stations learned the "mic flag" trick long ago. Mic flags are designed with television coverage in mind.

When your station is taking calls from listeners on issues of the day, it makes a good TV "public opinion" story. Many TV assignment managers have learned to send a reporter and camera in to tape live radio talk shows for multi-versions of hot news stories. Radio managers, don't be shy. Call up the TV stations in town when a particularly controversial or important subject is being discussed on your airwaves, especially if TV coverage on the story has been intense. You will find more about promoting your radio station on TV in Chapter 23, Promotions, of this book.

Benefit from All Information Media

People do not make distinctions about where they get their news. Television, radio, and the Internet are all part of their information network. Broadcasters should take a lesson from our audience and eliminate the barriers that keep us from using our resources to bring listeners and viewers the most compelling product we can produce.

Be generous with your airtime. If a TV station in your community has done something worthwhile, there is no reason for a local radio station not to mention it. If a radio station has made a contribution to the local community, then the local TV station should cover it. Anything that enhances the idea of your station as a "good neighbor" is useful promotion.

CHAPTER 20

Creating Powerful Radio
Public Service Announcements

"Artists who live and work with spiritual values cannot and should
not remain indifferent to a conflict in which the highest
values of humanity and civilization are at stake."
— *Pablo Picasso*

"It is better to give than to receive."
— *Acts 20:35*

It's generally understood that radio stations are licensed to serve the public. It can be radio at its best, or worst. In Europe, as well as in the United
States, some radio stations exist entirely to perform public service, but what
that means is open to interpretation. Most stations continue to solicit input
from the community to determine its needs. These information-gathering
efforts are called ascertainments.

Smart commercial broadcasters know that assessing the true concerns
of a community and addressing those issues can enhance a station's image
and raise its public profile. Public service works best when the entire station is involved and the campaign is tied in to news, features, sponsorships, announcements, liners, and long-form programming to achieve a
specific goal.

Fit Your Public Service to Your Target Audience

Let us say your target audience is adults twenty-five to fifty-four years old and you discover that their principal worry about their community is the school system. Your station might "adopt" a local school. Your promotions department, sales department, and even programming can put together a campaign to bring in volunteers, supplies, money, computers, and so on. Teenage listeners might have different concerns about their community. When you are deciding on content for your public service campaigns, try to find issues that not only are of importance to your listeners, but that also fit your target audience.

"Community service activities can be of tremendous benefit toward developing listener loyalty," says broadcasting manager Chris Berry. Here are some examples: WBBM-AM/Chicago, runs the "Wreath of Hope" campaign every year to raise money for a variety of local nonprofit agencies. The show's hosts broadcast live from shopping centers around the area while volunteers accept donations for the charities. Heavily promoted on air, the appearances help the charities, increase awareness of the station's personalities, and bring the call letters into the listeners' backyards.

At KGO/San Francisco, an entire programming day each year has been devoted to the "Leukemia Cure-a-thon." It raises money for research and victims of the disease. Producers and hosts design shows explaining the illness, the latest research findings, and the need for funding.

KGO's sister station, WLS/Chicago, has been holding its Cure-a-thon in a public place so listeners and organization volunteers can feel that they are a part of the event and meet their favorite personalities. Doctors, researchers, survivors, and families of victims are interviewed. The Cure-a-thon always has some very moving moments as family members describe the struggles of their loved ones. This special public service programming raises hundreds of thousands of dollars and the staff really feels good about participating.

WABC/New York is among many stations helping listeners fight fraud and wrongdoing by directly connecting them with attorneys or volunteer agencies such as Call for Action. Aggrieved listeners can call a volunteer-staffed consumer line with their complaints. The station then uses its firepower and contacts the business, employer, or other parties involved on the listener's behalf. They usually get results.

Years ago KFWB/Los Angeles made earthquake preparedness its issue. Entire broadcast days were turned over to reports and interview shows devoted to earthquake safety. The station published a free newsletter outlining everything from safety precautions to earthquake-proofing. The pamphlets were available free from the station or at sponsors' stores. Several stations in earthquake-prone areas have launched similar campaigns.

Take advantage of your staff's creativity. One way to encourage hosts to support your public service commitment is to have *them* come up with their own ideas for a promotion. Sam Walton, who founded the Wal-Mart chain of stores, said, "People always support ideas they help create." Most hosts already have a "pet" charity or cause they feel connected to or would like to endorse. If your host feels the organization or issue is important, he or she can really get listeners excited about joining it.

The key to community service is to approach it like all other forms of powerful radio. Powerful public service programming is interesting and relatable, and it *matters*. Bad public service programming is wasted airtime. Nobody will hear about your good efforts if the presentation on the air is boring.

Include public service events on your daily or weekly calendar. Hold up the mirror that is your station and reflect back the true needs and concerns of your community. Be known as the station that *always* has something going on. Radio executive and station owner Virgina Morris says she would not even consider hiring a manager who was not involved in the community—that is how strongly she feels strongly about it.

Local or Not?

There is no wrong way to do good work. Local concerns or issues usually work better, but stations that raise money for food drops in Africa or medical supplies in Bosnia also create good feelings.

Since the Internet makes it possible to see extreme emergencies and disasters around the world, stations can easily get involved in helping people in their town or on another continent. Whether your station is sending a truck full of supplies to hurricane victims ten states away or rebuilding a home for a burned-out family on the next block, you can use your station's Web site as well as its airtime to show need, organize help, and chart the difference your support has made. There are no rules here, but by finding a charity or cause about which your staff feels passionate, you'll do both your community and your station some good.

The Powerful Public Service Announcement

Most people hate "PSAs," and with good reason. They've traditionally been used as filler and treated that way. This need not and *should* not be. Every moment on the radio counts, even those devoted to public service. Here are two public service announcements on the same subject. They were heard within minutes of each other on different stations in the same market.

Which do you think is more powerful?

Station 1
St. John's Hospital needs type O blood. If you are type O, here's the phone number to call …

Station 2
There's a little girl, six years old, who's been badly hurt in a car crash. Both of her parents were killed. She's lying in a bed right now at St. John's Hospital fighting for her life. She might not make it, because she needs type O blood and the hospital has a shortage. If you're type O and want to help this little girl live, call us here at Z-97, and we'll tell you what to do. Z-97, the station that cares about our town.

If you can bring life to the story, your listeners will care about it, too.

You'll probably want to shy away from "produced" PSAs provided by outside agencies, unless they are great campaigns. For samples of some classics, you might want to listen to some of Dick Orkin's Radio Ranch spots or vintage Stan Freberg. If you can customize a campaign to make it sound like part of your station, you can make it work.

By being selective about the kind of public service announcements you use on your station, and by adding human and dramatic touches, you will turn what has long been perceived as a "tune-out" into an audience and image builder for your station.

CHAPTER 21

Creating Powerful Radio
Avoiding Burnout

> "What was any art but a mold in which to imprison
> for a moment, the shining elusive element which
> is life itself—life hurrying past us and running
> away, too strong to stop, too sweet to lose."
> —*Willa Cather*

In your quest to create powerful radio, it is important to look at what can move radio forward, as well as to understand what can hold Powerful Radio back. This is why creative burnout is worth talking about. Burnout is an occupational hazard that sometimes happens to a performer under the daily demand of public scrutiny and constant pressure for consistently original output. While burnout can be a type of exhaustion, or energy drain, it is different from genuine clinical depression. While burnout can *lead* to a performer becoming depressed, the good news is that it can also be fixed.

Talent

How can you tell when talented people are suffering from burnout? They complain, they call in sick, they are late for work. Ideas don't come to them

"IT'S COME TO OUR ATTENTION THAT YOU HAVE A LIFE OUTSIDE THE OFFICE."

as easily. They watch the clock, counting the minutes until the end of their shifts. They fear the blank page and begin to rely on other people's ideas more than their own. They want more guests, interviews, and "easy" stuff. Their shows aren't as good as they used to be, and they just don't seem too excited anymore.

Managers

Exhaustion can lead to burnout for managers as well as on air and producing talent. For economic reasons, many broadcast companies' resources have been stretched thin, making it necessary for individual managers to take on more and more responsibility. Even with improved time-management skills, many frustrated managers still feel overloaded with too much to do in a day. Unless companies provide realistic goals for managers, they can burn out as well.

Battling Burnout

When I wanted to learn more about ways to deal with creative burnout, I hosted a dinner party. Invited guests included actors, artists, a psychologist, a singer-songwriter, a film director, a textile designer, an architect, and some radio and TV people. Everyone in attendance made his or her living by facing the blank page and finding things to fill it. What did they do when the ideas stopped flowing? I gave everyone a pencil and paper. They began to write, talk, and argue. The following is what emerged.

Lower your expectations

No one is at his or her most creative all the time. Now may be the time to tap into the creativity of those around you. If your fire is burning low, try to rekindle your spirit and your ideas at the fires of others.

Are you doing the right work for you, right now?

Determine what you enjoy about what you do. If the list is short, it may be time to rethink your job and find something else. As scary as change can be, it's better to make the switch than burn out in a job that's not right for you.

Artists, on the radio or elsewhere, need the right environment to grow. Managers need to understand that creative people are sensitive, introspective, and insecure. Talent needs to understand that since you don't come with a list of "care and feeding" instructions, open communication with management is critical. Supervisors who don't take this into account will contribute to burnout.

Live a balanced life

It is easy to become driven to accomplish in this career and lose perspective on the rest of your life. Remember, you can love radio, but radio will not love you back.

Do not become your work. Do other things that make you feel good and give you a sense of accomplishment. Create a balance in your life.

Burnout occurs when you can no longer grow as a person. Don't let that happen. Challenge yourself to do new things outside of work.

Avoid energy vampires

You know the type, people who seem to suck the life right out of you by overwhelming you with their problems. Surround yourself with people who nourish you, who give, not just take.

Nourish your brain

Look at art. Go to a movie or attend the theater. Read. Talk to your kids. If you don't have kids, talk to someone else's or browse children's books. Play. Get out that set of watercolor paints in the closet and make some art. Listen to music. Try gardening.

Do something, *anything,* that will stimulate your own creativity and sustain you, even if you are not "in the mood right now."

Be inspired by reading

Take advantage of the plethora of books that inspire creativity. Important books for me include Julia Cameron's *The Artist's Way* and *Vein of Gold,* and Anne LaMott's *Bird by Bird*. You can also ask a friend to recommend a biography or favorite book that might inspire you.

Do what you want

On the air, whenever possible, follow your heart. Give others assignments that you don't particularly care about. Stick to what interests and matters to you. Look at what really makes you feel energized and passionate about life. Do those things. You'll minimize the risk of burning out if you maintain the integrity of your show.

Remember why you came

Rediscover your professional and personal roots. Take a look at what motivated you at the beginning of your career. What got you interested in doing this work in the first place? Why did you like being on the radio in the beginning? Why was it fun? Remember what led you down this long and winding road.

Take a break

The root of the word *vacation* is "vacate," to leave. Take some time away; a day, a week, a month, a year. You may just need a brief change of pace in order to get new input, have experiences, meet new people. Do something that will break the monotony of your daily routine and put it back in perspective.

Focus on the positive

One station manager found that the right attitude can make a big difference and set a good example for the staff:

> I could easily become consumed by budget constraints, destructive corporate directives, any number of distractions, and the ever-decreasing amount of decision-making latitude I have as a PD. But I try to stay focused on the positive elements of my job: I have the rare luxury of a large and talented staff to work with and we are still the number one station in this community. The way to survive is to stay focused on the positive.

Managing against Burnout

Program directors and other managers of artists and broadcasters have a special responsibility to guard against talent burnout. *Radio Sales Analyst* offered some worthwhile suggestions in this area under the heading "Principles of Motivation":

- The employee's behavior is functionally related to the way you treat them.

- People don't resist their own ideas.

- People will live up (or down) to your expectations of them.

- You must know the individuals you are trying to motivate.

- People will change only when they think they have to.

- Productive activity that is ignored will tend to decrease over time.

- Achievement and recognition are the top motivators at all levels.

Get a Life

The life of a performer is not always easy. A lack of stability can cause anxiety that can lead to burnout. Singer-songwriter Christine Lavin has lived through the ups and downs of the performer's life and offers this advice on what it takes to make it in a creative profession when times are tough:

> There is no dignity in starving. If you are not presently making enough money to support yourself with your [work], get a day job that will pay the bills while you work on your craft at night and on weekends.

Lavin worked temporary jobs for years while performing on weekends. Her final words of wisdom, "Don't borrow money if you can help it."

Lavin's experience is especially applicable for radio performers. Weekends are often the easiest route to getting on the air, trying out in a new format, or working with new partners on the air. Weekend shifts will not interfere with your "day job," whether you have one in radio or an entirely different field.

The Radio Life Can Be "Rootless"

If you have been in the business for any length of time, you may have heard some variation on the following:

"The only job security is the ability to 'secure' another job."

"Radio is like winning a video game. If you win, you get to play another round."

"You can always tell how well a broadcaster is doing by the size of the U-Haul trailer behind his car."

As you may be aware, commercial radio in the United States is not the most stable of careers. Often, you must move to a new city to have a chance to move up. You might find yourself out of a job at any time for just about any reason.

This insecurity adds stress and havoc to the already fragile life of the radio artist. A sense of humor helps, but some broadcasters can't take it and find other work. It follows that making your job a bit more secure would cut down on some of the stress-related burnout.

Writer, editor, reporter, and broadcast journalist Sheri Inglis warns: "To pursue a career in radio and live to tell about it, be a *whole person*, not just a radio or TV person." The following are Sheri's ideas for people who "want to work in broadcasting and survive."

- Look for a career in radio as you would a marriage partner. Don't get in because you think you can live with it. Get in only if you feel you can't live without it.

- *Diversify!* This is the single most important key to surviving the long haul in radio. Someone told me when I first began my career, "There ain't no gold watch in this business." Aside from a few rare exceptions, that is true. Resist the temptation to launch headlong into an "exciting career" as a disc jockey, talk host, news reporter or anchor, etc., and leave it at that.

  While you're pursuing your radio career, also learn and grow another professional skill. Whether it is public relations, marketing, script writing, real estate sales, flower arranging, court reporting, or giving scuba lessons, you need something else to fall back on. I don't know of a single radio veteran who hasn't nursed a bruised ego at least a few times following an ownership change, budget cut, format shift, or political fall from grace.

Pursuing a second career admittedly takes extraordinary determination, but you'll save yourself and your family added financial devastation if you have a backup plan up and running. By not putting all of your "eggs in one basket," you also empower yourself to move on and, often, up in your radio career rather than simply accepting a bad or unchallenging situation out of fear of unemployment.

- Be prepared. Always have your résumé and updated demo materials ready at all times, no matter how happy or popular you are in your present gig. New opportunities will often arise on short notice.

- Don't get involved in station gossip or politics. You increase your chances of being spared through ratings dips and managerial changes if you keep your mouth shut and your nose clean.

- Keep a good attitude about the station. No matter how messed up things are, avoid complaining to management or coworkers. Be very selective about the battles you want to fight, then fight them with the highest level of dignity, professionalism, and maturity possible. If you are unhappy at a given station, move on.

CHAPTER 22

Creating Powerful Radio
Airchecking

"No one can make you feel inferior without your consent."
—*Eleanor Roosevelt*

The Aircheck Session

Talent Is Hungry for Feedback

"Management rarely fails to let me know when I screw up, do something wrong, or make a mistake, but then they can't seem to tell me what to do to get it right." This is a typical complaint I hear all the time from on air talent throughout the world. Surprisingly, hosts often hire me at their own expense to conduct aircheck sessions with them, craving direction that their program directors cannot or do not have time to give.

Airchecking is more than just a show critique. One-on-one coaching, or airchecking, is a specific, focused way of working. It is not the only tool that can be used to develop, improve, and advance talent, but it is the best one. Airchecking is the process of listening to a show and, using specific criteria, determining what worked and what did not work. With a guide, airchecker, coach, or PD as your witness, you then decide what can be improved.

Even if you listen to archived audio of your shows religiously, you are likely to miss many nuances of the total performance. One air talent I work with says, "When I listen alone, I focus on how *I* did. I get critical of just me, not how the whole show went. When I listen with other people in the room, I focus on *everything* that is happening on the air: the guest being interviewed, sound effects, callers, and audio quality. I hear it all."

It can't be helped. Think of your school or family group photos. When you see one, the first thing you do is look at *yourself*. It is the same in radio. The natural thing is to pay attention to how *you* made a certain point or handled a particular caller. You are less likely to be aware of the subtleties of that caller's comments or the newsperson's clever contribution. There is something about listening to your show with a *witness* in the room that forces you to hear your work differently. Airchecking should be done in such a way that each talent sets achievable goals to fulfill his or her creative potential.

The Mirror

Talent, if you do not know what you sound like on the air, you are already in the danger zone. You are working with a handicap. Watch a child play by making faces in a mirror: "What do I look like if I'm mad?" "What do I look like with my tongue out?" "Can I see myself from the back?"

Airchecking is like a mirror. It allows you to determine the answers to the following: "How do I sound when I am sad or angry? How do I behave with a difficult guest? What happens when I try to sound smarter than my partner? Am I smarter than my partner? What happens when I pretend to know something about a topic I know nothing about? What happens when I'm bored on the air? How do I sound if I didn't get enough sleep? What kind of a show will I have if I have not been out of my house in a month except to go to work?"

Your audience knows, but without your aircheck as a mirror, you do not. Sitting alone with and listening to your show is like a single mirror. Working with a talented aircheck coach can give you multiple reflections of your work. There are other angles you cannot see with only one frame of reference. Viewing those other angles is the power of a good aircheck session.

What Exactly Is an Aircheck?

That depends. One New York DJ defines an aircheck session as "a way for the program director to yell at us periodically." Says another: "Isn't it like a report card?" From a manager: "Oh yes, we do that once a year with talent. We analyze audio of a past show. The meeting takes an entire day. You can read the report in their file." And one industry professional simply asked: "Isn't it some kind of postmortem after a dead show?"

These comments all have a grain or two of truth, but try thinking of your show as a garden and airchecking the show as a weeding process. In order to maintain its health, growth, and beauty, you should regularly walk through your garden and take note of which plants are thriving and which need attention. Some parts of the garden flourish, some struggle to survive. But always you check to make sure your plants have the right sun, soil, etc. Your aircheck is like that walk to see how well your garden is coming along.

When done correctly, airchecking can be a solution to the dilemma facing managers and programmers around the world who complain: "I can't find any good talent. I've listened to dozens of on-air auditions and shows and they are all bad or mediocre." Or, "This is a good station in a reasonably sized market, and the job pays a decent salary. Why can't we find the right people?"

Exactly where are all those talented and creative people hiding? Where is the next generation of talent? You may get lucky and find a genius on the doorstep of your radio station, but one important task of radio programmers and managers is to find and develop new personalities.

Anyone who has done it knows that it is hard work to develop on air personalities. Often it is less expensive and easier for stations to broadcast a syndicated national or network show than to have live, local talent on the air. But it is important to note that most syndicated programs were once local success stories. That is another reason it is important to work to develop new local talent now.

Even the strongest syndicated shows can be beaten by hot local talent. But looking to the future, what will stations do once today's syndicated shows run dry or move to television? Airchecking and developing talented people is one way to ensure that creative and powerful radio will continue.

> "One must be permitted to be clumsy and fail."
> —*May Sarton*

Basic Aircheck Rules

1. Always work from the audio of the show you are discussing. You may wish to transcribe it word for word to emphasize specifics. Keep in mind that a transcript can destroy context. Sarcasm, irony, and humor can all get left behind with the loss of vocal inflection. This often happens when a manager receives a nasty call or complaint letter with specific quotes included. Inevitably the context is missing. A discussion can degenerate quickly if the actual facts of the case are in dispute. Having a copy of the show on hand allows you to look not only at the content, but also the context of an event.

2. Focus on one thing at a time. Sometimes an aircheck session turns into a "dump" session, in which talent unburdens him or herself of a lot of thoughts having nothing to do with the show. A double standard applies here. It's acceptable, to a point, for the host to digress. After all, a PD is uniquely able to understand pressures talent may be under, and even, in some cases, to do something to alleviate them.

As a manager, however, you are there to aircheck, not to vent. Listen to the talent. Should you hear the makings of a great show taking place in your office, encourage the talent to put that on the air.

Don't let these diversions distract you from the aircheck session; just move the subject back to the archived show at the most appropriate moment.

3. Tell the truth. Trained communicators sense when you are fibbing.

4. Reinforce the positive by starting with the good stuff. Remember to acknowledge goals achieved.

5. Be fair. Criticism goes in very deep. No matter how angry you are, avoid verbalizing your negative reactions to a piece until you can express yourself calmly and rationally.

6. Let the talent discover along with you what needs to be improved. On air personalities are often their own harshest critics and can mercilessly rip apart their own programs during an aircheck session, recognizing and identifying specific areas where they can improve.

7. Outline strengths. Ask a lot of questions. What worked? Why did you want to do this on the radio? What were you trying to say here? Did this connect? Was the language visual? Did you talk to the individual and involve your listener? Did this make you laugh?

8. Have faith. Believe in your talent's ability to improve.

9. Always end an aircheck session with one or two mutually agreed upon "achievable goals." Pick at least one thing that can easily be accomplished by the next scheduled session. Try to let the talent initiate goal-setting.

10. Is there anything in the aircheck of your show that you could use as a promo?

"Managing creative people is an oxymoron. You don't manage
them at all. Instead you provide an environment in which
they can be simultaneously stimulated and protected,
challenged and encouraged, exposed and private."
—*Nicholas Negroponte*

The Method: How to Aircheck

Unfortunately, there is no airchecking school for programmers. You learn
by working with people, seeing what is effective and what is not. Some
aspects of airchecking will vary greatly, depending upon the individuals
involved. It is in the best interest of programmers and managers to learn
to aircheck effectively. If the talent wins, the station wins. There are a
few things one must *never* do, but the only *right* way to aircheck is the way
that *works*.

Without an understanding of what is required for an individual air talent to succeed, even the most gifted new hire may not reach his or her
potential. In a case like that, it takes a year or two for the talent to leave or
be asked to move on. What went wrong?

Let's go back to the garden analogy. You came home from the garden
center with some big, fancy bulbs. The picture on the box showed a huge,
exotic flower, but, unfortunately, the box was without instructions. How
much water was needed? How much sun?

There may have been nothing wrong with the talent you chose, but
when you have to play a guessing game, there is a good chance of damaging the talent, or at least failing to create an environment where talent, like
that fancy flower, can blossom.

If you found something you did not recognize in your garden, you
would not cut it back without knowing what it was. It could be something
wonderful. The same goes for air talent. Consultant Dan Vallie puts it well
when he advises programmers to "let talent go out on a limb as far as they
can. Do not restrict them until you find their range of potential and limita-
tions. It's better to reel them in after a while than to have to keep pushing
them out there."

Fix It Today

A great aircheck session with a trained program director or consultant can move talent along faster than any other tool. Progress may be painstakingly slow. Talent improves step by step, day by day. Frustratingly, the process may sometimes seem to be working in reverse. There is a period of intense growth, followed by what sound like patches of mediocrity, where all coaching seems to have been in vain. What you may really be hearing is the talent searching for ways to implement suggestions and ideas you have discussed. Have faith and continue the process. If you are on the right path, positive change will come.

Several other experts have contributed their aircheck rules and philosophies to this book, including consultant Dan Vallie, a big believer in spending time to coach talent.

Dan Vallie's Talent Development Steps

1. Talent is the product. You can't develop talent if you do not spend time together. The talent will improve more quickly if time is taken for coaching and direction.

2. Do not criticize talent or tell them something was poorly done unless **you** direct them on how to do it better. If you cannot give them a better way, at least approach the issue with a team attitude, working together to come up with a solution.

3. Make yourself part of the show, as the director. Directing involves making sure the talent play to their strengths. Help to assist and make up for their weaknesses. Give guidance in those periods where the talent is at a loss as to how to grow next or how to handle an immediate topical event on the air. If your feedback is useful, talent will not feel the session is a waste of time.

4. If the expectation is not clear, the delivery will not be on target.

5. You can learn from the talent, just as the talent can learn from you. Do not direct by doing all the talking. It is frequently more important to listen. Be sincerely interested in the talent's views and understand their perspectives.

6. Be a good facilitator. Draw talent out and get them to verbalize their feelings and thoughts. Watch their body language. Show them that you care about them and the show's success.

7. If yours is a music-intensive station with most of the personalities on the morning show, meet with them every day. It does not have to be an aircheck session. The format and length of the meeting can vary. If everyone sees it as helpful, you will all make time to meet. If any of you thinks it is a waste, the meeting will frequently be canceled or dreaded.

8. Do not try to impress the talent with how much you know, where you have worked, or the fact that you are the boss. Just be honest, encouraging, supportive, and consistent with your direction and approach.

9. Great coaches give talent credit when they perform, and share the blame when something fails. These are the people who can get you to the Super Bowl or World Cup, but only when you work as a team.

10. Praise often in public and private—but criticize only in private.

It Cuts Both Ways

Mistakes occur when an aircheck session is mishandled. Just as a talent can get a reputation for being difficult to work with, your reputation as a programmer can be severely damaged by a bad relationship with a host in your employ. These people do talk to one another and to managers. It is possible that the person whose aircheck session you botched years ago can keep you from getting your next job or warn a show you are actively courting.

There are a lot of ways to mess up an aircheck session. If you have worked in the business for a while, you are probably familiar with some of them. Consultant Lorna Ozmon provides an all-too-accurate picture of what can go wrong:

> Let's examine the state-of-the-art model for critiquing air personalities. Typically air personalities are critiqued, on average, monthly. The aircheck sessions are often canceled or rescheduled due to an "emergency" usually having to do with sales. The talent and the PD meet in the PD's office with all its inherent disruptions and distractions. The talent hands the PD a copy of a show the PD has never heard, which the PD plays.

As the show begins, the PD is thinking, "I hope I can come up with something to say and not look like I have nothing of value to offer." The talent is thinking, "I hope this is over soon and it doesn't hurt my feelings." After a few breaks, the PD stops the audio and, with a quizzical look, says, "There's something about that break that bothers me." At this the talent silently wonders, "What does that mean? and says, "Could you give me something a little more specific?"

Feeling slightly inadequate, the PD gives the talent a healthy dose of "don'ts" and sends the talent out feeling confused, unmotivated, clear on what *not* to do but clueless about what *to* do. This traditional approach to airchecks has done much to close the minds and hearts of talent at radio stations everywhere.

How Airchecking Can Damage Talent

Lorna Ozmon takes a psychological approach to airchecking and has developed her own techniques. She has found that before she can begin to make progress with a personality, it is essential to explore what has been said to him or her over the years that created both the good and bad habits he or she carries. Ozmon's cardinal rule for airchecking comes from Hippocrates: "Make a habit of two things—to help or at least to do no harm."

Ozmon explains:

Before talent can move forward, you've got to get rid of the unnecessary baggage, stuff they've been told by bad PDs or people who influenced them when they were just starting out. That stuff really sticks.

I usually ask them to make a list of all the "orders" they have been given through the years. Then we look at the list and ask, "What no longer works?" The idea is to get rid of the "old tapes" from previous programmers. Old-time journeymen broadcasters have been hammered by dozens of PDs. It is time to get rid of what no longer works for the talent. It is not enough to haul out the clichés and tell someone to "be an individual," "just be yourself," or "be more conversational."

In order to be effective, you have to be very specific when you guide talent. You have to ask questions and point out what you hear and what you think it means.

Ozmon particularly warns against the "Frankenstein syndrome," a persona copied from "pieces of others." She advises: "It is OK to use *tactics* learned from others, but do not cobble together pieces of what works for other people and imitate it. That *doesn't* work." Ozmon continues:

> There is much harm being done to the performances, psyches, and potential of broadcast personalities today. Management tends to forget that people who are asked to risk parts of who they are every day must be managed differently than those who work on the assembly line at an automotive plant.
>
> Many air personalities are now being managed by cops, not coaches. Cops punish people for mistakes and misjudgments. Coaches train, instruct, and inspire new behavior. Cops tells us what *not* to do. Coaches explain what *to* do and demonstrate *how* to do it. The result of the "cop mentality" in radio air personality development is a lot of time wasted in attempting talent development with disappointing on-air results.

What follows are ten complaints from talent who have expressed to Lorna Ozmon what they feel is wrong with the traditional aircheck or "critique" process:

- No, or too few, aircheck sessions
- Contradictory or inconsistent input
- Lack of praise for progress
- All negative feedback
- Lack of "how-to's" and creative input
- Vague input without specific examples
- Autocratic edicts without rationale to support or explain them
- Perceived personal attacks
- Criticism from a higher authority delivered as though it came from the program director
- Program directors who critique dishonestly, either because they do not believe a personality fits the station, or do not believe in his or her ability to succeed

Lorna Ozmon's list spells out the damage that can be done to talent. Clearly, air personalities who have experienced some of these difficulties will be less trusting of the process than those with positive airchecking experiences.

A Cautionary Tale

Here is what can happen when you ignore the preceding list: John considers aircheck sessions just this side of a torture chamber. He has good reason:

> I know my PD uses these aircheck meetings to jerk me around. He makes me feel small, and he gets off on belittling me. He keeps these stupid lists of minutiae. I dread these meetings. They wreck my whole day. I hate being airchecked. Even if I make a change, he never says anything positive about my work. I'm not convinced my PD knows why my show works when it does. I wish he would leave me alone. I get ratings, and I have been doing this for years.

If John works for you, you are either a sadist or something is terribly wrong with your airchecking technique. Because they are already in a very vulnerable situation, talent should be made to feel as much in control of their sessions as possible. Here is how:

- Let the talent choose the audio.

- If there are notes from the session, let the talent keep them.

- Give the talent access to positive feedback from anyone whose input is going to matter during the session.

- Always acknowledge progress and positive changes.

There are differing opinions as to the benefit of revealing research results to talent. Be careful. You do not want to withhold information, but you do not want to beat talent down with audience ratings so that they become discouraged. Consultant Randy Lane advises: "Keep the emphasis on the performance, regardless of the numbers." If there is a reason you are calling a meeting, let your talent know, if possible, what it is.

Why don't more programmers aircheck? Here are a few of the million reasons:

- **No time.** It takes as much as a two-hour session for each hour of programming.

- **Emotionally draining.** You are dealing with people's personal qualities and deepest feelings.

- **No confidence.** Most programmers have little training in this area and fear doing harm. Also, talent can get pretty defensive about their work. Lorna Ozmon counsels PDs to prepare for this using a tactic called "Objection Busting." She says:

    You must mentally prepare for every possible objection to what it is you are trying to sell. In the case of an aircheck session, it is usually a change in behavior. If you have a logical response to every reason why the talent does not agree with your position, you will be more relaxed, focused, and effective while conducting your aircheck sessions.

- **No crisis.** Some only aircheck when things go drastically (think lawsuit) wrong.

- **Burnout.** Most PDs are overworked and overwhelmed with demands for their attention. (See reasons No. 1 and No. 2.)

- **Don't like them.** Sometimes managers have a show or host that they find personally distasteful.

Using these reasons, many PDs recite an internal monologue such as this one:

Who am I to pick apart this show? These guys are professionals and have been doing it pretty well for a long time. I don't want to say anything to them that will break their stride. I know the show isn't as good as it could be, but I'm not sure why.
What if I'm just nitpicking on the little stuff?
What if I'm wrong?
What if I antagonize them? Then they will rebel and won't do anything I want them to do. I'm better off leaving them alone.

The end result of this internal discussion is that the aircheck session never happens, and the talent is deprived of an opportunity to improve his or her craft.

For program directors, the first step in making an effort at airchecking is acknowledging your areas of discomfort. Trust and truth must be established from both sides. This book cannot help you if you do not have good faith, a kind heart, and a desire to help your talent improve. If you are willing to overcome your resistance to airchecking, the rewards can be great. If you simply want a quick and easy way to strong-arm a performer into giving you the show you want to hear, this information won't do you any good.

Do not attempt to manipulate talent with false praise or threats. It is not right, it is not fair, and most of these folks are smart enough to know what you are doing. If you can only do one thing in your first aircheck session, pick out something you really did like and be specific about why. That would be an excellent start.

Knowing When the Time Is Right

Managers can aid talent by being sensitive to the right time for an aircheck. Educators call it the "teachable moment." Aircheck regularly at a mutually agreed-on date and place. As a guideline for newer talent, plan on a weekly session. Those getting started tend to require more attention from programmers, while more seasoned professionals may need only periodic airchecking to stay on track.

For talent who are not used to airchecking, the very idea of having to go through past shows with a PD can be unsettling. That is why consultant Tommy Kramer suggests: "Have your talent record every show. That way, you will always have access to a current show and your talent will get relaxed with the idea of being recorded. Plus, if something great happens on the air, you can have it on hand for a promo or sales presentation."

Lorna Ozmon feels strongly that full-time personalities should be airchecked once a month. She says:

People need time to process input and put it into practice for a reasonable period of time before they are ready to tackle a new concept or take the next step. Try to, as much as is operationally possible, make monthly sessions firm commitments. Although air personalities may say they dislike the aircheck process, nothing makes them feel less valued than canceling meetings with them.

For music program directors, Randy Lane uses this rule of thumb: "Have as much contact with your morning show as you do with the music and promotion directors." I agree with consultant Andy Beaubien when he says:

It is more desirable to briefly connect with an air talent on a very frequent basis than to rely on extended but infrequent meetings. The important thing is to maintain a continuing relationship. Some meetings should be in-depth discussions, while others may be brief and social in nature. Artistic growth can only come from the development of one's talent. Too often, once all the negatives in a person's style have been eliminated, there is nothing left but a bland and lifeless corpse.

Create a Safe Setting

For some, a "safe setting" may be a private office across a desk. Others prefer using more relaxed and casual settings away from the station with a glass of wine or cup of coffee. It does not have to be formal, but it does have to be regular and consistent.

Lorna Ozmon suggests:

> Get away from your phone, the sales department, and other distractions. Focus only on the air personality and the review. Go somewhere quiet and private enough to conduct the sessions effectively. Also, look for opportunities to be among people and observe life in your market at the same time. Meet over a meal if possible. People tend to be much more open to ideas when they are being fed.

Set the Scene

Tom Zarecki, consultant, programmer, and former Radio Computing Services (RCS) executive points out: "The goal is to get the talent to enjoy aircheck sessions." He agrees that the setting for an aircheck is crucial:

> If you don't have a private area, use your car. Sit in the parking lot or go for a drive and critique the show along the way. No interruptions, no calls, very private. In case the talent needs to raise his or her voice, other staffers will not hear yelling from behind a closed door, which fosters gossip.
>
> Never go through a host's work with other hosts present. The only time aircheck sessions should be in a group is with a team show, like a morning show, where two or more people interact. Otherwise, do not review airchecks at an air-talent meeting. It is fatal. Don't try it.

What Can Kill a Session?

The absolute worst thing you can do is turn a session into a personal attack. No matter what you have to say to an air talent, if he or she feels berated or treated disrespectfully, you will make no progress at all. Lorna Ozmon advises, "If you are not clear of the difference between an assertive and aggressive statement, remember it is easy to add the words 'you idiot' to an aggressive statement. Continually remind your air personalities that it is *what they do* on the air and not *who they are* that is being airchecked."

1. Avoid airchecking just prior to the show. It always takes some time to digest new information, and, if the session was disturbing in any way, it could hurt today's show.

2. Never ever, ever "hotline" a talent during his or her show. Resist the temptation unless your station's license is in jeopardy or lives are at stake. Receiving a "hotline call" from the boss during the show is a sure way to frighten the host and throw the remainder of the program off rhythm. He or she stops thinking creatively and begins worrying. This is to be avoided at all costs. The hotline is not a rolled-up newspaper with which you may strike the talent on his or her nose. Even if the manager is calling with praise (and he or she should), it destroys the host's concentration to hear it during the show.

The right time to aircheck or make any comments is once the show has concluded. It is best if the manager makes a note, considers the problem overnight, and then requests a meeting with the talent the following day. Try not to let a host worry for hours with an "I want to see you in my office" call that does not make the purpose of the meeting clear. If the show takes place outside of normal business hours, make an extra effort to aircheck at the host's convenience. Be flexible. Many top programmers are willing to come in on the weekends. An aircheck of the program in question should be available for the meeting. No matter how strong your feelings may be, come prepared to listen to a talent's reasons for handling something in a particular way.

3. Don't build unnecessary resentment. Be sensitive to your talent's schedules. For example, do not ask your overnight host to appear at a noon meeting when he or she would normally be asleep. If you aircheck the morning show, do not pounce on your team as they leave the studio. You are just getting to the station, but after several hours on air it is their lunchtime. They are probably hungry. They might be more receptive to your comments if their stomachs are full. Try taking them out or ordering breakfast. Hosts appreciate your willingness to take their odd hours into consideration.

4. Airchecking is hard work. All too often programmers hire and fire talent without ever having invested the time and energy that might have made a good host great, or enabled a talent to see the power of his or her work as well as its shortcomings.

If you are a radio program manager and your air talent asks you, "What did you think of the show?" and you didn't hear it; did hear it but didn't like it (but can't pinpoint *exactly* why. . .); or don't have time to deal with it now, *this* is the time to schedule an aircheck meeting.

Isn't There an Easier Way to Develop Talent?

Airchecking gets easier the more experience the talent and the coach have with it. Consultant Dan Vallie reminds us, "Coaching takes talent, too."

Airchecking is the power of one on one. It's being heard. It is someone rooting for you, being on your side. In sports it is the coach who pushes the athlete to maximum potential. Exercise makes sore muscles, but in the end it is worth it when you win.

Not only will you be pushing the talent on your staff to excel, but they will also be pushing you. A healthy aircheck session frequently features some strong differences of opinion. Most experts believe this should be encouraged.

Consultant Jaye Albright works with personalities who have differing styles and goals.

> At best, I hope to get the personalities talking about what they were trying to do. That way, I can base my feedback on how well they accomplished what they wanted to do in terms of my responses. I try to communicate one or two key reactions I had in as nonthreatening a manner as possible. It is not important to me that they always do what I suggest, but it is important that they know why I feel as I do.

I ask that they hold me to the same standard. Was I prepared or on autopilot? Did I offer clichés, or did I spend time thinking about the work? I hope they will be as direct about these things with me as I try to be with them.

The longer I have worked with someone and the better I know that person, the more I tailor what I do to his or her communication style. Some people are so controlling that critiques only happen on their turf, and they change very little over the years on the things I fervently believe would benefit the individual.

In these cases, I keep singing my song to them in hopes that eventually the air talent will realize that there is a recurring theme in my advice and perhaps some grain of my truth will imprint.

In other, more common situations, even the slightest word can injure. In those situations, I attempt to be subtle and always carefully watch for body-language indications of hurt, defensiveness, or misunderstanding.

It Does Get Easier

Sometimes a seasoned pro can be airchecked in a single word. A good example is an aircheck session that Los Angeles news presenter Susanne Whatley had with her news director.

> He was trying to get me to "brighten up" my performance. He gave me one word—"energy." Inside my own head I thought I was using enough energy, but when I tried it out his way, and then heard it back, my work sounded better! There is a lot of trust involved in doing what is suggested. When I first made the change, and pumped it up a little on the air, using higher energy, power, and pacing, it sounded silly to me inside my head, but when I heard it back on the tape, he was absolutely right.

Susanne is right. Things sound different in your headphones than they do coming out of a speaker. Encourage talent to grow independently by trying new ideas, experimenting on the radio, and "self-checking"; that is, listening to recorded shows on their own. You can also learn a lot from hearing others whose work you admire. You can even aircheck people you have never met by listening to their shows. It is a good way to see what qualities in their work are effective and might be adaptable to your individual performance.

Music radio consultant Guy Zapoleon "inspires hosts by playing a great talent example—past and present." A talent might wish to listen to a personality she looks up to in another market or, better still, someone who is on the staff who is philosophically aligned with her, and who can also be a mentor.

Every coach has a different method. Jaye Albright warns:

> Listening to your own work can be devastating. Seek objective feedback from as many directors as possible. Use what resonates truthfully with your own inner voice. Carefully consider the reactions of others, but do not ever take them personally. Their guidance is about their life experience and response to what you did. Try the things that seem sensible. Reject that which does not.

If there were an easier way, we would embrace it. Learning from others is something everyone does, but do not try to become someone else. Make it your goal to find your unique voice.

Getting It

The sections that follow contain some real stories of ways in which talent recognized and overcame obstacles using aircheck sessions.

"You Big Meanie!": Aircheck Success Story No. 1

Before her death, Mother Teresa, the nun who dedicated her life to caring for the sick and dying in India, was the subject of an hour's discussion. The host began the show by saying:

> I think Mother Teresa is a fraud. I have an article in front of me documenting her luxurious lifestyle, the money she has been given, private jet travel, and other perks of celebrity. It says here she accepted a huge contribution that turned out to be from stolen funds, and then, when asked, refused to give the money back. After all that, is she really a saint?

The host then took an hour of calls on what a fake he considered Mother Teresa to be. The following day, the program director was deluged with negative mail and angry calls. Much of the correspondence began by saying, "I usually love Dan's show but . . ." and ended with "I'll never listen to this radio station again!"

Why, the PD wondered, would this well-liked host generate such a heated reaction? The PD requested a copy of the show and found the problem immediately: Dan had introduced his supporting data only at the *beginning of the hour*. Listeners joining the program following the break, without having heard the show's opening, would have no idea what motivated him to say such angry things. It sounded like he was picking on Mother Teresa for no reason at all.

It would have been possible to listen to an entire half hour of Dan's show and hear him and the callers going back and forth about the saintliness or depravity of a prominent religious icon without ever knowing the revelations and allegations of her worldly shortcomings.

Using the audio from the program, the PD was able to explain to Dan that he had no problem with his opinion, however unpopular it might be.

But he pointed out that Dan had not been *heard* or *understood* by a majority of his listeners, because he had not reset the topic on the air for the new audience tuning in. The host was so busy being angry and outraged, he forgot to mention periodically what had sparked his initial reaction. Dan had failed to explain again the *reasons* for his anger. The result: To a majority of his audience, he just sounded mean. With the aircheck and letters from people who usually liked his show, the host could clearly see the result of not resetting a topic: He had been misunderstood.

Formatics Count

Resetting your topic at a minimum of every fifteen minutes is like giving your audience an on-ramp. Without resetting, it is like watching traffic on the freeway. You can see it go by, but you have no idea how to join in. Your show becomes accessible only to those who already got on the highway at the top of the hour.

Have you ever walked into a room where people were in the middle of a big fight screaming at one another? You wouldn't want to be involved and would either avoid entering the room or leave as quickly as possible. But if they stopped fighting and someone said to you, in a reasonable tone of voice, "Wait a minute. She says: 'Don't eat the butter, the bacon, the chocolate mousse; it will give you a heart attack.' But I say enjoying my life is more important than living an extra ten years. What do you think?" You have now been invited in and may be willing to contribute your opinion.

As for Dan's show, the reset could have been done this quickly:

I have an article that says Mother Teresa kept stolen money, demanded first-class air travel, feather pillows in hotel rooms, and gourmet food on the road. I have lost all respect for her. Some of you are telling me: "She is entitled to royal treatment for all the good work she does." What do you think?

Now the audience knows what is generating all that heat. They might not agree with the host or the callers, but they have a handle on what is going on. It no longer seems like an unfounded nasty attack against a saintly old lady.

"What Happened to You?": Aircheck Success Story No. 2

Rick had a weekend interview show covering serious issues. Around the station, he was charming and funny. Rick told such wonderful jokes and stories that management decided to give him a daily talk show of his own.

It didn't work. Although his weekend show hadn't been a lighthearted affair, this new job was meant to be a smart, yet entertaining program. Unfortunately, every time Rick opened the microphone, he sounded stiff and authoritarian. Gone were the offhand anecdotes, the wry commentaries, and the relaxed original humor that everyone had enjoyed in the halls.

We scheduled an aircheck session with Rick. Something peculiar happened. Rick visibly bored himself. He skipped over dull calls. He yawned, doodled on a scratch pad, and looked at his watch several times. At one point in the meeting, Rick actually dug around in his pocket for change and got up to buy a soda. Obviously if the host is bored with his own show, the listener is not likely to find it riveting entertainment.

There was another problem. Rick did not notice that his attention was wandering. This was the conversation:

PD: "Rick, what did you think of this program?"

RICK: "It's OK, it's fine, this is how I do my show."

PD: "Rick, anyone who spends ten minutes in a room with you knows how funny you are. How come that's not on air?"

Eventually, we got our answer. It turned out that the reason Rick was holding back was because he was concerned about his reputation as a journalist in the community. He was afraid to have fun or loosen up on the radio for fear of not being taken seriously as an intellect. What would people think of him? He was worried he would lose his credibility, look foolish, or fail altogether.

At the end of one segment, there was a traffic report. The reporter got the hiccups in the middle of her story. All of a sudden, Rick forgot he was on the radio. A simple body function brought out his natural humor, if only for a moment, as he suggested possible cures. We used those few seconds of audio to demonstrate to Rick how his spontaneity and storytelling humanized him and made him a more likable air personality. We explained that that could be a powerful connection to an audience. Once Rick understood he could be the same person on the air as he was in the halls, he was able to make the change.

"Look Out the Window": Aircheck Success Story No. 3

The sun was shining and flowers were blooming in Florida, and a weird weather phenomenon was taking place. During the night, strong winds from

Africa had blown sand from the Sahara desert to area swamplands, absorbing the usual stifling humidity in the air. On that day, the weather was dry, warm, and clear, instead of Tampa's usual unrelenting, sticky, tropical heat.

Blissfully unaware of the delightful spring afternoon in progress, the host on the air, a trained psychologist, broadcast two hours of carefully prepared and researched material on suicide and depression. The only people likely to have sat still for a show like that were probably incapable of physical movement. Great show. Wrong day.

During the aircheck session that followed, the host was very defensive. "I did everything I was supposed to," she said. "We had powerful stories from individuals involved in the experience, presented problems with solutions, painted word pictures. The show was personal without being too private, why are you on my case?"

"What did you do for the rest of the day after you got off the air?" I asked.

"Oh, it was such a wonderful day that I went sailing with my boyfriend, drank wine, had a picnic on our boat—it was bliss."

"Would you have listened to your own show out on the boat?" I asked her.

Silence.

When programming, producing, or hosting a show, it is always a good idea to literally take a look out the window and see what the day is like. It is part of what people are really thinking, doing, and talking about.

"Focus the Topic": Aircheck Success Story No. 4

PD Alan Eisenson relates the following story:

> We once had a talk host who found a great article in the Las Vegas paper. It was about a group of strippers bringing a class-action lawsuit against a chain of strip joints for not paying them the minimum wage, while also taking a portion of their tips. The host read the short newspaper article, but he never really *focused* it into a *talkable topic*. The show turned into a meandering discussion of stripping in general and ended up digressing into handicapped accessibility on public buses. (I still don't know how that happened!)
>
> When we were airchecking, I asked the host if he thought this would have been a great show had he only focused the issue into a tightly framed

talk-show topic—for example: Are strippers second-class citizens? Don't strippers deserve the same workplace rights as everybody else?

It is the job of the program director to coach and direct talk talent and producers into thinking this way. Most good hosts and producers can smell a hot issue; the challenge is framing it into a talkable topic. When a host mentions a topic or issue, I always ask, "What is the point, or what is the question?"

Sometimes it is not so easy to see the point or a question in a subject. Then you have to go deeper to find the talkable topic. Peel away the layers. It may take careful thought to get to the real heart of an issue.

"Did I Do That?": Aircheck Success Story No. 5

Syndication executive Denise McIntee has the briefest but probably most common aircheck success story: "I once played a tape of a host talking down and being curt to a lovely, articulate woman. The host was truly stunned when she heard herself and realized how bad it sounded. She never did it again."

"Who Cares If You Don't?": Aircheck Success Story No. 6

Here is another story from Alan Eisenson's files: "I worked with a talk host who brought up the issue of drug testing. In listening to him, it became clear that he really did not care about the topic. Because he had no opinion about it, he had no story to tell. In that case, he never should have brought it up. He failed to engage the audience in the issue."

When this happens, the programmer should use the aircheck method and ask why the host chose his or her topic. If a show failed to engage the audience, the answer to this question tends to be something along the lines of "Well, it was on the front page, and I thought it would be good."

The PD should then ask some key questions to determine if there was a reason the host cared which he or she failed to mention. If not, then this aircheck session can become an excellent opportunity to learn that you must, as Alan Eisenson says:

Always have a strong opinion about what you are discussing. Do not ever do a topic when you do not have an opinion, unless you have a *guest* on the show who has a strong opinion.

You engage the audience with your opinion/position or by telling a riveting relatable story about how the topic pertains to your life, or the lives of your audience. This is the *churn,* when your passion comes through and you can make your audience care about what you are saying. The show open or monologue is where you set the stage for your entire segment. If you do not care about your subject, you will not find a way to engage your audience.

It works better if the topic is something a host might easily discuss with a friend off air . . . and doesn't sound "manufactured" to fill a slot on the radio.

Make Time to Give Feedback

Programmer-turned-researcher Andy Beaubien warns that to neglect the talent may be just as dangerous and ineffective as bad airchecking. He recalls, "One person told me she made repeated attempts to arrange an interview with her newly appointed PD. After two months, she still had not succeeded. Various meetings had been planned, but the PD always canceled them. Feeling totally ignored and undervalued, she quit the station and took an on-air job with a competitor."

Randy Lane knows a DJ who says, "If you aren't getting feedback or being managed properly to perform at your best, tell your PD or GM what motivates you and what demoralizes you."

Talent Respects Talent

Sometimes an air talent will walk away from an aircheck session feeling as though he or she has been stomped by a big boot.

Seattle air personality Dave Ross has worked for several PDs. He admits he does not care to be critiqued in the traditional aircheck session. Understandably, he finds it difficult to be airchecked by someone whose judgment he does not respect. "I resent that it is just one person's opinion of my work. I much prefer to get up in front of a group of people at a live remote or performance and get instant, immediate feedback that way."

New Territory

The first time I airchecked a morning show, I was one of those nervous programmers. I thought, "Gee, who am I to tell these guys what is wrong with their show?" The night before, I had listened to hours of their work, made lists, taken copious notes, and been too anxious to get much sleep.

After the next day's program, our three morning team members walked in, sat down, looked me in the eye, and waited for me to say something. With sweaty hands, I put the tape in the cassette player. Before I could open my mouth, one host said:

No, no, no, let's skip over that part, wait until you hear the next part, now that was funny . . . and wait, back it up . . . here's where we had that boring caller! Wait, oh here I stepped on you guys and we screwed up the call letters, forget that . . . and here's the part where the caller started complaining about the prize because the dinner for two was at a restaurant that did not have free parking . . .

This went on for about an hour and a half. I had not uttered a single word. At the end of the session, the guys stood up and smiled. "Valerie," one of them said, "you are great at this. It's the best aircheck session we've ever had."

These three broadcast professionals had known exactly what was right and what was wrong with their show. They just needed someone to be a visible audience for them and to witness their self-critique.

I learned something valuable that day from those hosts. This was my lesson: People already know their own strengths and weaknesses. All we as programmers and managers need to do is to help them emphasize their strengths and conquer or play down their weaknesses.

Sometimes, as Massachusetts Institute of Technology Media Lab Professor Nicholas Negroponte says, "Management can be measured in its quality by its perceived absence."

Our areas of weakness are probably the things that are difficult for us or that we most dislike or avoid. That which comes easily is most likely our area of strength. This applies both to talent and to management.

Valerie Geller's Key Principles of Airchecking

1. **Define objectives and expectations.** Outline to the talent what you look for in a show. Make very clear what you expect of them, and who the target audience is.

2. **Do not lie.** If an on air talent does not trust you or respect you, he or she will not listen to you. If something is not your favorite bit or moment, it can still have merit. Be clear about this.

3. **Know why the show is there.** Remind yourself and the talent of the program's value to the station.

4. **Provide necessary tools.** Do not expect talent to make up for broken equipment, inept performances of others, or things beyond their control.

5. **Ask more than you tell.** Find out why something was done before you react. There may be a good reason why somebody did what he did.

6. **Respect the individual.** Performers are not interchangeable talking meat. Do not force your talent to fit into a format or structure that is very wrong for them. Jaye Albright feels it is impossible to get anyone to do anything he or she really does not want to do with any degree of commitment and conviction.

7. **Preserve privacy.** Do not put copies of aircheck evaluations in the talent's personnel files. Nor should you discuss an aircheck session with others. Record a session only if the talent wants to listen to it again later. For trust to develop, these sessions must be *private and confidential.*

8. **Look for and highlight powerful moments.** What had you wanting more? As you listen to the aircheck, try to be aware of comments both on the air and from others on your show. Remember, it does not always have to be the star talent having the "power" or "magic" moments; they just have to occur during the show. Denise McIntee searches out these moments: "If a host is able to bring out a poignant story in a caller who was hesitant to tell his or her story, I point that out and *praise, praise, praise.*"

Continued

9. **Focus only on the show.** This is not the time to take up other concerns. Tom Zarecki cautions: "Sometimes the aircheck session spins into a discussion of station issues the talent may be concerned about. Music, production, news, remotes, advertisers, other talent may all end up woven into your aircheck chat. But keep them short. Just like the classroom full of kids who keep the substitute teacher distracted so he or she won't get to the lesson, make sure your talent isn't just trying to get you off the track."

10. **Keep egos out.** It is tempting for talent to remind the PD that they are superstars in the market. Try to remember that the PD is really there to help. Programmers, lower your ego shields. Be willing to listen to talent's ideas. Perhaps they resist direction because they think it could work better another way. They might be right. Ask them what their ideas are. If they have feasible suggestions, throw out your ego and use them. Does it matter where a great idea comes from if it works?

11. **Set achievable goals.** As Lorna Ozmon puts it: "Avoid managing by minutia. When you focus on smaller sub-issues, you are perceived by talent as 'picking on little stuff,' which they see as meaningless to their overall success. To recognize a big-picture issue, ask yourself, 'Will this behavior significantly affect the station's ratings or revenue?' If the answer is yes, it is a big-picture issue. Pick your battles. Fight for the big-picture issues, and let the talent win the minor skirmishes."

12. **Acknowledge accomplishment.** Give authentic feedback for good work. This is Denise McIntee's strategy: "I do not use the session to point out 'faults,' but I might mention that when the host handled a similar situation in a different manner, it seemed to work much better." Ozmon says: "Most performers are 'pleasers.' When you tell them what pleases you, they will strive to do it again." Dan Vallie recommends following up meetings of substance with a memo to recap what was discussed. Internet news executive Bernard Gershon stresses that you must "try to make it clear that the memo is a reminder for them, and for you—not 'evidence' to be kept on file so that you can fire them if they screw up again."

Choosing a Show

You are about to read the wisdom of several veteran aircheckers. Notice how different they can be. Once again, the "right" way to select audio for your aircheck session is the way that works for you. There are several ways to do it.

- *Neither the program director nor the talent has heard the recorded show.* However, because it is advisable for the talent to select a program to work with, more than likely he or she has a pretty good idea of what is on it. Talent may have notes of problems or questions requiring a second opinion.

- *The PD can review the selected program before a session* and review it, making note of comments and questions he or she would like to go over with the talent.

- *The PD selects a specific show.* He or she may or may not choose to preview it. Often the reason for doing it this way is that the PD heard it live and noticed an area for discussion.

- *The selection is completely random.* For instance, you can send somebody back to the studio to pull any hour he can find. While at ABC Radio, then–news director Bernard Gershon used this as a part of his development technique: "We had our on-air talent choose a favorite segment, then one of our managers selected a different one, and then one was picked at random. Usually, the talent went first. Many times they were much harsher on themselves than you or I would ever be. They heard their inflections and imperfections."

How to Listen

Remember that the reference audio must *always* be available at the aircheck session.

Tom Zarecki suggests: "Listen with the person in front of you. The talent at some point will want to respond to you. Maybe not at first, but it won't take long." Jaye Albright draws a distinction between someone you have worked with before and someone who is on a first "aircheck date" with you: "With new people whose styles I do not know, I begin by listening to a full, scoped half-hour of the show without comment. Then I solicit reactions to what we just heard to learn how they communicate, what they try to do on the air, how prepared they are, and what skills I need to focus on first."

Transcription

Consultant Lorna Ozmon favors transcribing a show word for word. Why?

> If you just listen back to the show, sometimes the talent gets distracted by the sound of their own voice. If the words are written out, it works better. Listen to at least two hours of programming. Set time aside to focus on the show you intend to use for the aircheck. Do this away from other distractions, and make detailed notes. Look for patterns. If you have made good notes, you will begin to see one or two recurring areas for development.

I use transcriptions only when working in a language other than English, but Lorna has specific reasons for her method. She explains:

> Transcription provides talent with specific examples and depersonalizes the critique process. The "script" is less threatening than "what I said." Don't pick out one bad break. Look for and transcribe breaks which show typical problems. This will deflect the impression that you are trying to find the talent doing something wrong and show that your intent is to help him or her.

Randy Lane favors transcription for slightly different reasons. He says:

> Experience the show as a listener. Listen to at least an hour of the show casually (as listeners do) and get an overall feel for the show. Literally transcribe at least an hour of the show while you listen. This enables you to be amazingly specific. Jot down the elements that you remember from the hour. This will give you an idea of what elements might be cutting through to listeners.

Use the Pause

Using a pause is Tom Zarecki's method.

> *Try this:* Establish the tone of the entire meeting by listening for about thirty seconds, then stop. Talk about what you liked and didn't like about the way he or she introduced the hour. Pause mid-sentence to compliment the talent on something specific. Nobody minds this. You can't do it too much.

Nothing is more deadly and dull than pressing "play," then the two of you sitting and listening to a few minutes, or even the whole show, without anybody saying anything.

Ask Questions

Whichever way you decide to work with audio, there are some basic questions you can ask about any show that will help you evaluate its potential. This is my checklist of things I want to hear when I'm listening for powerful radio:

Questions about Powerful Radio

1. Are you talking to one person? Can the listener feel connected with the presenter, or is the host speaking to "all those listeners out there"?

2. Is the host using visual language? Can you "see" the story?

3. Is there passion, fun, or humor?

4. Does the host sound like he or she would rather be someplace else?

5. Is this a story affecting the listener's health, emotion, or money? Does the story inspire you to transform some aspect of your life?

6. Is there a "talkable topic" the listener can discuss later with others? Would the host talk about this off air?

7. Are there characters we can care about? Can you imagine this person?

8. Are you taking the listener on a journey?

9. Is this information that can't be found elsewhere? Is this information new?

10. Is it personal without being private? Do I get to know you as I listen?

11. Do I like spending time with this person? Would I enjoy a long car trip with him or her?

12. Does the show feel too long? If a topic is powerful, five minutes seems to pass in seconds. If a topic or host is dull—a one-minute piece will feel like it drags on forever.

13. Was the host in control of his or her show?

Questions to Ask at the Session

1. How does the talent want to be perceived by the audience? Have him pick three adjectives. Does she want to be seen as caring? Credible? Edgy? Funny? Intellectual? Is that happening?

2. Did the talent feel that the show worked? What parts were especially great? What bombed? Was there a talkable topic or engaging question? Was the topic or question focused?

3. Did the talent feel pressured to work with a subject from the front page of the newspaper even though he or she secretly could not have cared less about it? Did it sound "manufactured for air"? Did the show fit the day? Were there any breaking news stories or other events that should have been covered?

4. Was the talent nervous, unprepared, or anxious? Was the show accessible to people just tuning in?

5. Was the topic handled on our station in a way that was different or unique? Research shows that one of the reasons people leave News-Talk radio is that they find it presents problems that leave them feeling hopeless and depressed. Did your host or program offer solutions along with the problems?

6. Was the talent trying to persuade the listener to take a particular point of view? What are the tactics the talent used to attempt to convince the audience? Did they work? What drew the talent to this subject? Does the talent have some kind of personal experience with this topic? Did the talent reveal that?

7. If the host could redo today's show, what would be different? Would a listener speak about things heard on your station tonight with a spouse at the dinner table? Was there anything that could be used to promote upcoming shows?

Ensure that your station always has something real and compelling on air to offer your listeners—not something "manufactured for air" and boring—which will result in increased ratings for your station.

Don't Be a "Call Counter"

Some programmers tally up the number of calls a show took during an hour at the aircheck session as if that number alone tells them anything about the quality of the segment. Air talent also do this: "It was a great hour. I got tons of calls."

Programmers and talent new to talk radio are often surprised when a program gets a lot of calls but is not successful in the ratings. It seems that getting a lot of calls should be a logical indicator of listenership, right? Wrong. The amount of calls received by a show is *not* a valid indicator of how well a program is working. This can be difficult to understand for those who like to see immediate response. It just seems so logical: If a show is working, people will call. But radio isn't always logical.

Shows are successful when created and performed for the 98 percent of your audience who are *listening*, not for the 2 percent who fill the board with blinking lights. Personality Rush Limbaugh regularly reminds broadcasters about the importance of focusing on the content, without obsessing on the calls coming in. You could put a psychic on the air and you'll get the phone lines to light up, but the only people who will find the show interesting are the people on hold. Imagine a music radio station that gave concert tickets away for four straight hours every morning. The calls would be constant, but the ratings would be a disaster.

That's why programmer Jeremy Coleman refers to the full board of calls as "fools' gold."

Quality Callers

It's natural for some hosts to want to be polite to their callers, especially if they are worried about being perceived as "rude." But when a host allows a boring or inarticulate caller to wander on and on, that host is actually being rude to the thousands of listeners who are giving him their time. If a trade-off has to be made, choose your audience.

When airchecking, look for the quality of the calls that got on the air. Did the callers provide information, inspiration, or entertainment? Did they seem to know when you were kidding, when you were serious? Were they emotional? articulate? Are you pleased with the duration of the calls? If you think a call went on too long, where should it have ended? Air personality (and editor) Turi Ryder applies what she calls "the rule of 'one more thing.'" She announces her policy of hanging up on any caller who utters that phrase, but tells her listeners it's because she wants them to look their best, and the information they'll give first is usually their top material.

Do you feel you understood the callers' points? If the host didn't understand, did he or she ask for clarification? Did the callers add to the show's momentum or drag it down? Did the host feel or seem to be in control of the calls? Did the host change anybody's mind or the reverse? Were any of the calls upsetting? Humorous? Aggravating?

Are you getting a representative cross section of your targeted listeners to call in? Were any of these callers a potential resource for a future show? If so, did your producer get their contact numbers? Were you pleased with the mix of opinions and the number of calls you took? Do you feel the same way about all of this right now as you did during the show itself?

It is one thing to avoid confrontation between managers and hosts, but quite another to have a host who avoids it on the air. That is a sure way to a boring talk show. Tom Zarecki says, "Make the *listeners* like you, not the callers. Your greatest moments on the air may come from encounters with people who vehemently disagree with you."

Room for Risk

Ultimately, because the PD usually wins in a fight to the finish, it is important to allow talent to make a genuine mistake without getting beaten up. Talent will make mistakes, but, reminds consultant Andy Beaubien:

> Creativity cannot exist in a zero-risk environment. One of the PD's responsibilities is to encourage personalities to take calculated risks. Mistakes are a natural part of the creative process. That process involves dealing with unknown factors, the outcome of which is unpredictable. Conversely, making the same mistakes over and over again is not a sign of creative risk-taking but of carelessness and inattention.

If you want to show a talent what a bit could sound like if executed differently, you might try what consultant Guy Zapoleon calls the "before-and-after trick" of playing the original audio and then playing an edited version.

Jaye Albright uses the work of others on air to make her points: "It can be helpful to hear someone else successfully do the thing you are being asked to do."

Tom Zarecki's technique for listening includes the following points:

1. *Take notes during the meeting.* Have your own list of two or three points you want to cover. When talent comments on something *you* need to handle (examples: unreasonable demands from a salesperson, uncooperative screener, equipment problem), write this down and take care of it. Let the talent see you taking notes on their comments. This prompts them to make more comments.

2. *Create a short, numbered "what-to-work-on" list.* Your short list might be only one item! A typical list might say:
   • Make opening remarks shorter. Get to guest quicker.
   • Let callers provide the material. Don't be so quick to top them with your own lines.

3. *Make sure to date it.*

4. *Avoid the novel.* Focus on the important things.

5. *Agree on concessions.* You and the talent may each end up with your own short list of priority points to work on.

Tips for Teams

Here are some thoughts from consultants who work with team shows; Tommy Kramer advises, "Team shows have some special needs. The objective is to avoid 'train wrecks,' where the listener cannot tell what is going on." Here are his tips for teams:

1. Define roles. The funny guy has to be the funny guy. To use a sports comparison, the play-by-play person and the color announcer have separate, clearly distinct roles. Cast them as you would cast a movie, and then get the talent to stay in their roles. Nothing is worse than hearing two people try to top each other.

2. Listen to each other. It is horrible to hear two people who each pay no attention to what the other says. How can they hope to connect with the listener? Tiny things can spur great moments on the air. But if the talent is not listening to each other, they will miss the cue.

3. Use hand signals. Most teams think they do not need them. That is why so many teams talk all over each other. There is nothing compelling about hearing two people talking at once. Simply pointing at the other person right before your final word can correct this and make it sound seamless. It takes only a moment to point at the phone to signal that you are going to a caller or the computer for music. Point at yourself to signal that you have something to say. Use the slit-the-throat signal to show "cut this off." Most teams get away from hand signals after a while, but if the timing gets off, go back to them.

Tom Zarecki's Thoughts about Airchecking Teams

- The thing you should not do in these team sessions is severely criticize any one person, especially the primary host.

- Most of any meeting with teams should be positive, upbeat, and motivational. As in individual sessions, if something is great, react accordingly. Applaud. Play it again. Compliment specifics.

- Continue to meet with your primary host, and other team members, separately, to reap the benefits of confidential sessions.

- Before your meeting ends, make sure to set the date for the next aircheck session.

Finally, as Guy Zapoleon says, "Every great team needs to practice; you have to dribble before you can dunk."

Don't Rely on Unreliable Feedback

The news director and staff of one of the most dreadful and lazy newsrooms I have ever seen felt no need to improve or change because they received the occasional fan letter. Remember, even the worst show has one listener.

Consider the talk host who opens the microphone and asks for comments on his or her show. Sure, there may be some helpful ideas generated, but if your goal is to increase your audience, the people you really need to ask are not listening at all. The feedback you are generating is not germane. If you ask a retired community leader what he thinks of the big modern rock station in town, his comments may be heartfelt, but they are useless.

Untutored feedback sources can be deadly. I once worked with a station where the manager's wife was offended by a single remark on the station's morning show. As a result, the morning show was canned. That air talent walked across the street, got a job at the competition, and became No. 1 in the market!

There is also a phenomenon where people may have a strong reaction to a personality and *say* they hate him or her, *but they listen every day.* The same person who strongly claims not to like a show can often quote you chapter and verse what he hated on the air that morning, and the day before.

The *moral* here is this: Powerful talent causes powerful reactions, both negative and positive. If your goal is to get ratings, understand what you are really hearing. Don't react to unreliable feedback.

One general manager actually fired a top talent because the complaint he received "was a particularly well-written letter that made an excellent case." Again, the talent simply packed up his huge audience and went over to the competition.

When radio executive David G. Hall was a program director, he loved angry listener mail. On any given day, you could find the most vituperative letters tacked to his office door. You could hear the best irate phone calls by checking the station's Web site. Complaints, boycotts, and protests can also be a source of great free publicity for your station, ultimately generating new listeners.

Where Is the Line?

With creative performers, there is a real danger of stepping over the line. Andy Beaubien points out that unreliable feedback can encourage talent to cater to an ever-decreasing segment of their audience:

> Content must be judged not only in terms of entertainment and information value but by legal and public-taste standards as well. Many personalities constantly test these boundaries. The PD's job is to help personalities to stay within the necessary parameters without compromising the creative process.

For obvious reasons, content that is offensive to the target audience or portions of it is to be avoided. Content that is acceptable to your target audience but not necessarily to the overall market may be permissible and even necessary.

Personalities often find that certain kinds of "on-the-edge" material are very well received by a particular segment of their audience. In reality, that segment may represent only a small portion of the target audience. However, minority audience reinforcement can be very influential. If a personality is allowed to be swayed by this narrow audience segment, the overall cume, or cumulative audience, will be reduced to an ever-shrinking core.

This phenomenon is a silent killer. Because the active core can be quite vocal about its preferences, the departure of the greater cume can remain undetected until long after serious damage has taken place.

When you drive away your audience—that is the line.

It All Works Together

The aircheck process can actually help with show prep. Lorna Ozmon suggests closing the aircheck session with a discussion of new ideas, including prep. She says:

> Look at the next month's calendar, and brainstorm for ways to capitalize on holidays or special events within the context of the talent's work on your radio station. Bring new books, magazines, and newspaper articles that could serve as new sources of creative inspiration. Even if none of the ideas discussed are ever used on the air, this process helps keep the seeds of creativity alive.

Everybody's a Critic

Airchecking works best if there is only one person doing the feedback sessions. It can be very frustrating to hear comments from too many sources. The talent already gets feedback from his or her audience, producer, spouse, children, and people around the station. If you have clearly established your objectives and criteria for deciding what a good show is, adding the opinions and standards of others can only muddy the waters.

CHAPTER 23

Creating Powerful Radio Promotion

"Promotion is the exploitation of opportunity."
— Doug Harris

What Is Radio Promotion?

Simply, *promotion* is anything that puts the word out about your station. Promotion gets people talking about and listening to your product.

Promotions are events such as contests, publicity stunts, and outside advertising on billboards or TV. "Promos," on the other hand, are the spots or segments you run on your station that support your own programming.

Radio promotion has two goals: To draw in new listeners and to get current listeners to tune in more often. Promotion is also a sales tool for additional revenue while expanding the station's audience.

Doug Harris, marketing and promotions consultant, believes that marketing and promotion professionals are often the most misunderstood and underappreciated people in a radio station.

When operating budgets get tight, all expenses related to marketing become suspect, and because the effects of good advertising and promotion are not always immediately apparent, these funds are often the first to be cut. As the radio industry has become more cost conscious, traditional advertising campaigns for radio stations have become scarce, reserved for station launches, the debut of new morning shows, and the occasional cash contest. The current trend in the marketing and promotion of a broadcast property is to "get results with less."

That's not an impossible thing to do, but it requires a certain amount of creativity and planning. Doug has a couple of great stories of stations that launched successfully by "out-thinking rather than outspending" their competition:

Alternative rock station KPNT-FM, "The Point," launched in St. Louis, Missouri, with a special press conference. All the invited journalists were from local high school and university papers. At the "First Student Press Conference," these amateur journalists got the professional treatment, including interviews with the new station's personalities and a hot new alternative music artist. The station awarded a $500 educational grant for the best article, resulting in a great deal of press about KPNT in student publications around the city and an implied endorsement by the writers and their papers. Within two ratings periods, KPNT became a Top 10 radio station in a crowded marketplace, and a leader among school-aged listeners.

KTBZ-FM, "The Buzz," in Houston, Texas, was looking for a memorable way to inform its listeners about its scheduled move up the dial from 107.5 to 94.5. Reading from a supposedly "official" letter from station management, the station broadcast announcements that on a certain date, "The Buzz would cease to exist at 107.5." Panic swept through the loyal audience, and thousands of people called the radio station to protest. The station invited people to "Save The Buzz" rallies across the city, encouraging them to write, call, and e-mail The Buzz's management. Weeks later the station announced that because of the audience's support, it would be getting a new, stronger signal. Then the station invited the audience to a free "I Saved The Buzz" concert. Although the signal switch and even the free concert had been planned months in advance, the station was able to maximize the impact of these events by giving listeners credit for "saving The Buzz." What could have been a disaster (and indeed was for the station that took The Buzz's place on the dial) helped loyalty among Buzz listeners that has lasted for years.

Getting into Listeners' Minds

What does it take to earn a place in the mind of a radio listener? Harris says:

> People remember what is important to them, that which makes a profound impression. These are usually the things or experiences that they perceive to be either first, biggest, or best. As an example, many people can tell you that the name of the highest mountain in the world is Mt. Everest. Far fewer could give you the names of the second or third highest peaks. So, the trick becomes to convince your listener, or target listener, that your station is or has the first, biggest, or best of something.

What types of promotions make a lasting impression? Harris describes them with the amusing and memorable acronym "SAFO SHRIMPS":

The SAFO SHRIMPS Theory of Consumer Interest

Sex—also romance, love, and relationships

Achievement—songs in a row, award-winning programming

Fantasy—contest prizes or an experience with element of fantasy that cannot be bought

Outrage—edgy content, dramatic publicity stunts, and "shock talk"

Spectacle—uses "theater of the mind," station "roadshows," and live broadcasts; gives audiences something they've never seen before

Humor—major personalities, morning shows, comedy bits

Rescue—blood drives, fund-raising efforts, human interest stories

Injustice—news of the day; bad judgment calls by sports officials, politicians, etc.

Money—contest prizes, lottery results, stories on government spending

Patriotism—love or affection for sports teams, community, country, or home

Scandal—gossip, celebrity news

To decide which of the SAFO SHRIMPS tactics your station will use to lure listeners, Harris advises, "Learn as much as you can about your target audience and their needs." There are, of course, lots of research companies you can pay to provide this kind of information, but if you don't have the budget, your station can benefit from simply reviewing the news headlines that other media, like broadcast, print, and the Internet, are using to grab the attention of the same people you are looking to interest.

Keeping Your Promise

Doug Harris is also an expert on "branding" radio stations. "Branding" is often spoken of in hushed tones, as if it were a mystical phenomenon. But a one-word definition can simplify and clarify the meaning and importance of branding. In the world of broadcasting, a brand is a "promise." Every time a listener encounters a radio brand, that station's "promise" must be fulfilled. A station that promotes a safe haven for listeners and their families cannot allow its personalities to use racy or "blue" humor. Ever. If a listener lured by this "safe and fun for the whole family" promise tunes in to hear a dirty joke or even something slightly inappropriate, the "promise" has been broken. If a station does something out of character from its image, it risks changing that image in the minds of the audience and devaluing its brand. A brand is the collection of emotions and beliefs that comes to mind when a consumer hears the name of that radio station, sees its logo, or meets one of its personalities. A successful marketer protects his brand by ensuring that all of these contacts promote a single, pure image.

The same phenomenon works for radio stations. A radio station or station personality must do something significant in order to be remembered by a listener. It must be something that the listener cares enough about to form an opinion. Most markets have dozens of radio stations, and most listeners are "button-pushers". If the station, its personalities, or its programming are going to be remembered, they must send a compelling message, from a credible source, in a dramatic fashion. And this message must be sent with frequency and consistency.

Doug Harris breaks the process down into the steps described in the following subsections.

Define the Target

"The programming and marketing teams should identify a *primary target,* describing your intended listener's age, gender, and programming preferences." Harris continues:

> Your programming team may have purchased research to find the "hole" in your market, that segment of the listening audience which is not being served by another radio station or another piece of programming.
>
> The research may point out the radio stations from which your new station hopes to steal its audience. Your marketing team may visit some of these stations' events to see the audience in person. Other general information from research companies may reveal your intended listeners' tastes in reading materials, entertainment, automobiles, vacation destinations, and even food. Before you set your marketing strategy, look at all the research available. Know as much about your audience as possible.
>
> By knowing your audience, you ensure that you are promoting something that will be of genuine interest. Address a real need, giving listeners a real solution to a real problem. Offering a three-week vacation for two to another country may not be as useful to your target listener, a 33-year-old mother of two young children, as a weekend at Disneyworld. Promote the right thing at the right time to the right person.
>
> It may help you to follow the practice of many radio stations of creating a profile of a fictitious person with a name and a life story in order to imagine your target listener. Some programmers have even been known to place a photo of a stylized, fictitious family of this type in their broadcast studios to keep the on-air hosts focused on the target.

An additional tool for visualizing the target listener is "LifeStage Demographics." You can read more on LifeStage Demographics in Chapter 25. Whatever strategy you use to create and promote powerful radio, it is important to know who you're talking to.

Identify the Emotional Needs of Your Target

People remember the things they connect with emotionally. A message like "Ten songs in a row" or "More music in the morning" would seem to be a great selling tool because it is fact-based. It's true that claims like "The Rock Station" or "Hot Talk" tell the listener what to expect and can help differentiate a station from its competitors, if the audience cares about the claim. But emotional slogans like "We're with you" and "The sound of the city" often connect with a listener's lifestyle or feelings. Some programmers have found that this emotional imagery is more important than making an empirical claim about music or talk.

The very name of your station can add an emotional component to its positioning message. "The Edge" suggests a cutting-edge approach to music. "The Beat" connotes a rhythmic music presentation and hints that the station is in touch with the "beat" of the market. Monikers like "The Hawk," "The Colt," and "The Eagle" suggest that the station has the characteristics of those animals, like a feisty, proud, or playful spirit. And station names like "Jack" and "Alice" are meant to help promote a "we do what we want" kind of programming that appeals to a particular audience and positions the station as having a "personality" of its own.

The personality aspects of stations are an additional tool in positioning your station, as it works to compete with the flexible and individual choices listeners can make using their portable media players and custom computer music channels.

With micro-positioned formats on the rise, marketers and programmers may be best served by promoting an attitude, in addition to their music position and dial position, to earn a lasting place in the listener's memory.

Along with Doug's thoughts about building an emotional connection with creative and meaningful slogans and names, it's important to promote the on-air personalities at every opportunity. The emotional connection and relationship that a listener has to an on-air personality or presenter is a powerful incentive to select your station. For example, promoting your evening host taking requests for love songs at a set time builds an additional personal bridge to your listeners.

Give Me a Sign

To get the most use out of your station's logo as a marketing and promotional tool, Doug Harris makes these suggestions: "Your logo is part of building an emotional connection with your listener. Make sure that the artwork and the image it represents engage rather than offend or confuse your audience.

Take a trip to the grocery store. Companies spend millions of dollars researching which colors and packaging styles appeal to different sexes and age groups. Learn from their work. Compare a beer bottle or a can of charcoal lighter fluid with household cleaning supplies and shampoo. You'll notice a big difference that you may incorporate into your station's "packaging."

Be careful. Doug recommends that a logo be unique and distinctive but, more importantly, easy to read and identify. "Many stations make the mistake of using elaborate artwork that overpowers the call letters and dial position. It may look gorgeous, but if it is hard to read and or remember, you have not effectively promoted your station."

Doug mentions some other forms of "logo abuse" that include "use of colors that do not read well at night (a concern for billboards), or a font size that is too small or too fancy (how's your audience's eyesight?). Since logos are often reduced to black-and-white versions for use in some forms of media, good marketers must make sure it translates well. When it comes to creating a logo, stick to professional artists and a simple approach."

Even though Doug Harris is strong on research, when crafting a marketing and promotional identity, he still points out that "legions of successful stations have been launched on 'gut feelings' of brave programmers and marketers." There's no substitute for life experience. Research alone won't get you there. Your best asset for promoting a radio station is having a great product to promote.

Product, Permanence, and Promotion

Your product is what you do. Ideally, you have built a fine station with creative elements, good shows, interesting news and information, plus top personalities.

Permanence involves keeping those shows consistent by running them at regular times so the audience can develop the habit of listening.

Now comes promotion—letting the audience know where you are and what you are doing. You can promote any element of your radio station, as long as it's good, interesting radio. Don't knock yourself out barking people into the tent if the circus isn't great.

Promotions have to be as good and creative as the rest of your station. If your station is intense, dynamic, creative, funny, and passionate, your promos should be too. If they are not, you're missing an opportunity to generate revenue, get new listeners, and create powerful radio. A powerful promotion should:

- Promote the station's image as well as its product

- Build passion, emotion, and listener loyalty

- Involve your listeners

- Ensure that people who are not participating will still enjoy hearing the contest

Technology makes it possible to monitor listener's habits in real time. This is changing the way stations schedule promotions. In the United States, it has made sense to run promotions in connection with the big Arbitron ratings books. Many stations have had success starting their promotions on Thursdays because that's when listeners begin keeping track of what they're listening to in the Arbitron diaries.

Promoting the News

Your own airwaves can be one of the best vehicles available for marketing the news and information you offer. Take a small excerpt from a reporter's "magic moment" on the air, or a piece of a great interview on a breaking story, and create a powerful image-enhancing promo. It might sound like this:

If you weren't listening to Z-97 news yesterday at noon, here's what you missed: [insert audio of magic moment]. For news as it happens, it's Z-97!

This "performance promo" lets the audience know that if they're not listening to you, they're really missing out. This method applies to more than news programming. Record audio of *everything*. Save "magic moments" from callers, talk shows, contests, and monologues. They make great promos! Magic moment promos have an extra benefit. Often, listeners who hear the promo genuinely believe they heard the show from which it came. Your entertaining promo can get you credit for listening that didn't actually take place.

If your production director doesn't recognize a powerful radio moment when he or she hears one, or can't spend time listening during the day, it's something a good producer should save or note. Make sure your station has a system in place to get these creative moments into the production studio and back onto the airwaves with a minimum of delay.

You can also create promos around specific station personalities. At one Arizona station, a news promotion was built around individual reporters, including the then-morning police reporter. Here's the basic script:

> *While you're asleep, KTAR's Rod Petersen is out cruising the streets, looking for trouble... "And I'll find it too" [says Rod]. The best police and crime coverage on KTAR, Newsradio 620.*

A Scoop for a "Scoop"

Another way to engage your listeners while promoting your news product is to ask the audience to help you. Most news and talk TV and radio stations employ some version of the "tip line." And viewers or listeners may do more than just alert you to breaking news stories or events, they may be able to provide eyewitness reports or actual video or audio that you can use. Don't underestimate the attraction for many listeners in hearing their name on the radio or getting credit for a "scoop." This works for traffic tips as well. You will hear many radio stations thanking "mobile [or cell] caller Bill" for the information on the load of chickens that fell off a truck blocking the three left lanes of a major highway.

Many stations take this to the next level and thank listeners who participate with modest cash awards or gifts. A promotions director in San Francisco, with a limited budget, came up with the idea of "a scoop for a scoop," asking listeners to call with news tips. Whenever the station used one, the caller would receive a coupon good for free ice cream. Listeners from three counties called in to get those free scoops of ice cream. The tip line is not a contest, the "reward" or prize is a "thank you."

You can look at listener tip lines in one of two ways: as a lot of extra work screening the phone messages for veracity and tracking down leads, or as an opportunity to eclipse your competition by getting first crack at new stories that no one else has.

Let callers know on your outgoing message that this is not the place for anonymous sourcing. If a listener wants credit for letting the public know that a neighborhood grocer is storing toxic waste in the back room, he will probably receive it. If he wants to keep his job as a grocery store cashier at that market, the tip line is not the place to leave a message.

People who call in with news stories are likely altogether different than those who would enter a contest or competition. Instead of "winning," they want to be part of the station and believe they have something of value to share. And the station gets another promotional opportunity. When someone's story is on the air, he is going to get all his friends and family to listen. You could not ask for a better promotion for your radio station than a personal recommendation from one of your listeners.

"I Won! I Won!": Doug Harris on Creative Contesting

Contesting is about fantasy, big or small. We live in a cynical world, but many dream of winning big. In the best contests, everyone is a winner. Listeners get to play a part in an adventure or game, where nothing negative can happen, and even if you lose, people walk away feeling that it was fun to play.

The audience likes to imagine what life would be like if they met their favorite star, won a million dollars, drove a red Ferrari, traveled around the world, got their dream kitchen, or owned their own home.

The goal for an effective contest: to get people to believe that if they listen to this radio station, their lives could change.

Doug Harris breaks contesting into several different categories. He points out two factors controlling the likelihood that a listener will participate in a contest. "Generally speaking, the harder or more complicated your contest is to play, the fewer people will play it, and the bigger the prize or payoff, the more people are likely to enter.

The Pros and Cons of Contests

Designated Caller Contests

The on-air personality offers a prize or a chance to play a game to caller X. This is easy to do and easy to understand, but it limits participation to the most active audience members. Most people never call radio stations and believe their chances of winning are very small. Generally it is not exciting radio, unless the winner is extremely animated. However, many programmers believe that "teasing" the audience with an upcoming contest makes people listen longer.

Trivia Contests

The on-air personality solicits an answer to a question. Because the audience gets to "play along," even if they are not actually calling in, there is some added entertainment value. This is also a very simple contest to explain and conduct.

Recall Contests

This requires a bit more from your listeners. They are asked to tune in at a particular time of day to hear a code word, phrase, or song. They must then listen again later that day for a chance to call in and repeat the information to win a prize. The purpose of this form of contesting is to promote listening to a number of dayparts.

E-mail, Fax, or "Snail" Mail Contests

In all of these, a listener gets to choose his or her own time to participate. With a longer time frame, more people can participate. Mail-in responses require more time than fax or e-mail contesting, but all three remove the "run to the phone" or "stay by the radio" obstacle. These contests can be trivia or recall based, or can simply ask for a listener's contact information for a random drawing. Here you can also get more complex responses, such as for an essay or photo contest. (E-mail and instant- or text-message contesting can occur in real time and has produced some great talk radio. Personality shows can generate content in the form of audio for on-air use, photos and videos for the station's Web site, and stories or information that can be used in a variety of ways.)

Performance-Based Contests

Listeners may be asked to perform a stunt or a task over the phone or in person at a specific location. Of course, the more difficult, labor intensive, or potentially embarrassing the stunt, the smaller the potential universe of players becomes. In most cases, a substantial prize is required to get people to participate in these contests, but when they work, they can be a lot of fun. If they're theatrical enough, they can get your station covered on TV and in print.

Here are some examples of contests that got a lot of TV and print attention:

- To position its morning show as outrageous, contemporary hit radio station WZZU-FM in Spokane, Washington, conducted a search for the hairiest back in the city, inviting male listeners to come to a nightclub and show off their "pelts" while dancing. The winner got a cash prize and a laser hair removal treatment.

- That's the same feeling rock station KLOL-FM in Houston, Texas, was going for when it invited men who weighed over 300 pounds to enter the Fat Man's Dance Off at a local nightclub by offering a $500 cash prize. Over a dozen men participated and the winner got a standing ovation and left with a pretty blonde.

- For years, WEBN-FM in Cincinnati, Ohio, punned on the American national holiday of Labor Day by staging a "pregnant bikini contest." It drew huge crowds, and a lot of TV cameras.

All of these contests took advantage of the public's interest in the bizarre and unusual. In addition to all the free press, stations that can post photos of these types of spectacles on their Web sites can get more "promotional mileage" out of them.

Performance-based contesting can work over the radio, as well. KRBE-FM, in Houston, Texas, challenged listeners to have an on-air telephone conversation with their mothers during which the listeners would say something so outrageous that the moms would use foul language. "Make Your Momma Curse" has been used by dozens of radio stations around the world.

In both on-air and off-air performance contesting, this rule of thumb applies: The more difficult or more potentially embarrassing a contest is, the bigger the prize must be.

Can You Buy an Audience?

A Chicago radio station once ran a promotion called "The Million Dollar Minute." It threw a million one-dollar bills on the floor of a bank vault and a single listener was given sixty seconds to scoop up as much as she could.

The station calculated she would walk away with about $10,000. But, owing to a series of errors, the winner managed to grab $106,083. And *the station dropped in the ratings.* Many stations have tried giving away huge cash prizes, cars, and cruises, only to find listeners deserting when the contest is over.

While a powerful promotion can initially bring large numbers of new listeners "into the tent," unless you build a connection with them, no matter how big the prize, no matter how creative the contest, you cannot truly "buy an audience." Over the long haul, unless your station entertains and informs, providing a real sense of connection, you won't keep the listeners who have come for the contest. Listeners may love their prizes or sell them for a profit later, but providing content is ultimately the way to keep *your* prize—the new audience you have won.

The launch of a new station or show is one instance where a massive promotion or marketing effort can really pay off. Your objective is to bring people into the tent long enough for them to get a sample of your programming. Doug Harris calls this the "jet-assisted takeoff," resulting in a short-term spike in ratings.

Even though the majority of new listeners are coming to play the contest, if your programming is deserving, enough of them will stay to justify the expenditure. Another time to spend promotional or marketing dollars is when you've hired a high-profile show away from your competition and you want listeners to know where to find their favorite host. That expenditure nearly always gets a positive result.

Lots of small prizes often work better than one major prize. More people can win, and more importantly, more people *believe* they can win. These promotions can be less costly and they achieve the same goal of getting people to talk about what's happening on your station. Added up, the more winners, the more people are thinking good thoughts and spreading the word about your station.

The Bake Sale

Some of the best promotions in radio are spontaneous, developing from programming on the air. Here's a wonderful example: Dan's Bake Sale.

The idea for Dan's Bake Sale came from a conversation between talk show host Rush Limbaugh and one of his listeners. Rush publishes his own newsletter, available by paid subscription. "Dan the Listener" from Fort

Collins, Colorado, said he'd like a subscription but was short on money and couldn't afford one. In keeping with Rush's political philosophy of entre-preneurship and independence and his sense of humor, Rush decided to have a "bake sale," selling chocolate chip cookies to raise money for Dan's subscription.

It became a huge event. Newspapers reported all flights into Fort Collins booked for the weekend of the bake sale. People planned camping trips just to be there. Rush flew into town and thousands of fans turned out to meet him. It was huge, it was fun, it promoted Rush's show, and it created a news event covered by TV, radio, and the national press. It also sold a lot of subscriptions to Rush's newsletter!

Other Favorite Promotions

Some of the best promotions tie into public service, benefiting your com-munity while getting the word out about your radio station. They don't have to be expensive. A good promotion generates press that your station couldn't possibly buy. Here are a few success stories:

Orange Barrel Holiday

In the early 1980s, Albuquerque, New Mexico, was plagued by road con-struction projects. Traffic was a mess. Drivers were going crazy trying to maneuver around orange construction barrels, which were closing off lanes and streets everywhere.

The market's full-service station, KOB, decided to have some fun with a bad situation. The station contacted the company that made the orange barrels and devised the "Orange Barrel Holiday." Listeners signed up to win an all-expense-paid trip to the small town in Indiana where the barrels were manufactured. Highlights included a tour of the barrel factory and lunch in the plant cafeteria. The promotion worked by combining a sense of community involvement with a sense of humor.

The Ugliest Weed

One drought-stricken summer in California's San Joaquin Valley, radio station KFBK/Sacramento urged its listeners to send in the ugliest weed growing in their fields or gardens. This idea struck a chord in the largely agricultural area. Listeners responded in a big way. KFBK got so many tumorous growths, many of them enormous, that they filled up several storerooms and part of a warehouse.

The grower of the ugliest weed won a cash prize and some free gardening supplies from the sponsor and became a local celebrity. People in town talked about the contest, and it generated free publicity for the station on local television and in the newspapers. This is a great example of a promotion fitting a station and its community.

Mystery History

At the same time each day, WABC/New York played bits of audio from an actual historic moment. Listeners had to guess who was speaking to win prizes. Since politics, news, and discussion of current events fill much of the broadcast day, "Mystery History" works well on news and talk radio stations. It helps if a talented production director puts this contest together.

Singles Night at the Supermarket

This promotion combined knowledge of audience lifestyle with practical considerations such as sex, food, and revenue. The sponsor was the largest supermarket chain in California. The station, KIOI-FM/San Francisco, broadcast live from a store location and invited its target listeners, singles in their 20s and 30s, to meet the disc jockeys and each other. The station handed out free T-shirts with the station logo, and listeners wore them as they pushed their shopping carts through the aisles.

More than a thousand listeners turned out and several romantic relationships and one marriage resulted. The sponsor loved the promotion because it brought lots of people to the market. The event created great word-of-mouth publicity for the station and its client.

Go to Hell

This falls under the category of "geography joke" promotions. Stations often give away trips to the usual places. With a little creativity and an atlas, however, you can go the extra mile. WMIR in Lake Geneva, Wisconsin, created a Halloween promotion.

A check of the map turned up the town of Hell, in nearby Michigan. On-air promos promised listeners an all-expense-paid trip to Hell on Halloween, complete with dinner at the Devil's Den restaurant. The fact that this particular "Hell" was in Michigan was mentioned only once in each promo, and not very prominently.

The promotion set the town "on fire." Thousands of people signed up for the opportunity to go to Hell . . . and come back. A little research may turn up many such opportunities within driving distance of your station: "Win a free trip to Tokyo (Nebraska)," and so on.

A Promotion Checklist

"The promotions or marketing manager is the 'PD' of the off-air side of your radio station," says consultant Michael Hedges.

Michael Hedges's Tips for Creating Powerful Radio Promotions

- *Ask, "Does this promotion make sense?"* Every promotion must make sense within the marketing objectives of the radio station.

- *Less is truly more.* Choose your promotions carefully. When presented with five (major) promotional ideas for a month, choose the ONE that has the greatest likelihood of succeeding. Do that one.

- *They remember!* Every time the radio station is presented to the public, an impression is made. These impressions are cumulative in the mind of the listener. Listeners are equally likely to remember your faults or your merits. Your very polite listeners will never call to tell you how disgusting and dirty the remote van looked, but you can bet one will tell ten friends that your station looked tacky.

- *When designing a promotion, always ask yourself how it can be made bigger.* Radio is show biz. Show it to them!

- *Don't outsmart yourself.* Complicated promotions rarely succeed because listeners just don't have time to participate. You can build interest in a promotion only to the extent that the listeners see a payoff. The promotion will fail if the length of the rules promo goes over thirty seconds.

- *It's the details.* Think thirty times about each step through which the gentle listener must pass to play the game, attend the event, and win the prize. Use *their* eyes and ears, not yours. The wrong telephone number on an entry form is totally inexcusable.

- *Remember the payoff.* Sales promotions can work if, and only if, each and every listener-participant comes away from the event feeling that the time and energy he or she spent participating was in some way compensated.

- *Remember to get paid*. Plan for local media coverage. Think of ways to make your promotion interesting to them. Make sure that every local editor knows about your promotion well in advance. Have photos of every contest winner published in the local or community newspaper.

- *The promo is better than the bit*. Former Dallas radio personality Ron Chapman's "first and only law of promotion": The production must be the best element on your radio station. The writing must be tight, smart, and crisp. If a promotion, event, or contest doesn't sound exciting on your radio station, listeners will never *hear* it.

- *All promotions are equal*. Listeners don't necessarily know the difference between programming promotions and sales promotions and they don't mind being sold products or services compatible with their expectations of the radio station. Anything sold in an entertaining way is, well, entertaining.

Steer Clear of Contest Junkies

Warning: There is a group of people who live to play radio contests. Make sure your contest is legal and restrictions are clear. You can tailor your rules in order to weed out the contest addicts. Your rules should be structured in such a way as to give the average person the best chance of winning.

Avoid Disasters

Whatever your promotion, plan it carefully. Do a little informal research. Run your promotion idea by a few people around the office. See if they can spot any obvious flaws.

A storyline about a contest was dramatized on the 1980s TV show *WKRP in Cincinnati*. Although this contest played out on a network sitcom, it could easily be an example of a real station promotion gone horribly wrong: It was the standard American "Thanksgiving Turkey Giveaway," with a twist.

Instead of handing out coupons for frozen turkeys, the station would drop live turkeys from a helicopter to glide down to listeners waiting in a parking lot below. Unfortunately, the promotion department overlooked one important consideration—turkeys can't fly. As fictitious newsman Les Nessman reported live on the air, "Turkeys are hitting the ground like bags of wet cement!" Be certain your promotion will "fly" before you drop it on the public.

No Budget? No Problem

For some reason, many station managers do not believe in spending money on marketing. When faced with this challenge, Doug Harris says, "Use OPM." What is "OPM"? It's "other people's money" or "other people's media." How does one get hold of other people's money? Actually it is not very hard. As Doug Harris points out: "Clients of a radio station have cars, electronic products, restaurant gift certificates, trips, tickets, spa days, and access to places and people all of which can be incorporated into station giveaways." All those clients ask in return is airtime and maybe an appearance by you or one of your presenters from your station van. Here is where the sales department can be your best ally. Of course, they will expect advertising revenue in return, but that is fair.

If the sales department is unable to help, or if you are promoting a noncommercial radio station, you still have options. As a member of the media, you have access to cultural and entertainment events and items that your listeners do not.

One example of creative problem solving to promote a show in America came from public radio. A quiz show, just starting out, had no money for prizes, so the promoters talked one of their network's news presenters into recording an outgoing message on the voice mail system of each week's winner. And they made fun of themselves for not having money for better prizes. The audience got the joke, and now, several years later, though the program is a success, listeners still demand a chance to win that news presenter's voice on their phone answering machine. Now that bit is an integral part of the show.

Let's say you work at a noncommercial jazz station with no funds to spare. Ask a band that gets a lot of airplay from your station to put on a concert just for your listeners, and borrow a local jazz club for the venue. Everybody wins—the club gets exposure, the band gets airplay, your audience feels special and appreciated. Cost to you: zero.

Although you may not be spending any money on your event, it is advisable to detail in writing the value of the things your station is providing, and the value of the products or services you will receive in return. Make sure all the necessary people sign off on the event, and you can avoid some nasty surprises later.

Do not be afraid to use your contacts to arrange experiences for listeners that they would not otherwise have. Celebrities are often loyal to the stations that first recognized their talent and promoted them early in their careers.

"OPM" Programming

Make sure to use what Doug Harris calls "other people's media" (OPM) every chance you get.

> Listener polls, publicity stunts, and the traditionally wacky things that radio stations do are often attractive to television stations and print outlets, provided that they are sufficiently out of the ordinary to be of interest to the public. Of course, a good place to look is at your own company if it owns newspapers, magazines, TV, outdoor, or other media. But don't stop there. Create relationships and educate yourself on the needs of other media outlets in your area. And be prepared to give them content in a form that they can most easily use.
>
> Most cities have a media contact list published by the visitors' bureau, or you can do a little homework and create one. Then find someone on your staff who can write good press releases on a regular basis. Use this list to promote station activities, events, and personalities. Remember, these outlets and electronic media like the Internet are always in need of fresh entertaining content. If you can provide something interesting or exciting for them to cover, they will.

Approaching Television

How do you get a TV station to promote your radio station? As a New York City television assignment editor, Howard Price is the gatekeeper to getting stories on WABC TV. Here's what he says you need to know about pitching a radio story to television:

- Think about how you can break through the thousand or so faxes spewed daily onto the assignment editor's desk, the nine phone lines that ring constantly, and the 330 channels of scanner chatter that must be monitored.

- Don't get frustrated if you call a TV news desk and they are brusque with you or if you hear "no." It just means they are busy. Try again another time.

- Get a feel for what plays on the station you are pitching. Like radio's many formats, each TV station's programming targets specific audiences and demographics.

- Call once. Fax once. E-mail once. And never call when the newscast is on the air. Make sure your faxes and e-mails contain the facts—that's what the stations really need.

- Pitch things that dovetail with the day's news—especially if you are a news or talk station—and don't pitch a goofball story on a serious news day. It may work better to promote your "light" story to a TV station on a slow news day.

- Keep TV posted regularly, and with as much advance notice as possible, on your scheduled guests.

- Know the TV station's deadlines. Most coverage for morning news shows is locked in by 4 a.m.; for noon shows, by 10:30 a.m.; for the 5:00 and 6:00 p.m. news, it's about 3:30 p.m.; and for 10 or 11 p.m. newscasts, by about 9:30 p.m. The exception, of course, is for legitimate breaking news.

- Start your events on time, but run them long enough for latecomers to have a chance at getting some pictures and sound. Deliver what you promise on your press release or pitch to the newsroom.

- Plaster your call letters everywhere. To make sure your name, dial position, and images get the play you want, post them all over your studios and at your events. That way, even if they aren't mentioned, the audience will see them.

- No pictures—no story. TV is a visual medium. Compelling pictures are what drive it. A bunch of folks sitting around a radio studio don't make for exciting TV, unless of course they are high-profile folks making news exclusively on your air.

- Be "TV friendly." Create broadcast spaces inside and outside your studios that TV crews can easily negotiate to get the shots you want them to get. TV crews need extra time to put their trucks in place, string their cables, etc. Make sure there are electrical outlets in your studios that they can access. Giving them time to edit your story helps, but remember, "live" is TV's magic word.

- If your radio station is co-owned with a TV station, labor every day to strengthen that partnership. Share resources when it counts and each station will reap the rewards. If you are not co-owned but your station has a network affiliation, partner with your network's local TV outlet. Your network will love you, your TV partner will love you, and, most important, so will your audience.

Piggyback on Your Advertisers' Advertising

Doug Harris suggests "doing a little homework to find out which advertisers in your market spend the most money on television, print, and outdoor." He continues:

> Find a way to include one of the station personalities or a station logo in that client's advertising. The client might like to use one of your station personalities as a spokesperson for his product or service instead of an anonymous actor.
>
> This is a way to get exposure for your radio station's call letters, logo, or personalities at little or no cost to you. Of course, co-promoting a major event is a great way for your station to look larger than it would if it were doing this project alone. And if two media entities are willing to share the limelight, you can put your station's logo and personalities in front of a much bigger audience.
>
> Other resources—a branded Web site, an online newsletter, or an interactive phone system (such as a movie theater's recorded schedule on the phone message recorded by your afternoon host)—can all offer additional exposure for a particular personality, program, or promotion.
>
> These cost-effective examples of "other people's media" will enhance and amplify your marketing attack, especially if traditional, more expensive avenues of external marketing are closed.
>
> While on-air messages are usually short-form (10 to 60 seconds), more details and features of a promotion may be easily explained on the station's Web site. The Web site is also a great place to post photos of contest prizes, previous winners, contest rules, and other key information, too cumbersome for air.

Doug Harris' Action Plan for Success

Here is a seven-step process for planning in advance and putting things in writing to build an annual marketing plan for your station, personality, or program.

Step One: Each department at the radio station should prepare a list of goals, needs, and wants. The needs of the programming department are quite different from those of the sales department. Both are important. This list should include equipment upgrades, additional staff, and other expense-related requests. It should also include ratings and revenue goals and marketing targets and achievements. If your programming department wants to "own" the concertgoing public, then the marketing and promotion department needs to target concert venues and ticket outlets. Meanwhile, the sales department can target concert promoters and related activities and products such as soft drinks and guitar stores.

Step Two: Create an eighteen-month calendar beginning with the start of the next month. If that seems too big a job, try one year or even six months, but start planning now for the future. Keeping in mind the goals that have just been identified, here's what a planner might put on a calendar:

- National, regional, or local events and holidays
- Religious observations
- First day of school, university classes begin
- Days when banks, schools, and public offices might be closed
- Major sporting events
- Celebrity birthdays of interest to the target listener
- Station events or anniversaries
- Special station programming
- Ratings periods

A marketing manager should be looking for anything that might interest or distract the target audience. He or she should be looking for a "good parade" in order to "get in front of it." Promotion is the exploitation of opportunity.

Step Three: Marketing, programming, and on-air staff should meet to decide which of these calendar dates are most important and how the station will tie into them. If the team is not comfortable planning Christmas promotions in March, then at least acknowledge the need for a Christmas promotion and stockpile some airtime or station resources. For promotions during ratings periods, reserve funding and promotional airtime in an imaginary "war chest" for later use. You can decide later what your specific strategy and tactics will be. In commercial stations, talk to your sales department about their potential needs for these calendar periods. Ideally, the needs of sales should be integrated with those of programming to share costs and maximize revenue.

Step Four: Calculate your budget for each promotion or promotional period. If you know you'll be doing four concert remotes per weekend and giving away one hundred station T-shirts at $5 each, add that to the cost of having your staff at the event for two hours, special banners, etc., and budget the cost of running that promo each weekend. If you know that each weekend you send your staff out with prize packages costing $800, it's simple to put your budget together. Identify other costs like morning show giveaways and special opportunities as specifically as possible.

Be sure to leave some contingency dollars for "unscheduled" opportunities that may come up at the last minute. You don't want to miss a spontaneous moment to promote your station because you didn't leave any budget for it. For ratings periods, planning for a billboard campaign at one price and a TV campaign at another price will prepare you for either scenario.

Step Five: Defend and explain your budget by writing a story, or narrative, to go with your proposal. It should show the department's goals and how they work with the key periods you've identified. Your manager will review this budget, so requests need to appear reasonable, logical, and beneficial to the station. Financial managers are paid to keep costs down, but if you've done a good job with step four, your figures will not look like guesswork. Budgets are NEVER approved on the first pass, and you will be asked to reduce your request. A good marketer knows this. Ask for everything you need, but prepare to settle for less.

Step Six: When asked to reduce the budget, a marketing manager may wish to show the narratives to other department heads. There may be ways to cut expenses by sharing costs with other departments. The narratives explain marketing goals to everyone. Perhaps individual requests can be scaled back in order to meet group goals.

Step Seven: Review your progress and your spending every month. "Mid-course corrections" may be necessary if your plan is not having its desired effect. If you have launched something that is not working, the marketing and programming teams should take steps to correct it. At the end of the year, your station should be able to look back on a series of successes and a minimum of disappointments.

Remember, the most common mistakes in marketing and promoting broadcast properties and personalities can be avoided by following two simple rules:

1. *Plan in advance.* Why wait until the last minute to plan promotions? The dates for all national holidays, many sporting events, and the ratings periods that affect any market for the next year are all available today.

2. *Put everything in writing.* If a marketing manager must tell his tale over and over, it will slow things down and sap its strength. Have written rules about promotions and how they get on the air. Everyone involved in the process needs to know and follow these rules.

Use Your Own Airwaves and Web Site to Promote

Of course your station already has the two most powerful tools you need for keeping your listeners and attracting new ones. Since your Web site has the ability to be "searched" by anyone anywhere, it makes sense to add exciting content at every opportunity. Don't miss a chance to put up something great. Have a digital camera with you everywhere you go, not just at station events. Is your station's bumper sticker stuck on the back of the governor's limo? Get it onto your site fast. The most powerful tool to keep people listening longer or to give them an idea of what they can expect from your station is the powerful promo.

Up Next—Powerful Anticipation

One of the most highly paid positions at a major market radio station is that of production director. Radio stations are not known for throwing money around needlessly, so there must be something rare and special about a nonmanagerial position that can command almost as much salary as is spent on a morning show.

Creativity is the "X factor" that makes the production director such a valuable member of your team. Radio imaging pro Mark Driscoll says, "Your product is the station's package. Your promos are the wrapping paper and the bow on that package. Having great promos makes the listener want to open up the box and see what's inside."

Create Expectations

Innovatively produced promos for your station and your shows make the audience feel they will miss something if they tune away.

Maybe a listener is not interested in whatever is on the air at the moment. However, if you can create excitement and anticipation about an upcoming event, the listener may give you five or ten extra minutes of his or her time, or come back later.

Pick the Highlights

Promos can establish your station's "personality," or image. Some call it "stationality." You know you have a great station when you have trouble deciding which moments to promote.

Station promos are a lot like film promos. They incorporate peak experiences and show highlights to create excitement, energy, and, most of all, the desire to "be there." Like many movie trailers, the promos may often be better than the shows themselves.

Seize Opportunities

Anything from an upcoming appearance to the top-of-the-hour ID can become an opportunity to creatively promote your station. There's just one rule: If it is prerecorded, it has to be perfect. Make sure you have a good-quality, reliable audio recording system in place in order not to miss the chance to utilize a "magic moment" for a show promo. You may come across some of these moments during aircheck sessions, and it is very frustrating when the quality of the sound is too poor to use for a produced promo.

You do not need to have a huge budget to run great promos on your radio station. If you have creative air talents, you can harness their abilities to promote not only their own shows but the station itself.

Listen to some of the hundreds of audio feeds from various stations' Internet Web sites. There you will find a mix of hot promos, parody songs, and creative spots. In addition, many production directors maintain their own Web sites featuring examples of their best work.

Remember, when you make your promos, *formatics* count. Don't miss an opportunity to give call letters, dial position, and the station's name.

Promo Points: News/Talk Radio

Teases and Promos Are Best When Short

If you err, err on the side of brevity. It is better to leave the audience hungry than to overfeed them.

Cross-Promote Like You Mean It

Having each air personality enthusiastically mention other shows and events on the station promotes and personalizes both the hosts and the station. There is nothing like a word of endorsement from a listener's favorite host to make that listener give another show a chance.

If you are not a particular fan of the show you are being asked to promote, find one or two genuinely good things you *can* say, and say them. For example, "Sam's show got rated number one in the Reader's Choice Poll of City Magazine!" You don't have to lie; you just have to realize that when someone on your team succeeds, you win too.

If you are the number one show on the number seven station, it is not nearly as rewarding as being the number one host on the number one station.

Many of the biggest syndicated personalities in America take the time to cross-promote others on their local stations and their affiliates as well. Cross-promotion gives your schedule a feeling of continuity.

Do It Yourself—Get Your Own Outside Press

Promotions consultant Pam Baker says that talent shouldn't expect the station to do all the work:

> If you are a morning show personality and your show's events or antics are not receiving any press coverage, do it yourself. The sales team works hard to develop relationships with clients. You should do the same with the media. Be active on your own account. Positive public relations can not only boost your ratings, it helps establish you in the marketplace, making you more valuable. Consider the benefits of hiring your own public relations representative.

Throw Out Stale Bread

It is tempting to use great promos over and over again. I've heard stations use the same old promos for days, weeks, even years. Do not give in to that temptation! Even if you have produced the most hilarious promo—distinctive, memorable, and featuring seven of the biggest stars in Hollywood—after a while, it gets boring. In fact, if a listener hears the same promo over and over again for weeks, it can make your whole show sound boring. If a promo is really that fantastic, run it for a little while, store it for several months, and then recycle it.

Keep a library of stand-out promos that are not date-specific in the event you are unable to produce a fresh one for some reason.

Change your promos like you change your underwear. If someone complains and says, "But I did a great one last week," remind him or her that creativity leads to more creativity.

Stay "Up" for It

If you cut your promos last thing before you leave the station, there is a danger of sounding tired and unenthusiastic. After all, you have just spent three hours on the air, you want to go home, and you are holding your car keys. Try running into the production room prior to today's show and see what you can come up with to promote tomorrow's show. The promos will have that sound you have when you first go on the air—spirited and full of energy.

Get It Right

When you work with prerecorded elements, *make them perfect*. Live on the air, you cannot possibly control everything that happens. But when you record, you can. Make it flawless. Here you can create radio art.

Creating Powerful Promos

You can creatively "promo" anything. There's no excuse for a boring promo. TV "magazine" shows and tabloids make a business of promoting the most mundane details of stars' lives as if they were shocking new information. It's not until you've waited through 59 minutes of other news that you find that the "newly discovered nude photographs of today's biggest big screen star" are actually baby pictures. The purpose of the promo is to entice the listener to come back later or stay longer to hear what you've got.

Here is an example of a radio station bragging about increasing its transmitter power—something not usually considered exciting. Broadcaster Tom Bodett, a spokesperson for the Motel 6 chain, did the spot. Bodett made famous the Motel 6 tag line: "We'll leave the light on for you."

PROMO: KGO TRANSMITTER UPGRADE

[Soft country-style music plays behind the spot]

When a radio station has been around as long as KGO, some of that electronic stuff's bound to wear out. Well, since it did and not everyone can talk real loud like that Ronn Owens or Bernie Ward, KGO went out and got one of those new jillion-watt transmitters to squirt those sound waves out there.

[Electrical-sizzling sound effects]

Well, sure, it's a big deal to the baby harp seals up in Nova Scotia that are now getting a fuzzy earful of KGO at night, but what's it mean to you?

Well, not much except you might not need to use that microwave to heat your Lean Cuisine anymore and you probably won't have to actually switch on the lights either. Just turn on KGO and stand back...

I'm Tom Bodett, and we've cranked up the power for you on KGO News/Talk 810.

To write, produce, and create powerful promos, begin by thinking of how *you* could be enticed to tune in. A great promo will intrigue the audience with a promise of something interesting coming up. Although research shows they will be disappointed should the actual item not stand up to the promo, listeners tend to keep trying if the promo is really that good. There is a risk.

If you consistently fail to deliver what you promise, you can lose credibility and audience. Often, those tabloids really DO have amazing photos. Remember that promos are "the fancy bow you wrap around your stations' package." Your station needs to have something real to promote, or you'll have only a wrapped box, with nothing inside.

There are various styles of promos. If you want to experiment with your station's image and build continuity between shows, try to create the image that the radio station is like a family and all the hosts listen to and support one another. When done well, it really works. The "inside" promo is the method of one host promoting his or her show within another host's show. Your talkable topic or engaging question can make a good promo, as well.

Listen to your station's other programs. Then you'll really know the product you are promoting. For example: "Hi, I'm Sam on WKXW, The Talk Station. You are listening to the Dr. Paula Show, but I'd like to invite you to join me later on this afternoon. We'll be taking calls, the mayor will check in, and you'll get a chance to meet the number one singer in America right now. That's today at two p.m. here on the Talk Station."

Direct Promos

Example: "Up next with Bill Jones on WWXX, you'll meet the man who saved California's gray whales, and later in the show, Joe Jones's lawyer. He's defending a notorious author and death row inmate. Coming up, on WWXX."

That's an effective promo, but it took only fifteen seconds. It includes the name of the host, the station's name, the time coming up, and a teaser.

Parody Songs

Creating the Powerful Parody

Promos with parody songs can be a powerful way of getting a message across in a unique manner. If you're musically creative and you like to sing, this may be a method that works for you. Parody songs* can also be used to get your point across in a fun way.

To create a powerful parody song, find a current event, news story, or a celebrity *you* find humorous—then do one of the following:

- Pick a song that has a "hook" close to your topic.

- Pick a very popular current tune that is easy to sing.

- Use a nursery rhyme.

The Green Book of Songs by Jeff Green has song titles listed by topics; it is great for parody songs. You can also try working with karaoke music.

CHAPTER 24

Creating Powerful Radio
Sales and Commercials

"Do anything you want on the air ... but you still have to be able to sell it. If a sponsor is afraid to be associated with it, you lose."
— *The Greaseman (Doug Tracht, syndicated personality)*

Why should someone on air, working in commercial radio, care about commercials? Because they pay the bills. An understanding of the revenue side of the industry makes anyone a more valuable asset to the station.

It's remarkable how little some air personalities know or bother about the importance of commercials. They see the spots as a "break" in the programming instead of an integral part of the on-air package. A poorly done or boring commercial can be as much of a tune-out as any other bad programming, yet, if a commercial is done right, and creates powerful radio, it will keep listeners engaged.

Turn It Up!

Salespeople listen to and view the station differently than the rest of the staff. That became very clear to me one night on the way to dinner with friends in sales. The car radio was on. Suddenly the conversation was loudly interrupted: "Quiet, turn it up!" A client's spot was on. Sales people are just some of the people who turn the radio "up" during commercial breaks. That's their work. It's important to them. It's the way they and their stations make money.

Creative, effective, powerful commercials are important. And there's big money in making good ones. Televised sporting events like the Super Bowl or the Olympics are now watched nearly as much for the creativity of the commercials they carry as for the efforts of the athletes involved. But, in sales and advertising, as in sports, before you get to the big leagues, you have to practice, train, and learn the ropes.

Sales Is from Mars, Programming Is from Venus

Salespeople are a different breed from the on-air talent. We need both types to make a commercial radio station a success. For years I've been doing a seminar as part of the Creating Powerful Radio workshop (with apologies to John Gray): "Sales is from Mars, programming is from Venus."

For an on-air personality, the need to earn a living is there, but most chose their careers because of a need for creative expression, a love of performing, and a desire to be in the spotlight. It is essential to the happiness of an on-air talent to have an audience. But the motivation for a sales person is financial reward. Experienced account executives may have a background in selling products or services other than radio. It may not matter much to them what product they are selling. Nevertheless, a good sales person, no matter what he or she is selling, cares about the quality of the product and wants to see it succeed. They can be every bit as passionate about selling as air talent are about their shows.

Break Down the Brick Walls

The way sales and programming view one another can affect the success of a radio station. It's important that each side respects the work of the other. If key members of your sales department resent your morning host as the guy who leaves the building at 10:30 a.m., they probably don't understand his day began with show prep and a pot of black coffee at 2:00 a.m. Conversely, you have a problem if the morning personality sees the account executive as an unapproachable guy in Gucci loafers.

A lot of time is wasted in radio stations because there is distrust between sales and programming. Sales people often view talent, particularly on personality radio stations, as a liability. A sales person lives in fear of the one careless remark that will blow up an account he or she has been working for months to acquire. The talent, meanwhile, believes the sales staff would be perfectly happy running commercials fifty-nine minutes out of every hour. Hosts feel that sales have no respect for the product they are selling and little idea of what it takes to build credibility with an audience. With some effort, both sides can reach an understanding.

An opportunity presented itself one April Fool's Day. Station management agreed to an experiment: We made a switch. First thing in the morning the sales team were surprised to learn that instead of their regular duties, each was being given a shift on the News-Talk radio station. On-air personalities were handed a list of potential clients they would have to meet with and convince to buy advertising on the radio station.

The sales manager smiled. He thought it would be fun. "Going on the radio, how hard can it be? I talk all day long." After about an hour, mid-day host "Bob the Sales Manager" had sweat stains the size of soccer balls under each arm. His hands were shaking. Here is what listeners heard.

FIRST CALLER: "I want to talk about that ancient tree they are about to cut down on Main Street."

Silence from the host.

NEXT CALLER: "I want to talk about the verdict in the Lawson murder trial."

Silence from the host. Finally someone took pity on Bob and asked for some advice about getting a selling job.

At last, a subject Bob understood. He'd made it through the hour, but just barely. Here's what he said afterward: "You never appreciate how hard it is until the pressure is on, and you have to hit the ball yourself." Here are some excerpts from the talk show host's appraisal of his day:

I can't believe how hard it is. I hate wearing a suit. There's a lot of math, percentages, and numbers. I couldn't take it. I heard the word "no" more today than I have in my entire life. This is hard. If I had to do this every day for a living, I'd be miserable! I couldn't take the rejection.

After the experiment, talent showed a new respect for the efforts of the sales team. Now they bring in sales leads. Today, when this station's talk hosts meet someone with a business, product, or service or an executive who could be a potential advertiser, they collect business cards and hand them to the sales manager. This has led to new revenue for the station, based on relationships and connections with people who previously did not consider radio commercials as an effective advertising tool. The air staff now happily goes on sales calls to meet clients and the sales team has a new regard for what it takes to do the work. They like each other better now. That new respect has also paid off when talent are asked to do live copy or produce creative commercials.

The Live Copy Advantage: Credibility Sells

Some of the most effective spots are ad-libbed or "live copy" because there's room for fun, spontaneity, and personalization. Here's how it works: The host may be given either a fact sheet or a script. He or she highlights what is best about the product or service being advertised. Storytelling skills and personal experience are worked into the sell. If the host is credible, the spots are entertaining, and the product is decent, listeners are likely to buy. That, above all else, makes advertisers happy.

Credibility is paramount. American personality Howard Stern's sponsors pay enormous rates for his live spots, even though he sometimes seems not to be selling the product at all. Once in a live spot for a life insurance company, Stern created a brilliant show "bit." He advised male heads of households *not* to buy *too much* life insurance from his sponsor. As he explained it, after you die, your wife's new boyfriend will convince her to give him the insurance money to start a mail order business, which will subsequently fail, and then, bankrupt, your children will starve or wind up on the streets as teenage hookers.

The moral of Stern's commercial: You need this life insurance, but don't buy too much of it. That was an original and powerful commercial, and it was funny, too.

Many products in America are on the map today because of the personal selling and live copy spots done for them by personalities.

Another Live Copy Advantage: Job Security

Air personality Mike Siegel is quick to point out that tying air talent to advertisers through live copy spots makes it easier to ride out a couple of bad books. The advertiser believes it's the talent's personality that is selling the product. This creates financial security both for the station and the air talent. Even if numbers are down-trending, if you're bringing in big dollars for live spots, management will be reluctant to get rid of you.

Siegel also advises that if the account executive or the client writes a script for the campaign, the talent should have an opportunity to read the copy, give feedback, and give suggestions for modifications. Account executives: Make sure you record live copy spots and always follow up with the client to confirm not only that the script is satisfactory, but also that the spots are working.

Siegel believes that if you're selling a product, you'd better know it and use it. Eat at the restaurant. Drink the Washington State–grown cherry juice. Drive the car. Get the skylight installers to put one in your house. Siegel warns, "Don't endorse a product you don't know, and don't endorse a product you don't like. The spots won't ring true. The audience won't believe you, and they won't buy."

I remember a TV segment about legendary veteran commentator Paul Harvey, who is known for his innovative live commercials. Most of Paul Harvey's sponsors have been with him for decades, and listeners have come to associate these products with him. As a test of the listener's devotion, the reporter traveled to a rural factory and asked a group of women working on the production line to hold up their thermal beverage containers. Each woman proudly displayed the container manufactured by the company recommended and endorsed by their hero, Paul Harvey. That's the power of creative live copy selling.

Go Along on the Sales Call

Mike Siegel recommends going with the account executive to meet your sponsors, and getting to know them personally. Raise any questions you may have about any possible flaws or problems with the product or service at that time. Learn enough to be able to convey your personal enthusiasm. Consider including a brief interview with your client in the spot. Be sure you endorse only *one* product in each advertising category. (This is one of the reasons live spots demand premium pricing.) Follow up on any listener complaints. Again, Siegel warns, investigate thoroughly before endorsing.

If a spot doesn't work one way, be flexible and willing to change the approach. Don't treat commercials like a separate part of your show. The audience is sophisticated enough to know why the commercials are there. If the products and services are good, and properly targeted at your audience, you can make the commercials as informative and entertaining as the rest of your show.

All of this seems like a lot of work, but when handled properly, live spots can be a gold mine for everyone involved.

Produced Spots

Make the Commercials Powerful Radio

The Creating Powerful Radio principles apply to commercials: Does this product or service affect "health, heart, or saving money"? How does it benefit the listener? Remember to paint word pictures. Think and speak visually. Personalize, be a powerful storyteller. Keep the message on point. Be creative. You'll always win over your listener if you make him laugh. Make it matter, be truthful, make sure to always emphasize what is "in it" for the listener.

The Radio Advertising Bureau suggests these guidelines:

1. The most important rule in radio advertising: Mention the client often. Make sure the listeners know where to find the client.

2. Play up the advantage to the listener. What's the unique selling proposition of the product or service? What does it offer that is not available elsewhere?

3. Grab attention. Use noise, music, unusual voices, whatever is appropriate.

4. Zero in. Pitch directly to your target listener. "If you own an aging, overweight cat, listen to this!"

5. Be easily understood. Copy writers who use big words gratuitously (there's one now!) often lose the audience.

6. Get to the point! Don't delay the unique selling proposition.

7. Use action words—"Now" and "Today" when you're announcing a sale. Radio's greatest strength is its immediacy ... use it!

8. Make the listener part of a word picture. Don't just talk about that new car. Using sound effects and music creates a mood and puts your listener behind the wheel.

9. Avoid clichés such as: "We're known for our excellent quality and great customer service." Try, "Our quality sucks and we'll ignore you from the moment you come in until you leave in a huff." The audience will pay attention.

10. Be accurate. Make sure the spot is checked by the client or other responsible party before it hits the air. Nothing says "We're sloppy and don't deserve your money" more than a spot with factual errors that's rushed onto the air.

Selling the Talk

Broadcast executive David Baronfeld's decades of experience in sales and management have made him a believer in the benefits of selling News-Talk. "Although we have seen huge growth in listening options over the last few years, some of the most consistent performers have been the News and Talk formats. And while syndicated talk has become hugely popular, it is the local sponsorships like traffic, news, business reports, weather, sports, etc., that create premium revenue opportunities."

Baronfeld offers the following pointers, including techniques he has developed and learned through the years to sell radio, in particular talk radio, and live copy commercials.

1. Create promotional alliances. Identify twenty-five quality, high-profile local businesses. Multiple locations are preferable; however, a strong single location store can act as a magnet. Target one company per category and create an annual or semi-annual promotional event that you can do together for years. Examples would include: banks; casinos; home improvement stores; car dealerships; electronic, furniture, and jewelry stores; cosmetic surgeons; and sporting goods stores.

2. Create media partnerships. It is advantageous for radio to join forces not only with other TV and radio properties within your group or cluster, but also with competing media. Having a relationship with either the daily newspaper or leading TV station tells your advertisers that you are the "go to" dial position for breaking news, weather, sports, etc. Shared resources provide the opportunity to put your station's name in print or on the screen at no charge. You add name recognition and raise the level of your station's credibility with your listeners.

3. Think brand names. Brand selling is different than a co-op or non-traditional revenue deal. By prospecting for business generically, millions in potential revenue are never realized. Prospecting should be focused. When asked, "What's your favorite soft drink?" people don't say, "I'm a cola drinker." They say, "I like Coke."

For potential advertisers, paint a picture of your listeners with real-life examples of the products they buy and own: "They are Lexus owners who use Dell computers and stay at the Westin." Using brands as part of your presentation allows you to charge a premium for *your* brand.

4. Take a good look at your listener. Years ago, I worked with an AOR station to help improve their local sales effort. The sales people couldn't get beyond their image of the audience's 'band T-shirts and bad teeth,' but they had to make their budgets. So I brought a camera to the next station promotion and took pictures of their listeners. One visual emerged. No matter what they wore, their hair was fabulous.

Two days later, I walked into a sales meeting, showed the pictures, and suggested they call on the Conair blow dryers guy, the Aveda shampoo rep, and the distributor for Head and Shoulders. Less than 72 hours later, the station closed an annual contract, worth nearly six figures, with the area's largest beauty supply house."

That's just hair. Now think about how much money you could generate if you saw your listeners in a different light, as brand buyers and brand users of everything from mortgages to cars, phones, home improvements, travel, and so on.

5. Understand your advertiser's needs. The people I like to sell to are those accountable for hitting or overachieving their budgets. It makes most sense to talk about using radio directly with the people who are responsible for maximizing those sales. Shoot for the top. Call or write the company's president or CEO. Tell him or her you have an idea that can maximize sales and save them money. Nine times out of ten, you'll get the appointment.

6. Let your air talent sell for you—Part I. This is the sales perspective that Mike Siegel talks about. Everybody loves to meet the station's prime talent. Bring along a camera, and chances are good that a picture of them (ideally, wearing your station logo) and the client will occupy a prominent wall position. Do this in fifty companies with more than fifty employees. Soon you'll have thousands of "impressions" per week in the workplace. Make the goal to be in 540 offices in the next three years. That is a lot of exposure, and all you'll need is a digital camera.

7. Let your air talent sell for you—Part II. If you allow and encourage talent to earn income from revenue streams separate from salary (i.e. promotion fees, endorsements, live copy), you'll be viewed as talent-friendly, which is a good thing, especially at contract renewal time. Most on-air personalities understand that the better their relationship is with sales, the more the account executives will pitch them to clients, and the more money they'll make. Studies show that air talent who spend at least five hours a week with station salespeople can almost always equal and sometimes double their regular salaries.

8. Let your air talent sell for you—Part III. Perhaps you remember or have heard about the late talk personality Alan Berg. The movie *Talkradio* was loosely based on his life. We spent at least two to three hours per week making sales calls together. One day we had two calls to make. The first was with the owner of a Chinese restaurant. We walked in and made some small talk. In just minutes, Alan jumped in and said, "I can only endorse one Chinese restaurant. And if you'd like me to endorse yours, you'll need to buy a twenty-six week schedule." In less than thirty seconds we had the order.

Twenty minutes later, we're meeting with the owners of a rattan furniture store. As I begin my presentation, Alan says, "I can only endorse one furniture store. And if you'd like me to endorse yours, you'll need to buy a twenty-six week schedule." Again, within two minutes of the start of the meeting, we closed the deal. All I had said was, "Hello."

Selling Alan, or rather letting Alan sell, was truly extraordinary. Look around you. Your best salesperson may be a member of your air staff.

9. Hire a sales staff that lives a News-Talk lifestyle. Hire salespeople who use news and talk radio. At some clusters salespeople can sell most, if not all, of the stations. At others, there are separate sales staffs. In my opinion, that is the better way to go. As an example, Toyota has separate sales staffs and facilities for Toyota and their premium brand, Lexus. Don't hire a group of music radio listeners to convey what it's like to be a sports talk fan to your client.

Instead, assemble a staff of sellers who love the format, can describe its attributes, understand the variety of people to whom they will be selling, and share similar interests with the client. For example, hire a former business owner or someone who has sold the types of products your station will advertise. I'm not saying that non–News-Talk listeners can't sell this format, just don't have an entire sales staff of them.

10. Create as many premium avails as possible. Each week you have several hundred premium available spots for sale. Make sure your sales staff understands just how valuable these commercials are. Live reads, business and sports sponsorships, traffic and weather reports, news updates—don't let these golden nuggets go to waste. And don't give them away either. These are your "beachfront premium units." They are worth more, and you are entitled to charge more for them.

11. Have fun. If you sell News-Talk, you are involved in a format that appeals to more potential advertisers than any other in town. Your air talent is the best known. Your listeners are the most active. Welcome to radio utopia.

Making the Sale: Networking vs. Cold Calling

To excel at sales, just as on the programming side, it helps to be a good communicator. Your people skills and knowledge of how to make connections can lead to potential business and will serve you in all areas of life, not just broadcasting. Most people who gravitate toward sales are genuinely social individuals. Developing relationships is an important part of prospecting and growing sales contacts.

Business leads are all around you. The person exercising next to you, your uncle Dave, your kids' nanny; everyone in your circle can potentially lead to business. With the help of the Internet, you can make your own "coincidental meeting" occur by seeking out individuals who may already be inside companies you're looking to contact using online Social Networking Services (SNSs) to find business connections you may not have realized you had. Most of them are free or cost next to nothing to use. It may not be too long before the "cold call" becomes a rare event. It seems you may already be just a couple of acquaintances away from the person you thought you could never reach.

Pam Lontos, sales trainer, former vice president of Disney Radio, and author of *"I See Your Name Everywhere,"* now owns her own public relations company for speakers and authors. She suggests,

> It is much easier to approach prospects on the recommendation of their friends. But if everyone knows this, why aren't more people doing it? It's very hard to "cold call" a prospect, but if there is a prior relationship or connection in place, things become easier. Proper networking techniques are the secrets of the superstars in sales.

Tracking news sources and gathering clients are based on similar principles. The more people you know, the more ways you can follow a story or a business lead. Although there are effective shy sales people, the job is a more natural fit for outgoing personalities. You will find more about this in Chapter 2 under "Right Casting." I once watched "Michael," a top sales manager, work a room. Michael seemed genuinely interested in what was happening in the lives of each person he talked to, and he remembered everyone's name. All those people felt significant, special, and important.

If Michael had asked them for the entire contents of their wallets and purses at that moment, they would have cheerfully handed them over. He "works" his clients the same way. Michael understands that businesses are run by people. When you get the person on your side, you'll get their business.

Meeting the Right People

Pam Lontos advises: "Go meet the people who can make the sale. Attend charity events, or business social functions where the decision makers are. One salesman went to a local pub every Friday after work. He didn't go there to drink. He went there because all the advertising agency decision makers met there every Friday."

Once you've connected with the decision maker, Lontos suggests, it does no good to go up and say: "I'm Joe Blow with WXYO. Do you want to buy some advertising?" Instead Lontos advises:

> You must focus on and ask them about themselves to establish rapport. Find out how they got started in the business and what they enjoy most about their industry. Ask what they do in their spare time when not working. Put yourself in the prospects' place. Ask: "How would I know if someone I'm talking to would be a good prospect?"

How Can I Help?

Be of genuine help. For example, if you realize that two people you have met at an event don't know each other, introduce them. This is an easy way to be seen as a helpful person. Ask existing clients if they know anyone who would benefit from advertising on your station. Help them focus on a particular group. If they are golfers, ask about anyone in their foursome. If they belong to a civic group or organization, ask about the other members. It's not that people don't want to give you referrals; it's just that they truly can't think of anyone if you give them their whole world to choose from. You've got to help them narrow it down. After someone gives you a referral, ask what he or she thinks the referral will be looking to accomplish. This will give you a little preliminary information.

Also ask if you can use your contact's name. When you do call, say, "Susan asked me to call you and I promised I would."

Finally, Lontos reminds us, the secret weapon in sales is to be *genuinely* interested in other people:

> When you ask people about what they do, they will eventually ask you about what you do. Have a great benefit statement ready: "I help business-people with their advertising and marketing plans so they can increase their bottom line." Most people will respond by asking how you do that. Now you can start talking about what you do and how you can help them. That's a lot better than a cold call.

Pam Lontos's Sales Tips

- Understand your clients. Question and listen to the prospects and uncover and meet their true needs.

- Qualify the buyer. Always get to the top decision maker. Don't waste time with people who are not in a position to make a decision.

- Listen with the intent to understand. Only when you understand can you respond. Listening is more important than talking. The client will give you the information to sell him or her. The next thing you say should be based on what the client just said.

- Understand the power of questioning. You can qualify the buyer, establish rapport, eliminate competition, build credibility, identify needs, find hot buttons, get personal information, and close a sale, all by asking questions. Have powerful questions at your fingertips.

- Sell benefits, not features. Clients care only about what's in it for them. Sell the end result of what they want. You can find this out only by asking questions and listening.

- Use the power of testimonials. The best sales tool you have is a reference from a satisfied client. Use testimonials to overcome objections and build trust. Testimonials take the fear out of buying and make it easier to close.

- Learn to recognize buying signals. Prospects will tell you when they're ready to buy. You must pay attention.

- Remember, the best buying signal is: "How much does it cost?"

- Don't offer the price until you're asked. Also don't give price until you've first shown value.

- Know the difference between a stall and an objection. "I want to think it over" isn't an objection—don't waste time treating it like one. This prospect has an unanswered question. Find out what the prospect wants to think about, answer it, and continue selling more benefits.

- Uncover the real objection. Prospects usually won't tell you their true objections at first. Due to the fear of making a decision, they often give false objections at first, to stop you from selling them. Ask questions to find the real problem.

- Anticipate objections. If you've been selling for your station for two months, you already know the ten or so standard objections. Have answers to them written out and rehearsed. Create questions that eliminate objections before they are even mentioned.

- If you don't make a sale, make a firm appointment to return. Make some form of "sale" each time you call.

- Never argue with a prospect. If you win the argument, you still lose the sale.

- Redefine rejection. You're not being rejected, your offer is.

- Treat each client as though he/she is the most important.

- Satisfy client complaints in less than twenty-four hours. This will lead to added sales and a great reputation.

- Understand that hard work makes luck. Years of hard work went into making successful people "lucky." You can get just as lucky by learning how to sell and seeing more prospects.

- Use the power of persistence. Take "no" as a challenge. Learn from children how profitable persistence is.

- Have a sales call scheduled immediately after your sales meeting. Try out what you have just learned. Do it over and over, day after day, until that technique becomes automatic.

- Learn the ABC's of sales. Read, go to seminars, listen to CDs. Adapt the techniques you learn to your own personality. Use your car as a school. Play sales training or motivational CDs as you travel.

You've Made the Sale, Now What?

Your station may have the greatest production team in the world waiting to do your clients' bidding, but there's no rule that says a great car dealer is also a good copy writer, and you have certainly heard clients voice their own spots so poorly that their commercials sound like parodies.

Producing good commercials for your customers is where you'll really have a chance to win their trust and help them build their businesses. But what, exactly, makes a "good" radio spot?

Have you ever turned the radio *up* to hear a commercial? Audience research has taught us that when a spot is well produced and fits the station's target audience, listeners perceive that spot as new or useful information about products or services they may want to try, or special pricing on an item they may already use or need. They may actually pay special attention to that spot. Conversely, a bad or boring spot about a product or service that's not relevant or does not conform to the Powerful Radio principles involving health, heart, money, or transformation—that neither persuades, entertains, informs, nor inspires—will drive listeners away from your station.

For some people, creative ads that work seem to fall like rain from the sky. For the rest of us, there's Maureen Bulley. Bulley is president of The

Radio Store. Her books include the popular *Write Good Copy Fast,* and she holds seminars and workshops for industry professionals. She's managed to take what is often perceived as a highly creative and quirky process and put it in a form that anyone can use. Here she shares the techniques she teaches to create powerful ad copy:

> The correlation between audience tune-out and "commercial breaks" is no coincidence. But if we view breaks as an interruption of programming, so will our audience. Advertising jargon such as "stop set" or "commercial break" implies that we are stopping or breaking away from entertainment to broadcast commercials before we return to regular programming. Not coincidentally, it is also the time we lose listeners to the competition when they scan the dial to see who is *not* playing commercials at that moment.
>
> You can persuade your audience to stay with you for every minute of every hour. Commercials are a valuable part of your programming. You must treat them with the same respect as the rest of your show.
>
> Give careful thought to the placement of commercials in the context of the programming hour. Know when your competition schedules commercials and for how long. If they are about to lose their audience because of a commercial "break," be ready to receive and capture that audience with compelling programming.
>
> Be aware of how many spots in a row your station is airing. Not only will your audience wander, but long commercial clusters do a disservice to your advertisers. If no one stays to hear their commercials, no one can respond to them.
>
> Check computer-generated logs, paying attention to the sequence of commercials. Has the computer scheduled a hard-sell ad in the first position at 6:30 a.m. when the majority of your audience is waking up? Try a less jarring commercial in that important first position. Spots will often be an exit point for listeners, but don't hold the door open for them as they leave. Treat them like an old friend who came over for coffee and encourage them to stay for "just one more cup."
>
> If you are the talent for the spot, read commercials with a new attitude. Enter the studio in a positive state of mind. Prepare to focus, and contribute in a creative and meaningful way. Improvise in scripts whenever

possible to add a personal touch or to make an awkward script easier on the ear.

A well-organized session makes the finished commercials sound better. If a talent needs to run down the hall for a pair of working headphones, a bottle of water, or a functioning timer, you may lose the mood of the session or stop a creative process cold. If you're in charge of the studio where the commercials are produced, it's your job to make sure everything is in order ahead of time.

Scripts should be double-spaced and appear clean and uncluttered. NEVER include anything in the body of the script that is not meant for air. Copy writers should provide a pronunciation guide for words the talent may not know how to say, such as proper names and brand names. Show numbers as digits, not words. The eye recognizes "250" but stumbles over "two hundred and fifty." Scripts should be proofread and timed by reading aloud. This allows the writer to identify and correct word combinations that are difficult to say, or sentences that are too long to read in one breath. Focus on the end user when preparing a script for production.

The order in which scripts are read in a production session is also important. If the talent has just completed an airshift, his or her voice is warmed up and ready to perform. If production is scheduled *before* an airshift, allow time for the voice to warm up. Read easier scripts first, and build up to ones that are more demanding on the voice. A talent's voice is his livelihood. Treat it with respect.

Create Powerful Copy

The first step in creating powerful copy is gathering information and establishing clarity. What is this copy intended to do? What is its goal?

The advertising goal must be specific and measurable. Indicate precisely what you want to happen when people hear the commercial, and how often you want it to happen. Clarity will help you create a script that gets the desired result.

If your clients want to increase traffic to a Web site through their radio advertising schedules, advertising goals would specify how much more traffic they desire in measurable, quantifiable statements. By design, the script must include a call to action that sends the listener to the Web site. The script does *not* include a telephone number or street address, because that information would only distract listeners and would not help advertisers achieve their goals.

When writing scripts using the Copy Navigator designed by Maureen Bulley, brainstorm based on what you know about the product or service and the problem it will solve for consumers if they purchase it. Gather any other data that the advertiser thinks may be useful. If your station has access to research that may help position your client in the market or better target the client's ad, be sure to have it ready.

Perhaps you know that your listeners, twenty- to forty-year-old mothers, frequently use a certain city playground as a place to bring their kids and socialize. Perhaps you know that your client's car dealership is just a few blocks from this popular spot. Your automobile-repair client might not have thought: "We're just a two-minute walk to Playland" and that this could help sell auto tune-ups, but if *you* do, it can help that client get a result.

Broadcasters pay a lot of money for research about their listeners. Make sure your clients get to take advantage of that investment.

Maureen Bulley's "Copy Navigator"

The Copy Navigator can be completed by the copywriter, account executive for advertising copy, or the program director or promotions director if the goal is to write effective promotional copy. You may find it useful to ask additional questions to get the answers you require. Ask questions like, "Why should I buy from you? The store down the street has similar products?" Or, "If I bought one of your products and I wasn't satisfied, what would you do?" (A sample Copy Navigator follows.)

Write Good Copy Fast—Maureen Bulley's Copy Writing Techniques

All commercials *require* a beginning, a middle, and an end. In fact, some writers start by deciding how the commercial will end and work backwards. This is a style decision that you will make on your own.

One of the most common problems with scripts is that they introduce a theme or an idea at the beginning and fail to revisit that idea again at the end. If you state a problem at the beginning of a script, and then use the middle to state your client's approach to that problem, be sure to refer

Sample Copy Navigator

Date: _____   Account: _____

Marketing Goal: *What does the Advertiser expect to achieve over a specified period of time? That is, increase awareness/increase sales 10 percent over last fiscal year.*

_____

_____

_____

Advertising Goal: *What does the Advertiser expect to achieve with this advertising campaign? That is, increase inbound calls by 150 per week.*

_____

_____

_____

Best Potential Customer: *Describe the best prospect for this commercial. Include as much detail as possible.*

_____

_____

_____

_____

What's in It for Me? (Benefit): *What is the problem I am trying to solve with this advertising? That is, I'd love to take the whole family out for dinner, but it's too expensive. At Our Town Restaurant the whole family can enjoy a meal out, while saving money.*

_____

_____

_____

Why Should I Believe You? (Support): *This will back up the "What's in It for Me?" statement with reasons why the customer should believe what we say; that is, at Our Town Restaurant, children under 6 always eat free.*

_____

_____

_____

How Should It Sound?: *Describe the tone or manner of the copy, the same way you would describe the product's personality; that is, a sense of humor, a serious money-saving message.*

_____

_____

_____

Things to Include in Each Spot: *Elements that must be in every spot such as jingle, use of a specific announcer, or a slogan.*

_____

_____

_____

_____

your listeners back to the original problem and how your client will solve it for them at the end of the spot. For example:

> *If your car is acting a little sluggish lately, it may be time for a tune-up. It is time to save on a tune-up at Ed's Garage. Ed's will have your car running smoothly in no time with a fifty-six-point check and tune-up special for just $49.99. Ed will tune up your engine, and check all the fluid levels too. If they need topping off, he'll do it, all for under fifty bucks! Car a little sluggish? Perk it up with a Tune Up special at Ed's Garage. Call 566-CARS to book your appointment.*

Notice how we refer back to the opening "problem" of a sluggish car at the end of the commercial. This theme could be made even stronger by adding sound effects of a sluggish car at the beginning, and replacing them with sounds of a smooth-running car at the end.

Regardless of whether you are writing a narrative, dialogue, or any other style of commercial, review all of your scripts with the "beginning, middle, and end" concept in mind.

Writing Narratives

Maureen Bulley teaches thousands of people around the world how to write copy in a variety of styles. Here's an excerpt from her Certified Radio Copywriter© program that will give you an idea of how to write five basic types of advertising copy.

> Great narratives include all the necessary product information, but you hear it in a natural way, within the context of a story. That's the secret.
>
> A narrative is also known as a single-voice commercial. This is one of the most frequently used techniques in broadcast writing.
>
> One of the most common mistakes made with narratives is writing them too long. They end up being read so fast they lose all meaning. They become an irritant, compromising your station's programming and any results the advertiser had hoped to achieve.
>
> Write a narrative as though you were writing a letter to a friend, or speaking to someone on the telephone. Write the way people speak. People don't talk in complete sentences, and they do use slang. This will help you fit the entire thought in to the allotted time. Pick one theme or storyline to concentrate on, and then weave in the details as required.
>
> Another key to a good narrative is to know the skills and personality of your voice talent. If you write with a particular voice talent in mind, it becomes easier to develop the script to make it sound like something he or she would actually say. When you write your next narrative commercial, read it aloud the way you want your voice talent to read it. Then ask yourself if you can read it comfortably within the allotted time period, if it sounds natural, and if it convinces you that trying this product would be a good thing.
>
> Commercials that blend in to your programming and complement it, instead of intruding on it, are much more effective. If your station's

programming is high-energy, a narrative can mirror that programming without becoming a high-pitched scream-fest. Think about how one of your listeners might tell that story.

Writing Dialogue

They say that when two people really "click," they can finish each other's sentences or read each other's thoughts. That is how a great dialogue commercial sounds. In fact, allowing the talent to complete each other's thoughts is a great technique for writing and producing effective dialogue. Above all, dialogue, like narrative, should sound natural.

Prove it to yourself by writing your next dialogue commercial "short," giving the talent time to make it sound natural. Allow them time to pause and respond to what the other person is saying. If you don't have particularly strong acting talent, cast two people in the commercial who have complementary personalities, or appear to get along well in the halls or at the coffee machine. Your chances of achieving your goal of better dialogue will be greatly improved.

Let them work with the script by giving them only basic copy points, then ask them to converse with one another about the advertiser and the products. Your client may hand you a veritable grocery list of products to promote. Remember, though, that your obligation to your client is to achieve his or her goal. A dialogue ad that sounds like a list won't sound very natural, and is not likely to be effective.

Good dialogue makes the listeners feel like they're eavesdropping on a private conversation. So, try recording two people having a conversation about your client's product or service. You will probably get some great natural responses that make for a very realistic commercial. You can either excerpt portions of that session for your spot or use the actual dialogue as the "script" for your recording session with professional talent.

Finally, when you're choosing the voice actors for your commercial, be sure their voices are not similar. Otherwise it can be difficult for the listener to identify who is talking, and who is saying what.

Testimonials

A testimonial commercial could be from a satisfied customer, a celebrity endorsing a product, or a commercial voiced by the client. Whoever is doing it, the most important feature of a testimonial ad is that it must be believable. The other challenge with testimonials is making sure that they sound good in the execution. This can be achieved with good recording techniques, whether in-studio or on the street, and with people who simply sound good and give coherent, succinct comments.

If you and your client have chosen a local celebrity to be your spokesperson or to endorse your product, be sure you have explored all the positives and negatives of this type of approach. There's always a risk that the person you've chosen may do something later to embarrass the client or risk the reputation of the product. If you do involve celebrities, be sure to involve them in the creation of the script. Ask them what they would actually say about the product, and try to incorporate their honest feelings and words into the copy. This will give credibility and integrity to your celebrity testimonial spot, and the listeners do know the difference.

The final type of testimonial commercial is the client-voiced commercial. Before you cast a client in a commercial, be sure there's a perfectly legitimate reason for him or her to be there. If it's simply ego, that's not good business for either of you. If ego is at the root of your client's desire to appear in his ad, an ad that talks about your client can sometimes do the job. For example, John Jones might feel just as good about hearing a professional voice promote his business this way: "John Jones has been greeting customers at the door of his restaurant with a cup of his wife Mary's homemade chili for twenty-five years."

With endorsement commercials, it is always good to include the client in script development. If the client is in the spot, work to get the best possible voice delivery from him. Remember, your goal is to make him sound genuine, not like a professional announcer.

The Art of Storytelling

While all commercials require a beginning, middle, and end, it is sometimes difficult to express all of the important points within the prescribed time period. The key to successful storytelling is being able to complete it within the number of seconds provided. This is a challenging writing style, but with practice you can master it!

The best advice is to use fewer words. If you can say it in two words, don't use four. If you can make a statement with music or sound effects, it will help you to move the storyline forward without spending valuable time.

Never overlook your most important job of selling product for the advertiser. Ask yourself why you are using the storytelling technique, and decide if it's really appropriate. Do not tell a story for the sake of telling a story; make sure it introduces the product in a beneficial way, and "asks for the order."

One of the unique benefits of advertising with sound is that it gives us the opportunity to convey the story and have the listeners develop their own images about its details. Because they play an active role in completing the storyline, listeners tend to remember the message longer. They may also be able to relate personally to the story, or know someone who can.

When you work on your storytelling skills, begin by writing the story out, using as many words as it takes to tell it. Then go back and remove all unnecessary components that don't contribute to the storyline or sell the product. Once you have that first edit, look for places to economize on words. Look for opportunities to convey your message with sound. Even the voice reading your commercial will add to the story's overall texture. Keep paring down your script until it works within the prescribed time. Be sure to allow the announcer(s) time to tell the story at an appropriate pace. You'll defeat your purpose if you ask them to rush through the commercial to include all your copy.

Humor

Perhaps one of the most difficult techniques to master, humor is powerful when done properly. Humor is also a high-maintenance style. Humorous commercials tend to become tiresome fairly quickly and can go from being entertaining to annoying if the listener is overexposed to them. Humor is also culturally specific and differs from one target group to another. Use humor with caution, and be sure to have fun with the audience. Never make fun *of* your audience in an effort to sell a product or service.

The fundamental rule for writing a humorous commercial is to ensure that it stays true to the product. Many times people remember the joke in a commercial but are unable to identify the product or service advertised. So when you're deciding whether or not to use a humorous spot, ask yourself, "Does the humor serve to promote the product and encourage trial?" Remember, the job of advertising is to promote the product.

Common themes of humor spots include the following:

- *The human condition* — If the listener can say, "I have been there, I know about that," the humor is based on the human condition. These situations are funny because we can relate to them.

- *Incongruity* — This form of comedy consists simply of putting things together that don't belong together. Incongruity can be achieved either in the script writing itself or in the production style. Perhaps the music is completely the opposite of what people are expecting, or the voice talent is exactly the opposite of what the listener expects to hear.

- *Exaggeration* — Exaggerating or minimizing a situation can make for memorable comedy. Exaggeration can be achieved through words, but it can also be conveyed through the characters in your commercial, the selection of sound effects, or the choice of music. Think about what naturally belongs in the commercial for the product or service you're writing for, and then try using the polar opposite.

- *Puns or double meanings* — A pun or double meaning usually goes along with some type of misunderstanding. This launches the comedy and helps establish the humor in the situation.

Powerful Radio, as you can see from Maureen Bulley's tools for creating exciting and effective copy, can happen *in*, as well as *around,* the commercials on your station.

CHAPTER 25

Creating Powerful Radio
LifeStage Demographics

Are Traditional Demographics Still the Best Selling Strategy for the Future?

The pivotal moment came to me during a focus group. As the participants were leaving the room, I noticed a young woman in her early twenties saying "hello" to a 51-year-old lady on her way out. As they began to chat, the years between them melted away. Both had young children, attended the same "Mommy and Me" classes, were both buying minivans, and had stayed at the same hotel in Disneyworld. Although they were generations apart, they shared the same *LifeStage*.

That was the moment the light bulb in my head went on and the concept for LifeStage Demographics was born. We began examining research and focus group results and developed a system that could effectively tap into the listener's lifestyle and LifeStages. Armed with this information, stations could then make programming and marketing decisions based on what was important to their listeners. From a programming perspective, the ratings were astonishing. The stations working with LifeStage Demographics had huge listener increases and much more time spent listening. We then invited sales people to attend the workshops and explained the LifeStage

Demographics research. That helped the account executives better sell the station. It was a win-win for everyone.

I work with successful radio stations around the world, and one secret they all have in common is that they all cross demographic lines. Key elements to their programming successes are that their on-air personalities speak the truth, have a good sense of humor, provide new and useful information, and, most importantly, relate to the listeners. They cross demographic lines because good entertainment attracts listeners of all ages. But it is lifestyle and LifeStage that dictate what appeals to different groups of listeners. If radio managers and programmers begin to look at their audiences by life stages instead of by demographics, you will be surprised at the positive result.

Cable television found its market and makes a great deal of money, superserving, or niche targeting, people who belong to special interest groups or those who share similar lifestyle or life stages. On cable TV, you'll find special programming geared toward the health conscious or medically oriented, pet lovers, couples about to have a child, independent-film lovers, golf or home decorating enthusiasts, antique collectors, women, political junkies, gourmet food lovers, and more.

The magazine and publishing world learned about niche marketing over the past decades as it migrated from mass circulation "one size fits all" editorial publications to today's multiple smaller-niche special-interest markets. These focused publications set their foundations on the common interests of their readers. The Internet does a great job of superserving special interests and targeting those in various life stages.

Traditional demographic breakdowns we've worked with in the past are less and less relevant. Our society and culture are changing. The audience is changing along with it. If radio is going to continue to grow, develop and powerfully connect to the audience, it is time to rethink how we look at that audience. The old way of thinking about demographics just doesn't work anymore.

If you were to talk with account executives or program directors, they might tell you that the most coveted target demo for stations is adults, 25 to 54. In the radio industry, we've programmed and sold in terms of targeted demographics for so long that we have missed out on one thing: The way people live today is different from how people lived in the past, and traditional demographics of targeting 12+, 18 to 24, 25 to 54, 35 to 54, 55+ no longer strictly apply. Perhaps you have heard someone joke, "twenty-five to fifty-four, that's not a demographic, that's a family reunion!" It's true.

But what and who *is* the target audience? Does the 25 to 54 targeted goal reach out and appeal to the same audience? Of course not. Within each target and each format, there are very different audiences in different life stages, living very different lifestyles. To determine and superserve selected LifeStages while still keeping an open door to a mass audience is one of the benefits of using LifeStage Demographics.

Advertising has already noticed LifeStage Demographics. A recent evening in front of the television screen showed an arthritis medication ad featuring people in a variety of age and ethnic groups. The common thread was that all had been living with arthritis. This commercial showed the medication helping them resume their daily lives. Their LifeStage is ill health. Historically a drug company promoting a new medication for arthritis sufferers might have focused on the obvious market, elderly people. The information that is new here isn't only that there is a new drug discovery, it's that all kinds of people, including some over sixty-five, live with arthritis—and the pharmaceutical company is marketing its product to *all* of them.

Our culture is changing in other ways too. The old assumption was that people made buying decisions based on a common set of needs defined by age, income, sex, and ethnic group. To a certain extent, that is still true. But since people have more choices about the ways they live, they are making buying decisions based on a whole new set of additional criteria. That is what LifeStage Demographics is all about. If you look at a group of friends who are all in their thirties, you will probably find some contradictions in the conventional thinking about demographics.

Advertisers, programmers, and marketers tended to assume that a group of 33-year-old women shopped at the same stores, ate at the same restaurants, and saw the same movies as other women of their same race and income. But in reality, when a 33-year-old woman looks at her group of single friends, she sees that some of them are shopping, dining, and going out to movies together because they are enjoying the single life and each other's company; others are weary of being on their own and are actively seeking partners. Some are meeting at the playground with their kids talking about preschool, and renting movies. Others are planning vacations to islands in the Pacific with their husbands or boyfriends. It isn't so much their paychecks or their ages that are dictating their lifestyles as choices they have made.

Let's follow that subgroup of thirty-something women to the playground and see who else is there. There are some older women, some ethnically diverse women, and some men. The age range is 16 to 65. The unifying LifeStage demographic here is that they are all taking care of children at around 2:00 in the afternoon. They are all making buying decisions and lifestyle choices based on the commonality of responsibility for children.

You might think that the 65-year-old grandmother at that playground, with her high disposable income and her status as a retired person, would buy a certain kind of car, perhaps a sporty, luxury convertible. Instead, she has a Volvo wagon with toys in the back and cereal embedded between the seats.

You might think the 40-year-old man pushing the 5-year old on the swing is completely out of place, but he is one of three men on that playground today who works from home and cares for his children. His wife, a physician, is attending to her medical practice. Today he will also stop by the grocery store and take his child to a fast-food restaurant for a treat. Choices these men will make include: public school vs. private school, soccer camp vs. camping vacation, bottled water vs. juice boxes, washing the kids' hands with Purell vs. Handi-Wipes, computer class vs. music lessons, McDonalds Happy Meal vs. a granola bar, video vs. art project. And of course those same people are making decisions about which TV station is on in the family room and which radio station is on in their cars.

A 44-year-old single female professional might be living the same lifestyle as a 23-year-old single woman working in a big city. A recently divorced man of 51 might spend his cash on designer clothing, a sports car, meals at expensive restaurants, and premiere seats at sporting events. His lifestyle could mirror that of a 26-year-old single executive who spends his or her time and money the same way. The chronological age of the listener does not matter as much as the LifeStage.

Because people are living longer, enjoying active lives and good health, the stereotypes defining people's lifestyles have been pitched out the window. The stereotypes of roles of men and women have changed. Older women have young children. Healthy, fit women are watching and playing sports. Men start new families at sixty. Since people are living longer because of advanced medical breakthroughs, with emphasis on leading healthier lifestyles, those who are 55 and over may have more disposable income to spend on leisure activities, vitamins, exercise equipment, travel, clothing, cars, gadgets, and more. And here's big news: The older audience doesn't *consider* itself to be an "older" audience anymore.

Ironically the very people who ought to be aware of this, often the young people making key marketing decisions and agency advertising buys, are doing so without an awareness of how listeners/consumers in different life stages actually live. Traditional categories like 12+, 18 to 34, 25 to 54, 55+ no longer give us the information we need to make accurate programming and marketing decisions.

If broadcasting does not redefine the way in which we view and understand audiences, and plan our marketing strategies accordingly by acknowledging special interests and LifeStage Demographics, radio may miss the boat.

In reassessing what works for sales, advertising, marketing and programming, it is time to look at using LifeStage Demographics as a strategy.

Using LifeStage Demographics

When I teach LifeStage Demographics to programming, marketing, or sales departments at radio and TV stations, what most people want to know is: "How can I use this? How does this help *us* get ratings, market our station, or sell more advertising?"

A thorough knowledge of LifeStage Demographics helps you draw a far more accurate picture of your target audience by giving you a practical understanding of the listener's various life stages. Here's how.

Sales

Having an understanding of LifeStage Demographics helps effectively target sales presentations for clients, with proven results. Knowing your audience and specifically targeting a life stage is invaluable when presenting your station's listener profile to prospective clients. If, for example, you understand through LifeStage Demographics that most listeners without children do not buy life insurance but buy as much as they can afford as soon as they have their kids, that is useful information in pitching a prospective insurance agency and helping get the sale.

A sales force armed with the knowledge of LifeStage Demographics can better explain your station's value to a potential advertiser: "Our classic rock station has an audience of dads packing lunches for their twelve-year-old kids before those dads go to work. You'll sell a lot of life insurance to these fathers because every day they think, 'What would happen if I didn't get home from my job? How would my family cope?'" Those who are single don't usually buy life insurance, nor do young couples without kids.

Most recent homebuyers, regardless of their ages, tend to defer luxury spending. They spend weekend time and spare money not on restaurants, but on the house. They might make several trips in a day to hardware or home repair shops. You'll do a lot of business with the big home "do-it-yourself store" because you'll know those listeners are spending fixing their own houses instead of hiring others to do it for them. Younger homebuyers may simply not have the extra money to hire help once they buy the house, more mature homebuyers may be worried about saving money to send their children to college.

Commercials

LifeStage also helps production directors at stations create better and more successful commercials that net results for the clients, particularly when you can define special interest groups. Common interests elevate awareness for commercials. Advertising in *special-interest media* is as interesting to the audience as is editorial content. That support means less of the ad dollar is being spent on simply getting attention and more of it is going into defining the message.

If radio ignores this new audience fragmentation, we may very well hand over receptive consumers to other media. It's time to redefine demographics as a sales and marketing strategy and to go with special interests and life stages instead.

LifeStage Demographics – Help with Promotions and Marketing

Marketing campaigns specifically designed to target the LifeStage of your desired audience will net better results along with increased word of mouth. You will achieve more effective planning of contests, product tie-ins, and events. The result: Your listeners will feel more connected to "their" station and believe, "They are talking to ME." Here is one example of a perfect LifeStage Demographic promotion: An adult contemporary station that had chosen to specifically target young mothers, between twenty-five and thirty-five, held a circus with clowns and prizes for the children. During the event, the station also offered a five-dollar oil change and lube job for the busy moms. Members of the station's target audience could attend the radio station function, get a bargain on necessary automobile maintenance, and save the time it would take to bring the car into the mechanics shop, all while having fun at the circus with their kids.

Programming and On-Air Talent

Hire staff in various stages of life. It helps if most are in the LifeStage of the target audience you wish to attract. Learning LifeStage Demographics not only helps your on-air talent, in selecting content and in show prep, but also helps managers in hiring decisions for new on-air or behind-the-scenes producing talent. Through the use of LifeStage Demographics, you will create more powerful, relevant, and surgically targeted programming which will benefit the station by growing and developing the listener base and extending the audience's time spent listening.

Music and Imaging

Using LifeStage Demographics aids your music and research departments in selecting songs, liners, and jingle packages.

Get the Audience You Serve

In other words, LifeStage Demographics helps to make sure you are speaking to your audience at every opportunity in a language that they can fully understand, and that you fully understand their needs in order to serve them. There is no part of your station, from its logo to the coffee in your breakroom, that is not affected by LifeStage Demographics.

LifeStage Demographic research shows that race and age do not play as big a role in defining audience interests as do education level and social class. According to this research, upper-middle-class educated Asians, African Americans, Native Americans, and Hispanics have more in common with upper-middle-class Anglo-Saxons than those with lower income levels or less education. Like it or not, defining interests solely by race and age will soon be a thing of the past.

As LifeStage Demographics developed, we applied the concept to both sales and programming with very good results. Ratings increased at several stations, as did revenue.

Every successful radio station must appeal to a broad range of listeners who are experiencing various life stages. However, by gaining an understanding of the various LifeStage of your listeners, you will have an opportunity to eclipse your competition and win a larger share of the potential audience.

Life-stage categories can and frequently do overlap. For example, a person can be a homeowner without being married, a woman who is looking to find a partner, may also have children.

LifeStage Demographics Categories

"Kids"

There are as many kinds of kids, teenagers, and young people as there are people. Kids are divided into four subcategories:

- *Academic fast track:* "I want to be a doctor, so I study all the time."

- *Trendy:* "I spend all my free time at the mall hanging out with my friends. I'll worry about my future later on."

- *Sports fanatic:* "I play football, baseball, soccer, basketball—any sport whenever I can—and I go to the games."

- *The "perennial kid":* These "kids" can be eighteen or thirty-five years old! They may still be attending college. They are making important independent spending decisions. Some are young people who are done with school. They may have tried living on their own, gotten jobs, or attended college, but, whether due to practical economic or emotional reasons, these kids have returned to the "nest" and are living a LifeStage of prolonged adolescence, remaining at home with their families. Research is showing that the expected age of reaching adulthood has now moved to people's late twenties.

Young Men

Amazingly, we also found similar life stages in the category of "young men." Again, here were different generations, but similar lives. We discovered a 38-year-old man living an identical lifestyle to a 17-year-old. Here were men of significantly different ages, almost different generations, living similar lives. Both worked in music/video stores, both rented apartments, both drove sports cars. Both of these men were "not sure what they wanted to do with the rest of their lives." Both were single; dated a lot; got regular, expensive haircuts; ate out frequently; attended concerts; and visited their families each week for a home-cooked meal. Both the 17-year-old and the 38-year-old also brought sacks of dirty clothes home each week so their mothers could do their laundry!

Young Women

As we learned from our earlier virtual trip to the park, chronological age does not matter as much as life stage. A woman could be 17 or 46 and still want to shop at trendy stores, purchase lacy underwear, or have an interest in romantic gossip about the latest pop stars.

Working People

There are several types of LifeStage Demographic breakdowns in the working world. Among these, we found two main categories: (1) People who had made a career commitment lived a very different lifestyle than (2) those who still had major career decisions pending.

1. Just a Job: This group admitted that their "real" lives were outside of their jobs. Someday they hoped to find their true calling and on that day would step into the role they were meant to play. At present, they were not committed to or deeply involved in their work.

Whether in retail, the corporate world, the public sector or in fast-food services, these people were still trying to "find themselves" and were working at their jobs merely to make a paycheck.

2. Career Commitment: Those who had made a career commitment lived a very different lifestyle than people who were in the "Just a Job" LifeStage, who still had major career decisions pending. The committed career people were struggling to get ahead in their chosen fields. They spent long or extra hours at work, and many went into the office on weekends.

Some traveled extensively for their jobs. The career commitments cut into their time with family, friends, and leisure activities. Many said they spent time thinking about their work, even when they were not on the job.

Renters

Renters lived a vastly different lifestyle than homeowners did. Because they were not under the financial responsibility of maintaining a home, often there was more disposable income available. They also tended to have more flexibility. A notable characteristic of this LifeStage is that if need be, renters could relocate more easily for work or personal reasons than those who owned their homes.

Homeowners

As noted, it was not uncommon to find new home buyers making several trips to a home repair shop in one weekend (and not always to buy items, but sometimes just to ask questions!). Extra money that was once used for vacations, luxury items, and evenings out often went into paying extra costs or expenses for the house.

Solo

If someone lived alone, his or her listening, viewing, travel, entertaining, and spending habits were different from those of couples.

Couples

Couples tended to make decisions together, and with more compromising. This included everything from which radio station was played in the car to the choice of vacation destinations.

Couples with Kids or without Kids

Those with children lived a different lifestyle than those who did not have them. Again, age was irrelevant.

Good Health/Ill Health

Age was not necessarily a factor here. We found that the lifestyle of an 80-year-old man, spending most of his days in bed, watching TV or listening to the radio, wearing a bathrobe and pajamas, wasn't all that different from that of a 38-year-old woman recovering from a difficult back surgery.

Special Interests

We found other categories of LifeStages, with people who had special interests in common, including pet lovers, sports fanatics, gourmet chefs, etc. Here, neither age nor sex mattered as much as the common interest. Although there were generational commonalties that could not be ignored, age was not necessarily a factor here either.

When you are formatting, programming, and marketing your radio station, it is not enough to say, "We want an audience of 25- to 54-year-old men." A programmer must also ask, "Which LifeStages of 25- to 54-year-old men does our station want to serve?"

Life Stages Are Fluid

Life stages are more fluid than traditional age/sex/income-based demographics. After all, your own next age-defined demographic group, if you are in your twenties, is your thirties, then your forties, and so on; however, if your LifeStage is "With Kids," you may raise a family of young children, live in a child-free house for awhile, divorce, remarry, then start all over again with a new house full of small children.

It takes a little more effort on the part of researchers to get used to the idea that we cannot just park people into an age, sex, ethnic, or even income group and expect them to live a certain way. It takes research and effort to market yourself to the various people in different LifeStages, but the payoff is worth it.

A Station Should Hire People in the Life Stages It Wishes to Attract

There is no substitute for life experience. Your imagination can take you only so far. Most of us base our understanding of the world on direct experience.

It's no longer enough to say we want our audience to be men 25 to 54. Whatever your LifeStage target, "With Kids" checking out schools,

"Couples" planning vacations at an exotic resort, "Solo" singles looking for spouses, or active people training for a marathon, if you have not experienced it, it makes sense to have people around you who have.

If you are running a station or hosting or producing a program whose target audience doesn't look or live like you (and it is possible that you are), surround yourself with people who are like the audience you wish to target. Then you have to trust these people. Listen to them. They may have insights that do not show up in conventional research.

"They say the early forties is the new late thirties."

CHAPTER *26*

Creating Powerful Radio
Research

"Better products don't win, better *perceptions* win."
— *Jack Trout*

"You know the station is a success when people
who don't listen lie and say they do."
— *Overheard at a National Association of*
Broadcasters Convention

People love to look at research. We open the newspaper or watch TV and gobble up those Gallup polls, pie charts, and percentages of who is doing what. We like statistics, finished products, *results*. Most of us know it's not the data, but how one interprets it that counts.

Applying research to radio is a challenge. It's easiest with music radio. You ask a group of people what they think about a song, a performing artist, or a jingle. Interpreting "Personality" or News-Talk research is tougher. The reason? You can research only what has gone *before*. There is no way to predict in a research study what people are going to respond to *tomorrow*.

Working in talk radio is not for the faint-hearted. It elicits strong reactions. Your listeners will love you or hate you. They're active, and they'll let you know how they feel with calls, faxes, flowers, e-mails, boycotts, and threats.

311

There is one clear difference between News-Talk programming research and music programming research. In news and talk radio, polarization can be a good thing. Strong listener reaction, to a news-talk personality—be it positive or negative—is good, provided there is a *balance*. Don't be afraid of this intense reaction, it's one of the strengths of talk radio.

In talk radio, negative reaction *can* be a good thing, if balanced by an equal and opposite positive reaction. There is cause for concern if 97 percent of the audience hates your host or show and only 3 percent love it.

If you have an equal number of positively and negatively polarized opinions, that is a sign that whether they love it or hate it, they're listening.

Take strong personalities Rush Limbaugh and Howard Stern, for example. People either love them or hate then, but each has *millions* of listeners. The natural instinct of programmers is that they want their stations to be liked. They do not enjoy calming angry listeners or spending their work days answering e-mails from irate audience members. If a programmer can fight his or her instinct and override the pressure, it bears keeping in mind that it takes a while to grow a show. Stick with programming you believe in. Even if it is controversial, it is worth it. You will have a valuable product in the end.

Listeners are creatures of habit. They do not like change. They like it the old way. While behavior can be immediately changed, according to Dr. Evian Gordon from Australia's Brain Resource Company, it can take a thousand repetitions before a human brain is "rewired" to change, and this includes changing listener's habits.

It's only when the new way has a chance to "kick in" that it becomes a habit for them. So, (1) if they don't like the host today, they might tomorrow; and (2) if they hate him but they listen (and write it in their diary), that's OK. Don't be alarmed when your research shows that the audience has strong opinions about the hosts on your station. Controversy is not necessarily a bad thing. At a station I once worked with printed on its T-shirts, "Listen to talk radio because all great minds *don't* think alike."

Just about every radio market can tell the story of a beloved host whose name is known to all in the community but who is listened to by very few. Conversely, the mention of certain hosts causes dramatic negative response among many who would never miss a show. Music radio is both morning-show and music driven. In America, news and talk are very different formats. Obviously both benefit when there is a lot of news happening:

a natural disaster, a political crisis, a war, a huge trial, or an election. But talk radio tends to be personality and opinion driven, while news radio is information based and current-events driven.

A hybrid of these two—News-Talk—has splintered into several specifically targeted formats. Under the News-Talk umbrella, you can hear hot talk, self-help talk, sports talk, right- or left-wing political talk, Christian talk, male- or female-oriented talk, and FM or youth-oriented talk, among others. Clearly, talk radio programmers have taken a clue from their music-oriented counterparts and fragmented the format, targeting specific demographic groups for their stations.

What research *can* do is help you understand your audience and its lifestyles. It can answer questions like: How can my station better serve my audience? Or, What have they responded to in the past?

One of my favorite research projects came from Frank Magid and Associates in Marion, Iowa. They did a presentation years ago on the topics people would always listen to on the air. Those main topics include:

- Health (safety)

- Heart (emotional stories that touch the "heart")

- Pocketbook (money)

When you look at the content of stories that people remember over a week, this list remains fairly accurate, though now there is a fourth category to add, which is *transformation.*

Transformative topics can include anything that gives a listener hope for the future, how his or her life can be better tomorrow than it is at the moment because of something they've heard on air. The current trend of self-help advice, or fix-it programming, proves this.

Research can also be an incredible tool for programmers and managers when working with on-air talent and sales people. One project I took on involved a Religious Talk station on which a minister, a priest, and an attorney all hosted shows. They were dull. Even people with a lot of faith were tuning out. I was called in to "fix" the shows.

Here's what was going wrong: The hosts were talking *at* the listeners. They were lecturing, orating, and preaching, but not communicating. These men held themselves above their audience. Although each considered himself to be a good listener, not one of them really cared what his audience was saying. As a result, it was not personal, intimate, interesting, or meaningful. It was very boring radio.

I met with these hosts as a group, then one on one and just could not seem to get them to understand that they were not communicating powerfully. Well-educated, always treated with great respect, and with fairly high self-images, these men refused to believe that they were not getting through.

It was a focus group research project that saved these shows. We hid our hosts behind a two-way mirror and watched the proceedings. The focus group put on headphones and began listening to a recording of the first radio program. Within minutes, most had removed their headphones and were talking amongst themselves.

The priest was outraged. "But I'm just getting to the important part. They're not paying attention!" He was shocked that people had tuned him out. I pointed out that in church no one would dare to get up and leave on a Sunday morning, even if the sermon was dull. Parishioners would all sit politely, quietly bored, though pretending to listen. But alone in their cars, at home, or in a listening focus group, listeners do what they please, which is to tune out if a show is boring or irrelevant to their lives.

It was only after all three of the hosts experienced the tune-outs that they were ready to learn the techniques of creating powerful radio: storytelling, showing their hearts, being more personal, and listening. All three hosts have successful shows today because they were led to understand that they must become more powerful communicators.

Research is a necessary tool of modern business. Can you imagine a car manufacturer putting out a new car without test-marketing it first? Big money is at stake. People in business want data before they introduce a new product. They need a realistic sense of how the audience or consumer will react. Radio is no different.

Many products we don't think twice about today are in our lives because of quantitative research: single-serving frozen dinners, zipper-lock plastic bags, automobile cup holders, a tire patch in a can.

In the United States, there are pages and pages of names of broadcasting researchers in the radio directories. Anyone can hang out a shingle and call him or herself a researcher. Be careful which company you choose. It's a combination of skills and personality that makes good research.

If done right, research can help you get ratings and learn the habits of your audience.

No Crystal Ball

Researcher Steve Apel emphasizes that market research can't predict consumer behavior. "If it could, no product backed by research would ever fail. What research can do, if used properly, is identify public trends and tendencies." In radio, this means giving your listeners something they've been missing or more of what they say they like. There is no crystal ball.

Remember that while there are many research techniques, the basic process involves:

- Asking the right questions

- Compiling the data

- Analyzing and interpreting the results

Don't get intimidated by the language of research.

Apel advises that if you've hired research professionals using advanced analytical techniques to interpret a study, ask them to *explain* the techniques they are using. Be sure you're comfortable with the logic. After all, you need to understand and have confidence in this interpretation if you are using it to make changes to your station.

Researcher and consultant Matt Hudson warns that research alone is no way to make your programming decisions. He says: "[Research] does not prove or disprove anything. We still need creative minds to understand, interpret, and implement the findings."

Here, Hudson defines some research terms and talks generally about radio research. In some cases, I've provided examples to illustrate Matt's definitions.

Qualitative vs. Quantitative

"*Qualitative* studies, such as focus groups, involve ten to twelve people and are used to collect indicators that will be tested in a more statistically reliable research project, for example, a phone study. *Quantitative* studies, such as format searches or perceptual telephone studies, are large sample procedures which yield quantitative results. These can be generalized to the population from which the sample was selected."

In other words, you've got only twenty-eight people at your station and you already know their opinions about everything anyway. So, you get twelve people, strangers who really like talk radio, gathered in a room, then you ask them in great depth and detail about whatever you need to discover. These twelve people are a flashlight in the dark. They will illuminate new areas and point you in the direction you need to go for your larger or quantitative study.

This group is like gold. They can teach you things you never believed possible about your radio station; and the deeper you go, the better it gets. Just as in the focus group that taught the religious broadcasters how to communicate, when you really listen to these twelve people, powerful things can happen. However, you shouldn't make big decisions like firing someone because twelve people don't like the person. That calls for a bigger, quantitative study.

The questions based on the insight gained in the qualitative study can lead you in a direction of seeking trends in the quantitative study.

Let's say a station's evening talk host is the subject of a small focus group study. Turns out, some of the listeners find him so irritating that they put up with static to hear another host on a station hundreds of miles away. Up until then, the station's management had no idea the distant station could even be heard in the market. Thanks to the small focus group's *qualitative* results, *quantitative* questions about the distant station can be asked in the larger perceptual study.

Some researchers say you should never base programming decisions on qualitative research, and all agree that unless designed to do so, results from qualitative research should not be the sole factor in decision-making. Let us say you wanted to build a new bakery in New York City. If you ask nine people which bakery has the best bread in New York, you'd get nine different answers. They could give you some great ideas on what they like to see in the bakery, or whether they prefer store-bought bread.

But you certainly wouldn't want to use the results of your nine-person study to determine where you'd put your new store, what types of bread you would bake, or how much you should charge. To make these kinds of decisions, you'd have to ask many more people than that.

Phantom Cume

In the United States, radio measures listening using diaries. Listeners either write down what they hear on the radio in a diary or remember what they've heard and then relate this information by phone to a data collection company. Neither of these methods captures "real-time" listening, that is, listening as it is happening. So, every radio station has a number of listeners for whom they'll never get credit. This phenomenon is called *phantom cume*. It's the percentage of your cume that does not mention your radio station when asked to recall which stations they have listened to in the past week.

A healthy phantom cume seems to be around 25 to 30 percent over your reported cume. However, we are seeing many stations with phantom cumes reaching 70 percent of reported cume! Radio stations are presently experimenting with some new techniques to lower their phantom cumes and get the ratings credit they deserve.

Phantom cume may soon be a thing of the past, as new audience measurement technologies emerge, such as Arbitron's People Meter, though these new methods may also bring on their own problems or challenges.

Often research confirms something you already suspect about your station. I once used a research study to verify my instinct about a station I was consulting: that we had many more listeners to the station than we were getting credit for in the ratings diaries. Working with a research company, we were able to objectively verify that we had huge unreported listening (phantom cume) and easily fixed the problem by having the on-air personalities identify the station's name and call letters more frequently. That way the audience knew *whom* they were listening to and could later recall and identify the station when asked.

Validity

A test or study should measure what it is intended to measure. The ideal research situation is to have a valid test or study that is also reliable. It is actually possible to have a valid test that is unreliable or an invalid test that is reliable.

As an example, you can ask all the morning host's friends if they like the show. You can do everything right. You can make sure the responses aren't influenced by one another and your demos are properly sampled, but your sample is still a group of your host's friends. The study is perfectly valid, it's just not reliable. If you really want to know what the community thinks of your morning host, don't recruit a group of his biggest fans.

Because you know your market, work with your researcher to ensure validity. Ask about the criteria your research company uses to select the group. Do a mission statement for your study, then make sure you ask questions that will give you the answers you need. Even though they may not be the answers you want, ask yourself: Is it skewed or biased in any way? Does it really measure what we want?

Prestige Bias

Respondents tend to give answers that they think will make them seem more educated, successful, hip, financially stable, or otherwise prestigious. A good researcher can control this problem by asking and directing the questions correctly.

Researcher Bias

In this case, respondents provide specific answers because they believe these are the ones the researcher wants to hear. They want to impress and please the researcher. Again, this is easily managed by a skilled professional.

Random Sample

Every person has an equal chance of being selected to participate in a focus group, music test, or telephone perceptual study. A station database is NOT a random sample. If someone has volunteered for your study, he or she could not really have been chosen at random.

Size Is Important

What is a "statistically reliable sample size?" It depends on the error rate you are willing to accept. Generally, between 75 and 100 people should participate in your perceptual study for each demographic group, or "cell," you want to measure. For instance, if you want to do a study measuring adults 25 to 44, you'll want approximately the following number of participants:

- Women 25 to 34 (at least 75 respondents)
- Men 25 to 34 (at least 75 respondents)

- Women 35 to 44 (at least 75 respondents)
- Men 35 to 44 (at least 75 respondents)

This yields a total of 300 participants, generally considered adequate for this type of study.

How to Use a Focus Group

These results should NOT be used to make major decisions. This small sample research technique gives you an indicator; it helps you to devise the next set of questions you will need in your larger group for a telephone perceptual study.

When Should We Do Research?

Hudson concludes that conducting research to coincide with the start of a ratings period is not logical. Listeners don't try a new station when the ratings book begins. Broadcasters should think of research as a preventative strategic weapon. While the results of your research can be had almost immediately, it can take several months for the effects of the programming changes to show. It bears repeating that brain research demonstrates that it can take as many as a thousand repetitions to make a lasting impression.

Programming changes should be in place long before you enter a ratings measurement period.

What to Find Out

Steve Apel suggests: "Through questions that probe listener knowledge and impressions, you can get a feel for whether people perceive your station's programming the way you intend." What he means by this is that by asking the same question in a number of different ways—using, for example, different descriptive terms—you can get a clearer picture of what listeners really think. The picture "enable[s] you to assess whether or not your station is on target and provide[s] a basic guide for modifying the station to better suit [your] listeners' needs, tastes, and expectations."

For example, during a perceptual study, you might ask the following questions: Which station plays the best rock? Which station plays the widest variety of rock? Which station plays the hottest rock? Which station plays your favorite rock? A skilled researcher will be able to interpret the differences in the responses to give you more than just a simple "call letter" answer to the question.

Finally, those who call radio stations or write to you are NOT necessarily indicative of who is listening to your station. Research has shown that only between 1 and 3 percent of your audience will ever call the station. To best serve your audience, create programs for the 97 percent who are listening, not those who call.

Ask Your Own People

In the beginning of *USA Today,* Gannett's publishing division did a smart thing. It developed a concept of a "fast food" newspaper targeted to, among others, travelers, business people, and TV viewers. This would be a paper for people without a lot of time to read who just wanted the news headlines, sports, and gossipy "water cooler" features. The publishers chose an easy-to-read style accompanied by photos and colorful graphics.

Gannett used demographic research of the U.S. population and hired well-qualified reporters in proportion to the ethnic makeup of the United States: 52 percent women, 48 percent men, 18 percent African American, and so on. They hoped and speculated that the staffers would bring their own background experiences and unique perspectives to the stories they covered, as well as to story selection and story ideas. The concept worked. *USA Today* is omnipresent in airports, hotels, offices, and newsstands around the world.

A lesson can be learned here for radio. It never hurts to have your target demographic represented in your workplace, and it can't hurt to ask anyone with an opinion to spend a few minutes giving his or her thoughts to you. Be aware, however, of who's speaking. If your chief engineer, a known classical music buff, can't stand your afternoon sex therapy advice show, don't be surprised or make any programming decisions as a result. If, however, your chief engineer is a twice-divorced woman known for her romantic prowess and she finds that same afternoon show dry or pompous, you might want her to elaborate.

Remember: *Research is just a tool.* It is one of the many weapons in your arsenal for creating a powerful radio station. You can have all the research results in the world, but it always comes down to people. You have to use your judgment every step of the way—not just in hiring your airstaff but also in choosing your researchers and the participants in your research project. Apply all your creative skills. The rules for Creating Powerful Radio apply to research as well.

CHAPTER 27

Creating Powerful Radio
Final Notes

> "Our greatest glory is not in never falling, but in
> rising every time we fall."
> — *Confucius*

> "If at first you don't succeed, try, try again."
> — *Proverb*

Working in radio is a great job, with no heavy lifting. In what other profession do you get paid to tell the stories of life, chronicle the times we live in, find the most interesting people alive, meet them, and talk to them?

It is easy to get disillusioned and jaded when concern for profit seems to make creativity a luxury, if not a vice. But those who run the business side of radio need you. They are basing their station's financial future on one idea: that people will listen to what they have put on their radio stations. Your thoughts, your ideas, your words, and your personality are the product they are selling. You matter. It is up to you to use your creativity to make what is on the radio powerful.

Don't waste a minute of your time on the air. Say your station's name or call letters with pride! Make it matter. Be glad to be there. Tell the truth as you know it to be. Do every show with the same enthusiasm as you did your first, knowing it could be your last. Do not get caught up in pettiness at work.

In the 1700s Denis Diderot made this plea to artists: "Move me, surprise me, rend my heart, make me tremble, weep, shudder, outrage me, ... then delight me if you can."

In talk, as in all radio, do not forget the important things. Be yourself. Use your life experience. Even though you are talking about the personal events of your life, do not divulge what is private. The Powerful Radio you create should be as unique as your DNA, but always engage or involve the listener.

Prepare, do the formatics, state your opinions, be courageous, and use humor. Remember, it is never about you, it is always about the listeners. They are the people who are giving you the most precious thing they have on earth: their time.

Resources

Contributors

Jaye Albright
Consultant, Albright & O'Malley
Email: radioconsultj@aol.com
www.radioconsult.com

Steve Apels
Research Consultant
Email: steve@apels.net

Dave Baronfeld
MetroNetworks
Email: Dbaronfeld@aol.com
www.metronetworks.com

Andy Beaubien
General Manager/Consultant
Broadcast Programming & Research
Email: Andybpr@earthlink.net
www.bpr.com.au

Jerry Bell
Managing Editor/Reporter
KOA, Clear Channel–Denver
Email: jerrygbell@clearchannel.com

Mervin Block
"Writing Broadcast News"
Television Newswriting Workshop
Email: merblo@aol.com
www.mervinblock.com

Ross Brittain
The Ross Brittain Report
Email: ross_brittain@compuserve.com
www.rbreport.com

Maureen Bulley
The Radio Store, Inc.
"Write Good Copy Fast"
Email: doradio@total.net
www.theradiostore.com

John Catchings
TV Production and Consultation
Email: JC@johncatchings.com
www.catchingsandassociates.com

Jim Chenevey
CBS Radio News
Email: jch@cbsnews.com
www.cbsnews.com

Alan Eisenson
Operations Manager
KFBK/KSTE
Email: alaneisenson@clearchannel.com
www.kfbk.com

Caroline Feraday
Air Personality
Email: caroline@feraday.fsnet.co.uk
www.lbc.co.uk

Nic Gaunt
Photographer
Email: nic@nicgaunt.demon.co.uk
www.nicgaunt.com

Bernard Gershon
Vice President/General Manager
ABC News.com
Email: bernard.l.gershon@abc.com
www.abc.com

Dr. Evian Gordon
Chairman/CEO
The Brain Resource Company
Email: evian.gordon@brainresource.com
www.brainresource.com

Jeff Green
Author, Green Book of
Songs by Subject
www.greenbookofsongs.com

Doug Harris
Creative Animal International
Email: dough@creativeanimal.com
www.creativeanimal.com

Lee Harris
News Anchor
1010 WINS New York
Email: lee@harrismedia.com
www.1010wins.com

Michael Hedges
"Follow the Media"
Email: newsletter@followthemedia.com

Mark Howell
News Director, Journalist
KUZZ Radio
Email: mhowell@buckowens.com
www.markhowellnews.com

Matt Hudson
Music Test America
Email: musictestamerica@comcast.net
www.musictestamerica.com

Lynn Jimenez-Catchings
News Journalist
KGO Radio
Email: lmcatch@hotmail.com
www.KGOam810.com;
www.sehabladinero.info

Michael C. Keith
Assoc. Prof. Boston College
Author, The Radio Station
www.michaelckeith.com

Tommy Kramer
Talent coach
Email: tommy@tommykramer.net
www.audiencedevelopmentgroup.com

Christine Lavin
Artist/Singer-songwriter
www.christinelavin.com

Warren Levinson
Journalist, NY Bureau Chief
Associated Press
Email: wlevinson@ap.org
www.ap.org

Pam Lontos
President, PR/PR
Email: pam@prpr.net
www.prpr.net

Melissa McConnell Wilson
General Manager
KVHS-FM Radio
Email: wilson143@aol.com
www.kvhs.com

Denise McIntee
President
Powerful Radio Productions, Inc.
Email: Denisemac1@aol.com
www.powerfulradio.com

Jeremy Millar
Group PD
Australian Radio Network
Email: jeremymillar@arn.com.au
www.arn.com.au

Mackie Morris
The Magid Institute
Email: Mackie.morris@magid.com
www.magid.com

Lorna Ozmon
Consultant
President, Ozmon Media, Inc.
Email: lozmon@aol.com
www.ozmonmedia.com

Deborah Potter
Exec. Director NewsLab
Email: Potter@newslab.org
www.newslab.org

Howard Price
Assignment Editor
WABC-TV News
Email: Howard.B.Price@abc.com

Sean Ross
VP/Music and Programming
Edison Media Research
Email: sross@edisonresearch.com
www.edisonresearch.com;
www.theinfinitedial.com

Turi Ryder
Air Personality
Email: turi@shebopsproductions.com
www.shebopsproductions.com

Scott Shannon
PD/Morning Personality
WPLJ Radio
www.trueoldieschannel.com;
www.scottshannon.com

Dave Sholin
Astralwerks Records
Email: yourduke@aol.com
www.astralwerks.com

Mike Siegel
Major Attractions
Email: mikesiegel2000@yahoo.com
www.mikesiegel.com

Dan Vallie
Vallie/Richards Consulting, Inc.
Email: valliedan@aol.com
www.vallierichards.com

Guy Zapoleon
Zapoleon Media Strategies
Email: info@zapoleon.com
www.zapoleon.com

Tom Zarecki
Jetcast, Inc.
Email: tomz@jetcast.com
www.jetcast.com

Index

Notes

Notes

Notes

Notes

Notes

Notes